UNDERSTANDING TROUBLED AND TROUBLING YOUTH

OTHER RECENT VOLUMES IN THE
SAGE FOCUS EDITIONS

UNDERSTANDING TROUBLED AND TROUBLING YOUTH

Edited by
Peter E. Leone

Foreword by
Thomas M. Skrtic

SAGE PUBLICATIONS
The International Professional Publishers
Newbury Park London New Delhi

For information address:

SAGE Publications, Inc.
2111 West Hillcrest Drive
Newbury Park, California 91320

SAGE Publications Ltd.
28 Banner Street
London EC1Y 8QE
England

SAGE Publications Pvt. Ltd.
M-32 Market
Greater Kailash I
New Delhi 110 048 India

Printed in the United States of America

Library of Congress Cataloging-in-Publication Data

Main entry under title

Understanding troubled and troubling youth
  edited by Peter E. Leone
      p.   cm. — (sage focus editions : v. 116)
  Includes bibliographical references.
  ISBN 0-8039-3442-4. — ISBN 0-8039-3443-2 (pbk.)
    1. Juvenile delinquency—United States. 2. Juvenile delinquents-
-United States—Psychology. 3. Juvenile delinquency—United States-
-Prevention. I. Leone, Peter (Peter E.)
HV9104.U48   1990
364.3′6′0973—dc20   90-8228
                                                   CIP

FIRST PRINTING, 1990

Sage Production Editor: Amy Kleiman

Contents

Foreword

Power/Knowledge and the Professions

THOMAS M. SKRTIC

The normative view of the professions places the responsibility for determining a valid foundation for professional knowledge and practice in the hands of professionals themselves. It assumes that the validity of professional knowledge is unproblematic, and that, with the growth of knowledge generally, incremental refinements will be made to update what is at bottom a solid foundation of neutral, objective knowledge about reality. But this view of professional knowledge is changing, not to any great extent in the professions, but in the larger intellectual community from which the professions draw their knowledge claims. At that level, and particularly in the social sciences and humanities, there is growing recognition that, ultimately, knowledge production and utilization are moral and political acts with implications for human development and social justice. Thus, because knowledge is power in the information age, the professions have emerged as the most powerful class in society, particularly the professions that define and classify human beings.

During their ascendancy, roughly 1870-1930, the professions extended their influence to virtually all departments of life and consolidated their authority as the exclusive bearers of the scientific knowledge necessary for the good life. Not only were professionals viewed as capable of releasing nature's potential, they were understood to do so in the interest of the common good (Bledstein, 1976). As such, professionals were viewed as the personification of the victory of science over superstition and fear, and professionalization as the institutionalization of the ethic of service as a restraint on self-interest and greed. However, since then, and particularly since the 1960s, the perceived utility of professional knowledge and the legitimacy of the professions themselves have been eroded by three waves of criticism: sociological, philosophical, and political.

The sociological critique centers on the contradictions implied by the dynamic nature of society and the institutional context of professional service. As society has become more dynamic, and as social needs and values have changed, new problems have been created, many of which are so complex that no single profession can address them effectively. Although this trend has required professionals to think divergently and to work collaboratively across disciplinary boundaries, the professions have become increasingly convergent and specialized, which has worked against the type of thinking and interdisciplinary effort that is necessary (Gilb, 1966). In addition, the fact that virtually all professionals work in organizations creates ethical problems when the needs of the organization are in conflict with those of the client (Schein, 1973). As a result of these and other problems related to the interaction of the convergent and bureaucratic nature of the professions and the divergent and democratic character of society, some of the most pressing problems faced by society are the direct result of the application of professional knowledge to prior problems (Freidson, 1988; Schein, 1973). Ultimately, however, the most troubling aspect of the sociological critique is that it calls into question the normative notion of the ethic of service to society. Whereas turn-of-the-century intellectuals characterized professionalization as "a grand cultural reform, capable of restoring sanity to a capitalist civilization intoxicated with self-aggrandizement" (Haskell, 1984b, p. 177), it is commonplace for contemporary analysts to characterize it as merely another form of self-aggrandizement (Collins, 1979), "a capitalist remedy for the defects of capitalism" (Haskell, 1984a, p. 219).

The philosophical critique of the professions is a logical outgrowth of the epistemological and moral critiques of positivism and of science (Bernstein, 1976; Rorty, 1979). The professions are implicated in the critique of positivism because the model of professional knowledge is premised on the positivist theory of knowledge (Schon, 1983; Shils, 1978). That is, the practical knowledge required for the performance of services to clients is presumed to be grounded in a foundation of theoretical knowledge that is produced in the scientific disciplines and is assumed to be objective knowledge about reality (Schein, 1973). Moreover, the critique of science rejects the traditional image of science as a technical undertaking that yields objective knowledge. The emergent view is that, rather than a neutral, technical activity, science is a form of engagement between an object of study and an observer who is conditioned to see it in a particular way by his or her paradigm or frame of reference (Kuhn, 1970). As such, what is observed or "discovered" in the object is as much a product of this interaction as it is of the object itself. And because it is possible to engage an object of study in different ways, "the same object is capable of yielding many different kinds of knowledge. This leads us to see knowledge as a potentiality resting in an object of investigation and to see science as being concerned with the realization of potentialities—of possible knowledges" (Morgan, 1983, p. 13). The idea that science produces possible knowledges rather than objective knowledge has profound implications for the professions because it means that the knowledge that grounds thought and action in any given profession is not inherently correct. It is only a particular type of knowledge based on a particular frame of reference. It is not objective knowledge about reality; it is merely one of many possible knowledges.

The general trend in both the physical and the social sciences is away from objectivism and toward subjectivism (Bernstein, 1976; Schwartz & Ogilvy, 1979). But, as significant as this trend has been philosophically, the political critique of the professions is based on a more important development: the reconceptualization of the nature of knowledge itself. Since Descartes, the general conceptualization of knowledge has been foundational—the idea that there is a fixed set of foundational criteria against which all knowledge claims can be judged (Bernstein, 1983). But the emergent view is antifoundational, a conceptualization of knowledge as interpretation, a distinctively human process in which no single interpretation ever has enough cognitive authority to privilege it over another (Derrida, 1982; Feyerabend, 1975). Although, historically, debate in the social sciences and humanities has been premised on the foundational view of knowledge, which has led to arguments over the best methodology, theory, or paradigm for social analysis, today scholars in the social sciences and humanities are calling for dialogical discourse—an antifoundational, reflective discourse about, and appreciation of, the variety of possible interpretations of social life (Bernstein, 1983; Ricoeur, 1981; Rorty, 1979). A related development has been a series of revisions in the metaphor for social life: from an organism to a game; from a game to a drama; and finally from a drama to a text (Geertz, 1983). The text metaphor implies a mode of social analysis that views human action as discourse, a discourse that can be read or interpreted in many ways, none of which is correct in a foundational sense, but all of which carry with them particular implications for human development and social justice. Social analysis under the text metaphor is the study of what conditions, limits, and institutionalizes discursive formations, or human actions; a form of analysis that "concentrates on the relations of power, knowledge, and the body in modern society" (Dreyfus & Rabinow, 1983, p. 105). The basic question is how power comes to be concentrated in the hands of those who have the right to order, classify, exclude, and, generally, affirm or deny true or false propositions; that is, the power to interpret.

No aspect of modern life has received more critical attention under the text analogy than the professions, for it is this group in modern society that has accumulated the power to interpret normality, and thus the power to define and classify those who are abnormal and to treat their bodies. And there is no one who has devoted more energy or attracted more attention to the question of power/knowledge and the professions than the French philosopher Michel Foucault (e.g., 1980). Foucault turns social analysis on its head, in that, rather than looking for deep meaning, which, of course, is the customary mode of social analysis, he looks for surface practices. As such, his primary interest is the different modes by which, in our culture, human beings are turned into subjects. His analyses of the professions of psychiatry (1973), medicine (1975), and criminology (1979) are classic examples of the power to interpret normality. Although on the surface his work is indistinguishable from that of a historian, the key difference is that he is far less interested in events than in the modes of understanding that produce the events. Ultimately, he wants to know what, in a particular time and place, leads people to believe in what they were doing.

Understanding Troubled and Troubling Youth emerged out of a recognition of the lack of utility of professional knowledge to address the problems faced by youth in the United States today. It documents the overwhelming complexity of the problem, and is premised specifically on the need for divergent thinking and interdisciplinary collaboration in addressing the multitude of interrelated factors that contribute to and sustain it. Moreover, its multidisciplinary format clearly illustrates the fact that the problem takes a different form depending on the disciplinary perspective one uses to frame it.

Beyond its potential to initiate a dialogical discourse among the professions concerned with the problem of troubled and troubling youth, this volume's larger contribution is what it has to say to a society that continues to alienate more and more of its young people. As Foucault (1983) has argued, the most insightful way to understand society is to consider it from the perspective of the professions that have emerged to contain its failures. As such, the real value of *Understanding Troubled and Troubling Youth* is that, by exposing the reader to the ways of seeing of the various disciplines that contain the failure of modern society to nurture its youth and to make culture meaningful to them, it provides profound insight into what it means to come of age in a society like ours, and, more important, what it means to do so in a just and meaningful way. Finally, by refocusing our attention on factors external to youth themselves, the authors of the chapters to follow hold out the possibility that, rather than seeing troubled and troubling behavior simply as a target for manipulation, we may yet come to see it as a form of strategic consciousness, as a way coping with the world, as a narrative on what is so troubling to our sons and daughters about us and our society.

References

Bernstein, R. J. (1976). *The restructuring of social and political theory.* Philadelphia: University of Pennsylvania Press.

Bernstein, R. J. (1983). *Beyond objectivism and relativism: Science, hermeneutics, and praxis.* Philadelphia: University of Pennsylvania Press.

Bledstein, B. J. (1976). *The culture of professionalism: The middle class and the development of higher education in America.* New York: W. W. Norton.

Collins, R. (1979). *The credential society.* New York: Academic Press.

Derrida, J. (1982). *Dissemination* (B. Johnson, Trans.). London: Athlone.

Dreyfus, H. L., & Rabinow, P. (Eds.). (1983). *Michel Foucault: Beyond structuralism and hermeneutics.* Chicago: University of Chicago Press.

Foucault, M. (1973). *Madness and civilization: A history of insanity in the age of reason* (R. Howard, Trans.). New York: Vintage/Random House.

Foucault, M. (1975). *The birth of the clinic: An archeology of medical perception* (A. M. Sheridan Smith, Trans.). New York: Vintage/Random House.

Foucault, M. (1979). *Discipline and punish: The birth of the prison.* New York: Vintage.

Foucault, M. (1980). *Power/knowledge: Selected interviews and other writings, 1972-1977* (C. Gordon, L. Marshall, J. Meplam, & K. Soper, Eds.). Brighton, Sussex: Harvester.

Foucault, M. (1983). The subject and power. In H. L. Dreyfus & R. Rabinow (Eds.), *Michel Foucault: Beyond structuralism and hermeneutic*e (pp. 208-226). Chicago: University of Chicago Press.

Feyerabend, P. (1975). *Against method*. London: Verso.

Freidson, E. (1988). *Professional powers: A study of the institutionalization of formal knowledge*. Chicago: University of Chicago Press.

Geertz, C. (1983). *Local knowledge: Further essays in interpretive anthropology*. New York: Basic Books.

Gilb, C. L. (1966). *Hidden hierarchies: The professions and government*. New York: Harper & Row.

Haskell, T. L. (1984a). Professionalism versus capitalism: R. H. Tawney, Émile Durkheim, and C. S. Peirce on the disinterestedness of professional communities. In T. L. Haskell, *The authority of experts: Studies in history and theory* (pp. 180-225). Bloomington: Indiana University Press.

Haskell, T. L. (1984b). *The authority of experts: Studies in history and theory*. Bloomington: Indiana University Press.

Kuhn, T. S. (1970). *The structure of scientific revolutions*. Chicago: University of Chicago Press.

Morgan, G. (Ed.). (1983). *Beyond method: Strategies for social research*. Beverly Hills, CA: Sage.

Ricoeur, P. (1981). *Paul Ricoeur: Hermeneutics and the human sciences* (J. B. Thompson, Ed. and Trans.). Cambridge: Cambridge University Press.

Rorty, R. (1979). *Philosophy and the mirror of nature*. Princeton, NJ: Princeton University Press.

Schein, E. H. (1973). *Professional education*. New York: McGraw-Hill.

Schon, D. A. (1983). *The reflective practitioner: How professionals think in action*. New York: Basic Books.

Schwartz, P., & Ogilvy, J. (1979). *The emergent paradigm: Changing patterns of thought and belief* (Analytic Report 7, Values and Lifestyle Program). Menlo Park, CA: SRI International.

Shils, E. (1978). The order of learning in the United States from 1865 to 1920: The ascendancy of the universities. *Minerva, 16*(2), 159-195.

Acknowledgments

A number of colleagues were influential in shaping my ideas concerning troubled and troubling youth. Bruce Fuller, Bill Rhodes, Tom Skrtic, and Ed Trickett, through their research, writing, and discussions, have helped me understand the multifaceted nature of human behavior and inquiry. I am also grateful to the contributors to this volume, from whom I learned a great deal as I read and reread their manuscripts and who most often responded positively to my editorial suggestions.

Ten of the chapters contained in this book were presented at the Seminar on Troubled and Troubling Youth, held May 3-5, 1989, at the Donaldson Brown Center in Port Deposit, Maryland. The seminar, sponsored by the Center for Educational Research and Development (CERD) in the College of Education at the University of Maryland, College Park, provided an opportunity for contributors to discuss and respond to one another's papers. I thank John Guthrie, director of CERD, and the CERD advisory group for supporting the seminar.

Many of the Community-Based Research Staff at the University of Maryland, especially Kathi Keppler, Ellen Spero, and Mary Walter, were supportive of this project. They critiqued my ideas, were patient with me when deadlines for other projects were missed, and were good listeners. Within the Department of Special Education, Phil Burke, Lani Florian, and Michael Powers provided valuable feedback and support for the development of this book.

I would also like to acknowledge the contributions of Jeff, Tammy, Rex, Doug, Rocky, Roger, Debbie, and many other former students. They helped me to understand their life experiences as I struggled to teach them how to cope with junior high school. Finally, Diane, Andy, and K. A. have been and will always be my collaborators.

—*Peter E. Leone*

1

Toward Integrated Perspectives on Troubling Behavior

PETER E. LEONE

Children and adolescents who engage in behavior that is labeled deviant receive treatment and services from a range of different professionals and agencies. Frequently, integrated services for those children who experience multiple problems such as school failure, drug or alcohol dependency, and emotional distress, or those who violate the law or are neglected by their families and communities, are impeded by a limited understanding by professionals. Too often, disagreement regarding the nature and ownership of problem behavior, appropriate treatment, and means of systematically investigating those children and the contexts of their behavior interferes with appropriate responses to problem behavior.

As families, professionals, and communities struggle to respond to troubling behavior, too often conceptualizations of the problem are limited by disciplinary, professional, or theoretical boundaries. While disciplinary boundaries may frame problems and responses to those problems in personally satisfying and professionally appropriate ways, they limit our ability to understand the social, political, and historical contexts within which all behaviors occur. Similarly, our biases concerning the proper modes of inquiry for investigating troubling behavior inhibit our ability to understand the complex nature of the phenomenon. Ultimately, youths themselves, their families, and society

AUTHOR'S NOTE: Thanks to Diane Greig, Joe McCaleb, and Tom Skrtic for suggestions made during the development of this chapter.

15

suffer as problems are marginally understood and inadequately addressed. Often, in frustration, we collectively cite schools, families, communities, and other parties for exacerbating or ignoring the roots of problem behavior. In short, the problems of troubled and troubling youth transcend the conceptual, disciplinary, and service delivery boundaries established by researchers and professionals who attempt to understand and respond to deviant behavior.[1]

The Language of Deviant Behaviors

Discussion of deviant behavior is impossible without reference to popular and professional language used to describe individuals and actions that conflict with an established order. Our choice of terms reveals a great deal about how we construct and define the concept of deviant behavior and the underlying assumptions we make about youths or behavior under consideration. Typically, terms used reflect the contexts within which we observe or experience specific behaviors and the cultural biases we share. Educators, for instance, employ terms such as *truant, dropout,* and *disruptive* to characterize patterns of behavior that interfere with or are at variance with the functioning of the school. Special educators in keeping with state regulations governing identification and provision of services to exceptional students use terms such as *serious emotional disturbance* and *behavior disorder* to refer to troubling students from their perspective.

In contrast, juvenile justice professionals label behavior as a *status offense* or an individual as a *status offender, repeat offender, child in need of assistance,* or *delinquent.* In general, these terms reflect the rule-violating nature of specific acts or patterns of behavior. Clinicians or therapists use a wide range of terms to describe youths who exhibit deviant behavior. Labels range from general terms such as *client* and *substance abuser* to terms based on clinical nomenclature such as DSM III-R (American Psychiatric Association, 1987) that label particular clusters of behaviors with terms such as *oppositional deviant disorder* or *conduct disorder—group type.* While these varied labels may have technical meanings within professional groups, they can convey negative connotations to others and may impede communication across groups.

Issues related to labeling, definition, and assessment of youth, and the effects of labeling have been discussed from educational (Wood &

Lakin, 1979), sociological (Gove, 1975), psychological (Achenbach, 1985), and multidisciplinary (Hobbs, 1975) perspectives. While terminology serves administrative functions and is essential for some research purposes, all labels are limiting when they give us the sense that we know or understand a particular phenomenon and imply a primary problem, cause, or response. While specific behaviors or clusters of behaviors may be defined as a primary problem from a particular disciplinary, professional, or analytic viewpoint, too often we reify the concept of deviance from a particular perspective. In doing so we forget that disordered behavior, like the perspectives used to define or label it, are social constructions and, as such, have historical and political antecedents. Further, problems experienced by many youth encompass more than a given label can suggest.[2]

Professional and Disciplinary Perspectives

Not only do labels and terms vary, but individuals in the professions and scholars in the social and behavioral sciences have constructed different conceptualizations of deviant behavior (Hobbs, 1975). Understanding these differing viewpoints is essential if programs, policy, and research are to be guided by more than a unidimensional or monolithic orientation toward troubled and troubling youth.

Professional and disciplinary perspectives emanate from the training that individuals receive, their personal experiences, and the roles they assume: educators, social workers, attorneys, criminal justice professionals, psychologists, researchers. The parent disciplines of many of the helping professions, psychology or sociology, also provide convenient and comfortable frameworks for understanding troubling behavior.

Educators, for example, are most concerned with academic, social, and vocational skill development of youth and with the ability of the community to provide appropriate educational services or employment. Educators view students who consistently act out in school as disruptive, maladjusted, or emotionally disturbed (see Nelson & Rutherford, Chapter 3 of this volume, and Fink, Chapter 4). While social workers may also be concerned with the academic or vocational skills of youths, their primary foci are problems related to poverty, substance abuse, or teenage parenthood or the ability of families to nurture and support their sons and daughters (see McAdoo, Chapter 11). Criminal justice professionals view youths who exhibit troubling behavior as products of a juvenile subculture whose norms are in conflict with larger societal norms. Probation officers and jurists are often concerned about whether youths can disassociate themselves from peers with whom they have engaged in delinquent acts and meet specific standards for behavior in the community.

Primary concerns of psychologists or counselors might be the ability of troubled youths to cope with a range of problems, including poorly developed interpersonal skills, negative feelings about themselves, and limited school and employment opportunities. Clinicians or therapists may view disordered behavior as a manifestation of individual or family pathology (see Dishion, Chapter 7, and Snyder & Huntley, Chapter 10).

All of these traditional conceptualizations of troubled youth may make sense within their respective professions and disciplines. While some professionals and social scientists understand the multiple contexts within which behaviors occur, often administrative structures and the dominant conceptualizations of our discipline or profession make collaborating with others and developing appropriate responses to troubling behavior difficult if not impossible. For example, when service criteria, caseloads, or staffing patterns for a particular agency result in the exclusion of youths whose problems extend beyond traditional service boundaries, those youths, their families, and society bear the costs.

Micro, Meso, or Macro?

Often accompanying professional or disciplinary perspectives are analytical perspectives concerning the proper level at which to respond to troubling behavior. Differing beliefs typically involve issues of causality, responsibility, and remediation of the problem; perspectives on these issues can involve a micro, meso, or macro level of analysis (Everhart, 1987).[3]

Micro, or problem- or person-centered perspectives, focus on maladaptive, rule-violating behavior exhibited by youths. From these viewpoints, troubled or troubling youth have not learned appropriate normative behavior in the community and need to learn adaptive, prosocial skills. Problem- or person-centered perspectives direct attention to youths exhibiting specific behaviors, the topography or contours of their behavior, or strategies to alter or suppress behavior.

On a second level, *meso or social ecological perspectives* focus on the social interactions between troubled youths and others in their environments. From these social ecological perspectives, it is essential to view troubling behavior in its social context. Deviant or troubling behavior occurs when there is an imbalance between a youth and the other members of his or her social system. Dynamic, ecological perspectives place the onus for change on both the troubled youth *and* the other members of his or her environment. These perspectives suggest that although behavior exhibited by troubled youths may be learned, that behavior and the responses to it by members of the adolescents' social networks are maladaptive.

A third set of perspectives on troubled youth includes *macro, structural-, or cultural-level analyses*, which involve examining the institutions, culture, and other societal forces that give meaning to daily events and influence behavior. From these viewpoints, troubling behavior can be seen as a function of the roles that adolescents play within society and the unanticipated purposes that deviant behaviors serve. For some, acts of delinquent behavior illustrate inherent conflicts that exist among adolescents, families, schools, and society. Others, from a macro-level point of view, see deviant behavior as symptomatic of the lack of challenging, meaningful roles that schools, families, and other institutions provide for adolescents. Macro perspectives can also help us understand how systemic problems such as racism, poverty, and homelessness create conditions in which certain adolescent behaviors viewed as maladaptive within the larger cultural context are quite adaptive within specific subcultures.

Modes of Inquiry

In addition to terminology, disciplinary or professional boundaries, and differing analytical perspectives that impede our ability to understand troubling behavior, differing research methods can also be divisive forces that interfere with our ability to work collectively to respond to serious problems experienced by youth. Currently, much of the research on troubled and troubling youth is empirically based. These methods frequently are based on unquestioned assumptions that what we study is tangible, that pieces of what we perceive can be studied independently of the whole, and that our methods are value free (Jensen, 1984). While empirical or positivist methods have yielded and will continue to yield useful information, other legitimate forms of inquiry—based on differing assumptions about reality—and other ways of knowing—based on interpretive and critical research methods—are infrequently understood or employed (Leone, 1988; Soltis, 1984). Often, the underlying assumptions upon which research, practice, and knowledge are built remain unchallenged and unquestioned (Skrtic, 1986). Differing methods of research or inquiry yield different types of information. The "correctness" of a particular method of inquiry is not the question; rather, we need to understand the underlying assumptions being made by those conducting the investigation, the tools being used to direct attention to different aspects of troubling behavior, and the contexts within which behaviors occur.

New Directions

Understanding these different perspectives has implications for those providing appropriate services to and investigating troubled and troubling youth. Collaborative relationships and collaborative responses begin with understanding and respecting differing professional and analytical perspectives and research traditions.

This volume attempts to bring together scholars from a number of different disciplines who are concerned with troubled and troubling youth and who represent diverse points of view. The chapters are organized according to the levels of analysis employed by the authors in approaching problems associated with troubled and troubling youth. The contributors to Part I have adopted person- and problem-centered perspectives; that is, the level of analysis and perspectives focus on issues related to prevalence, identification, and services for troubled and troubling youth.

Chapters in Part II reflect social ecological perspectives on troubling behavior. Accordingly, authors in this section focus on the nature of the relationships between youths and the social contexts and individuals in their daily lives.

In Part III, the authors employ structural and cultural perspectives on disordered behavior. While these authors, like other contributors to the volume, are concerned with troubled and troubling youth, their primary foci are the institutions and the cultural and social forces that contribute to the creation, maintenance, and attenuation of troubling behavior.

The book concludes with a review of problems currently facing adolescents and a description of a few projects that have attempted to intervene on behalf of troubled youth and to create innovative multidisciplinary responses to their needs. In sum, the contributors have attempted to provide a glimpse into the myriad ways in which we can conceptualize, research, and ultimately respond to and understand troubled and troubling youth.

Notes

1. The Study of Child Variance explicated a number of the dominant theoretical perspectives on emotional disturbance and related disorders in children (Rhodes & Tracy, 1972). Rhodes and Paul (1978) further examined deviant behavior and the scientific and philosophical structures that support current conceptualizations.

2. Achenbach (1985) eschews current assessment practices and taxonomies in behavior disorders and has proposed a multiaxial taxonometric approach to child and adolescent behavior problems for clinical and research purposes. His schema for classification of disorders involves assessing parent perspectives, teacher perspectives, cognitive functioning, physical conditions, and clinical judgments. Although broader than current and highly unreliable assessment and classification procedures, his proposals are fairly rooted in the dominant microanalytic (the child as source of the problem) view of deviant behavior.

3. Bronfenbrenner (1979), from a social ecological perspective, identifies four different levels of analysis for understanding the contexts that we experience: micro, meso, ecto, and macro.

References

Achenbach, T. M. (1985). *Assessment and taxonomy of child and adolescent psychopathology.* Beverly Hills, CA: Sage.

American Psychiatric Association. (1987). *Diagnostic and statistical manual of mental disorders* (3rd ed., rev.). Washington, DC: Author.

Bronfenbrenner, U. (1979). *The ecology of human development: Experiments by nature and design.* Cambridge, MA: Harvard University Press.

Everhart, R. (1987). Understanding school disruption and classroom control. *Harvard Educational Review, 57,* 77-83.

Gove, W. (Ed.). (1975). *The labeling of deviance: Evaluating a perspective.* New York: Halstead.

Hobbs, N. (Ed.). (1975). *Issues in the classification of children* (Vol. 2). San Francisco: Jossey-Bass.

Jensen, A. R. (1984). Political ideologies and educational research. *Phi Delta Kappan, 65*(7), 460-462.

Leone, P. E. (1988). Rethinking our assumptions about troubled and troubling youth. *Behavioral Disorders, 13,* 134-136.

Rhodes, W. C., & Paul, J. L. (1978). *Emotionally disturbed and deviant children: New views and approaches.* Englewood Cliffs, NJ: Prentice-Hall.

Rhodes, W. C., & Tracy, M. (1972). *A study of child variance* (Vol. 1). Ann Arbor: University of Michigan Press.

Skrtic, T. (1986). The crisis in special education knowledge: A perspective on perspectives. *Focus on Exceptional Children, 18*(7), 1-16.

Soltis, J. F. (1984). On the nature of educational research. *Educational Researcher, 13*(10), 5-10.

Wood, F. H., & Lakin, K. C. (Eds.). (1979). *Disturbing, disordered or disturbed? Perspectives on the definition of problem behavior in educational settings.* Minneapolis: University of Minnesota, Department of Psychoeducational Studies, Advanced Training Institute for Trainers of Teachers for Seriously Emotionally Disturbed Children and Youth.

PART I

Person- and
Problem-Centered Perspectives

2

Protecting the Rights of Troubled and Troubling Youth

Understanding Attorneys' Perspectives

LOREN M. WARBOYS
CAROLE B. SHAUFFER

It's a common scenario: Two high school faculty members discuss a student as they leave the principal's office. One teacher says: "I can't believe the problems I'm having in class with Peter X. He acts out, he's uncooperative, and he encourages the other kids to be equally disruptive. He's been suspended for a few days twice this year, but it doesn't seem to have any effect on him. So I went to talk with the principal about it and asked if he could suspend Peter for the rest of the semester to teach him a lesson. I think if he were out of school, the other kids would get the message too. The principal says that the kid has due-process rights and can't be suspended without a full hearing. He says I have to gather evidence on each of these incidents. I'm too busy teaching to gather evidence, and I certainly can't expect the other kids to talk about what happens in class. I don't know who these lawyers think they're helping with all this due-process stuff. It certainly isn't helping Peter. He thinks that he can get away of any kind of behavior. He's not learning anything and all the other kids are losing out too. We are going to destroy these kids with all these rights."

The hostility expressed by this teacher toward the legal profession is shared by many people who want to help troubled youth. The operating principles of the legal profession seem foreign to those of the "helping professions." Teachers, social and mental health workers, counselors, and other professionals cannot understand why lawyers thwart their efforts to help by erecting seemingly insurmountable legal barriers to providing treatment or controlling unacceptable behavior. Unfortunately, lawyers and other professionals too often end up as adversaries unable to resolve their differences for the benefit of their mutual client. These differences are not merely superficial, nor do they result from ill will on the part of either group. Rather, they are based on fundamentally different ways of looking at the world in general and at children in particular.

To understand the attorneys' perspective on troubled and troubling youth, one must look at certain elements that are basic to the legal worldview. First, attorneys are concerned with categorizing and line drawing. Attorneys look for clear legal definitions so that similar situations can be treated in similar ways. Precedents are of the utmost importance. They help ensure fairness and provide a level of predictability that people can rely on to plan their affairs.

Second, attorneys are trained to think in an adversarial way. An attorney vigorously represents a client and acts under that client's direction. The traditional role of the lawyer is to advocate for what the client wants, not to make judgments about what may be in the client's best interest. The attorney's basic function is to assure that the client's viewpoint is clearly articulated and fairly considered, and, ultimately, that the client's aims—right or wrong—are achieved.

Third, the legal system as a whole is designed to determine who is right and who is wrong rather than to act as a problem solver. Litigation, in particular, assigns blame to one party and vindicates the other. For this reason, a lawyer may resist what seems like a reasonable compromise and strive to prove that his or her client is right and blameless. (This applies not only to lawyers for children, but to lawyers for school districts and treatment providers as well.) Even litigation that obtains a result that benefits all parties can cause bad feelings because of this aspect of blame.

Fourth, lawyers often focus on procedure over substance. This is entirely appropriate since attorneys usually have no training in the substance of the dispute (e.g., identifying mental illness, providing educational services), while they are trained to judge the fairness of the process. For lawyers, "due process" means that everyone's interests are protected when a fair and rational decision-making system is in place and followed in each case. The complexity of the procedural safeguards varies depending on the importance of the interests at stake and the potential harm resulting from error. The procedures are designed to reduce the risk of mistake and to give all parties a fair opportunity to present their positions.

Finally, attorneys seek to limit discretion. While it might be ideal from a treatment professional's point of view to have unlimited discretion in setting behavioral consequences or choosing a course of treatment, the attorney tries to protect the client against potential abuses of that discretion by limiting that professional's freedom to act without outside, often judicial or quasi-judicial, review. Put another way, treatment providers usually seek to increase discretion so that they can do the most good; attorneys usually seek to decrease discretion to avoid the greatest harm. Unfettered discretion presumes total good faith, professional competence, and a right to supersede the decision-making authority of the individual most directly affected. The legal profession rarely will grant such presumptions.

Application of these basic principles underlying the legal world becomes complicated when one is dealing with children and troubled youth. Within the legal system there has never been clear agreement on young persons' proper legal status. Are they akin to property and therefore subject to the whims of their possessors (e.g., parents or legal custodians)? Are they defenseless beings in need of protection and nurturing—either from their parents, or, if that's imposition, from the state (the *parens patriae* doctrine)? Are they independent persons entitled to rights of their own? At various times in U.S. legal history each of these views has been ascendant, and elements of all three views are present in legal decisions being written today. The lawyer's (and the court's) view of children's legal status directly affects the way in which the lawyer represents the child.

This chapter examines how the legal profession views children and the resolution of disputes involving children. We concentrate on those areas that have caused the greatest conflict between lawyers and treatment providers. In particular, we look at four basic issues: (a) how the law draws the line between childhood and adulthood and the significance of that distinction; (b) the problems encountered when others assert a right to act for the child; (c) the types of and reasons for legal limitations on the discretion of treatment providers to make decisions affecting a child; and (d) the impact of the adversarial nature of the legal system on treatment efforts.

Who Is a Child?

The treatment professional looking at an individual who has ongoing emotional problems is not as concerned about general issues of definition as about responding to that individual's needs. The legal system, while also concerned with the individual's needs, is first concerned with establishing coherent, consistent definitions. For example, there are substantial differences in the legal rights and responsibilities of adults and children. The law grants adults full freedom to make their own decisions. The state may deprive an adult of this right only if a state agent meets a very high standard of proof in establishing extraordinary circumstances. This is the essence of a citizen's "liberty" interest, protected in the Constitution. At the same time, the law has long recognized that certain persons are incompetent to exercise this freedom. Children are a classic example. Therefore, the question of who is an adult and who is a child is particularly important to attorneys. It is really a question of legal competency.

Chronological age appears to be an objective measure of adulthood and, therefore, a reasonable criterion to use in defining childhood. However, age-based definitions of childhood are not the same in every instance. For example, most states allow persons to drive a car at age 16, vote at age 18, and drink alcohol at age 21. In addition, relying purely on chronological age is inadequate for many purposes. It is obvious that an individual does not cease being a child one day and become an adult the next. In addition, different persons mature at different rates. Therefore, considerations other than age must be taken into account by the law in determining when the rights of an adult accrue to an individual.

In some situations an individual's emotional or cognitive maturity is more important than chronological age. For example, in determining when a young woman should be permitted to decide to terminate a pregnancy without parental consent, chronological age is only one factor used in assessing maturity and legal capacity. The U.S. Supreme Court has decided that while states can use chronological age as a preliminary guide for determining whether a young woman is capable of giving informed consent to abortion without parental input, they also must allow for a "mature minor" exception (*Bellotti v. Baird*, 443 U.S. 622 [1979]). This exception must take into account cognitive and emotional maturity. The courts are therefore required to define what maturity is in each case and to try to do this in an equitable manner. In these situations, the law is attempting to recognize reality as a treatment professional or a parent or the person in the street sees it. However, flexibility is achieved at the cost of precision and efficiency. Someone must make case-by-case decisions about whether individuals have reached a sufficient level of maturity.

The importance of resolving the question of who is a child and the seriousness of the consequences of such a determination are most dramatically demonstrated in the juvenile capital punishment cases before the U.S. Supreme Court. In 1988, the Court overturned the death sentence of an Oklahoma boy who was 15 at the time he murdered his brother-in-law. As do many states, Oklahoma had a statute that allowed young persons to be tried as adults and to be subject to adult sanctions in certain cases involving serious crimes. In the case of first-degree murder, these sanctions included the death penalty. A plurality of the Court ruled that imposing a death sentence on a youngster who was under 16 at the time his crime was committed violates the Eighth Amendment to the U.S. Constitution.

> It is likely cruel, and certainly unusual, to impose a punishment that takes as its predicate the existence of a fully rational, choosing agent, who may be deterred by the harshest of sanctions and toward whom society may legitimately take a retributive stance. (*Thompson v. Oklahoma*, 108 S.Ct. 2687, 2693 n.23 [1988])

An adolescent's "inexperience, less education, and less intelligence," "lesser culpability," and "capacity for growth" and "society's fiduciary obligations to its children" make the death penalty for one under 16 years of age an unconstitutional punishment.

The dissenters in the case rejected the notion that it is "a fundamental principle of our society that no one who is as little as one day short of his 16th birthday can have sufficient maturity and moral responsibility to be subjected to capital punishment for any crime" (*Thompson v. Oklahoma,* at 2712). Although the dissenters agreed that at some age a line does exist below which it would always be cruel or unusual to impose the death penalty, they rejected the notion that the line exists at age 16.[1]

This case demonstrates the tension between relying on a fixed constant like age as a determinant for when childhood ends and recognizing that subjective factors such as experience, education, and intelligence are an essential part of the determination. The case also demonstrates the tremendous consequences that can be at stake. Ironically, it is the dissenters, who would have voted to uphold the death penalty, who take what appears to be the more humanistic view that all individuals are different and so should be subject to different standards. In this case, the conservative, legalistic view that requires clear line drawing and a predictable consistent result is, ironically, more protective.

Ultimately, the legal system, like other social institutions, must settle for a compromise. Consistent objective standards must be set for determining when childhood ends and when an individual assumes the rights and responsibilities of adulthood. These standards must remain relatively inflexible, particularly when they involve rights and responsibilities such as voting, driving, and school attendance, which are generally applicable. The system would be overwhelmed if it attempted to make decisions based on individual circumstances in these situations. On the other hand, the law allows some ability to make exceptions, particularly when very personal and individual rights, like the right to reproductive freedom, are involved.

Who Speaks for the Child?

Once an individual is defined as a child, he or she is deprived of the right to make certain choices independently. The law must therefore designate a substitute decision maker. In our legal system, under ordinary circumstances, parents fulfill that role. The integrity of the family is one of the most fundamental principles of American law. Only in extreme circumstances, such as cases of child abuse or legal incompetence of parents, will the state intervene and abrogate to itself or delegate to another the right to make basic decisions about a child's life.

The Supreme Court summarized this principle in the *Parham* case, which dealt with the power of parents independently to commit their adolescent child to a state psychiatric hospital. The Court observed:

> Our jurisprudence historically has reflected Western Civilization concepts of the family as a unit with broad parental authority over minor children. . . . The law's concept of the family rests on a presumption that parents possess what a child lacks in maturity, experience, and capacity for judgment required for making life's difficult decisions. More important, historically it has recognized that natural bonds of affection lead parents to act in the best interests of their children. . . . Most children, even in adolescence, simply are not able to make sound judgments concerning many decisions, including their

need for medical care or treatment. Parents can and must make those judgments. (*Parham v. J.R.*, 442 U.S. 584, 610 [1979])

In the *Parham* case, the Court held that the Constitution required only minimal procedural safeguards to review such psychiatric admissions.

On the other hand, there are situations in which it is unclear who should make decisions for the child. For example, who decides what position a child should take in a child custody dispute between his or her parents? Who decides what placement or forms of treatment are appropriate for a child who is a ward of the court? What happens when an adolescent is strongly opposed to a decision made by a treatment provider or educator and the parent is unavailable or unwilling to take a position on the appropriateness of the treatment? What happens if a treatment provider, such as a physician, believes that a parent's decisions are endangering the child or are self-serving and not in the child's best interest?

In most of these cases, a court will appoint an attorney to represent the child. However, that is only the beginning of the problem. The attorney must decide what position to advocate on behalf of his or her client. The attorney's perspective on this decision often brings him or her into conflict with treatment providers. Treatment providers believe that they are working in the young person's best interest although they may not be acting in accordance with the desires expressed by the youth. An attorney, on the other hand, except when working with very young children, is responsible for representing the expressed wishes of the client.

In practice, this means that the attorney will often be thwarting the plan of treatment professionals and may, in the view of the treatment professional, be acting against the clients' best interest. For example, a child who is a ward of the court may wish to be discharged from a psychiatric treatment facility. The child's therapist may strongly and sincerely believe that discharge will damage the child and interfere with the child's ability to regain moral functioning. Even if the therapist is right, the child's attorney has an obligation to advocate for the child's expressed position and to use every legal means to secure the child's release. It is the job of the court, not the attorney, to mediate between the client and the facility and, where appropriate, decide what is in the child's best interest.

There are two exceptions to this principle. The first is when the child is too young to express a coherent or reasoned point of view. Even then, however, the attorney is obligated to seek a neutral evaluation of what is in the child's interest rather than uncritically accept the view of professionals whose interests may overtly or subtly be opposed to those of the client. The second exception, which also occurs primarily in cases involving young children, is when the opinion the child expresses is not, in fact, the child's real opinion, but has been influenced by some outside consideration. For example, a sexually abused child may cover for a perpetrator in order to protect other members of the family. Again, in this case the attorney has an obligation to obtain neutral professional assistance in ascertaining the child's real views.

The question of who speaks for the child becomes even more serious when the child's point of view conflicts with those of the parents. An attorney faces a dilemma when a parent insists that a child take one course of action and the child resists. Parents—particularly those who are paying the attorney's fee—resent the fact that the attorney takes direction from the child rather than from them. Even more resentment is generated when the client cannot express a point of view, but the attorney concludes that the client's best interest is served by something other than the stated goals of a parent or a professional. For example, the parents of a developmentally disabled client may want that client placed in an institutional environment. The professional operating that institution may agree that the child can be well served there. The attorney, on the other hand, may conclude that the child can benefit from and is legally entitled to placement in a less restrictive environment. In that case the attorney is ethically obligated to argue for the less restrictive placement. It is important to realize that, in these situations, the attorney does not claim to be entitled to make decisions for the child. The attorney claims only to be representing the child and so the child's point of view. It is the court or other arbitrator who will decide what action should be taken, after considering not only the child's view, but also the child's interest and the views and interests of the others who are concerned. In these circumstances, it is the court that has taken the role of the parent, not the attorney.

How Are Decisions Made?

Another potential source of misunderstanding between attorneys and other child-serving professionals is the attorneys' focus on procedural fairness. To justify permitting one individual to usurp the decision-making authority of another, a system must be in place that assures the fairness of the decisions that are made. Unquestionably, such systems have costs. Balancing the conflicting interests is extremely difficult. The complaint of the teacher quoted at the beginning of this chapter is typical. Attorneys are comfortable with and insist upon a formalistic procedure in meting out rewards and, particularly, punishments. Treatment professionals usually favor the spontaneous, immediate imposition of consequences.

There is a reason for this focus on procedure beyond an attorney's comfort and familiarity with procedural issues. While immediate, flexible consequences may in most cases be effective, they also lend themselves to discrimination and abuse. The requirement that formal procedures be followed helps ensure that children will benefit from fair and impartial decision making in which all the facts are considered and the effects of prejudices of the individual imposing the decision are minimized. While treatment providers generally seek the broadest discretion, lawyers are cautious by training and would rather overprotect most clients than leave even a few clients in danger. Procedural due process is necessarily conceived with the most abusive, least competent or effective treatment person in mind. It is designed to protect against that person's inefficiency or unfairness. Unfortunately, some attorneys may act as though these negative assumptions reflect reality in each case. Conversely, an educator or therapist may feel that the procedural protections are a personal insult, that they imply that he or she is incompetent and abusive. Both parties fail to realize that these procedures are simply general safeguards that can be applied to any situation.

Although the attitude of the teacher in the opening vignette reflects the view that youth have too many procedural rights, the law generally gives less weight to the legal interests of a young person than to those of an adult. Even in the context of the potential loss of freedom in a delinquency case, the Supreme Court has said that a juvenile's interest "must be qualified by the recognition that juveniles, unlike adults, are always in some form of custody" (*Schall v. Martin*, 467 U.S. 253 [1984]). In this respect, the juvenile's liberty interest may, in appropriate circumstances, be subordinated to the state's *parens patriae* interest in preserving and promoting the welfare of the child.

In determining the scope of procedural protections required, the courts consider a number of factors. One of these factors is the reason for the action that is proposed. Generally, this breaks down to a discussion of whether the purpose is to benefit the young person or to advance a separate social interest, such as protection of society or discipline in the schools. The more the proposed action is truly advanced to promote the best interests of the child, the more leeway the law gives decision makers. Naturally, many actions have mixed purposes, or their purported purpose is different from their real one. In these circumstances, a court will look closely at the real consequences of the proposed action.

The classic example of this is the *Gault* case (*In re Gault*, 387 U.S. 1 [1967]), which imposed detailed procedural protections on juvenile delinquency adjudications. For years, prior to *Gault*, juveniles did not have a right to counsel or other hearing rights comparable to those in the adult criminal justice system. The rationale was that the juvenile justice system was designed to help young people, not punish them; therefore, even though juveniles lost their liberty, full procedural safeguards were not needed. The Supreme Court closely examined the actual workings of the juvenile justice system and observed that the child seemed to "receive the worst of both worlds: he gets neither the protections accorded adults nor the solicitous care and regenerative treatment postulated for children" (387 U.S. 1, 18 n.23). The Court concluded, "Juvenile Court history has again demonstrated that unbridled discretion, however benevolently motivated, is frequently a poor substitute for principle and procedure" (387 U.S. at 18).

Another factor that the law considers in determining the scope of procedural safeguards required is the risk of error. One aspect of this is the ability of the decision makers to make the type of judgments needed. In *Gault*, the court was highly skeptical of social workers and juvenile court personnel's ability really to know what would be of benefit to troubled youth. The Court quoted approvingly from an article that stated that "few fields exist in which more serious coercive measures are applied, on such flimsy objective evidence, than in that of juvenile delinquency" (387 U.S. at 19 n.25).

Gault led the way for a series of cases that mandated procedural protections for children. In doing so, the Court presented a lengthy analysis on the importance of procedural protections:

> Failure to observe the fundamental requirements of due process has resulted in instances, which might have been avoided, of unfairness to individuals and inadequate or inaccurate findings of fact and unfortunate prescriptions of remedy. Due process of law is the primary and indispensable foundation of individual freedom. It is the basic and essential term in the social compact which defines the rights of the individual and delimits the powers which the state may exercise. As Mr. Justice Frankfurter has said: "The history of

American freedom is, in no small measure, the history of procedure." . . .
It is [the] instruments of due process which enhance the possibility that
truth will emerge from the confrontation of opposing versions and conflicting
data. "Procedure is to law what scientific method is to science." (*Gault*,
pp. 1439-1440)

School disciplinary procedures are an example of the legal system's
efforts to harmonize conflicting interests when dealing with troubled
adolescents. Minor sanctions, such as verbal reprimands, detention, and
other forms of in-school discipline, are left almost completely to the discretion of appropriate school personnel. Short-term suspensions from
school require some procedural protections, including verbal notice
of the charges and an opportunity for the student to explain his or
her version of the facts to a somewhat neutral arbiter (usually a principal). Long-term exclusions from school (more than 5 or 10 days)
require much more elaborate procedures, including written notice of the
charges, presentation of evidence, the right for the student to be represented by counsel, and other safeguards.

Who Wins and Who Loses?

Perhaps the greatest cause of conflict between attorneys and treatment providers is the adversarial nature of the legal system. In representing a client, the attorney is ethically obligated to try to obtain the
result that the client wants, regardless of the effects of that result (unless
the result would be illegal or in itself unethical). In addition, the
achievement of that result becomes a victory for the lawyer and his or
her client and a defeat for "the other side," those who opposed that
result. Once the legal system is brought into play, the situation often
ceases to be a problem in which everyone will benefit from an appropriate resolution and becomes a contest in which one party will be
proven right and the other wrong. Unfortunately, this is one aspect of
the legal system that treatment providers also sometimes buy into, and,
rather than defusing the conflict, they set out to vindicate their own
position.

The maintenance of an adversarial posture does serve a valuable
function in juvenile cases. It corrects the tendency that adults have to
disregard the child's point of view entirely and in effect to conspire with
treatment professionals to force the child to do what is good for him or

her rather than what he or she wants. When the attorney takes this role the due-process protections become empty form. They really are, in that case, only red tape without any purpose. On the other hand, an unyieldingly adversarial approach on either side stands in the way of effectively resolving the differences of opinion and securing for the child the most appropriate, acceptable, effective treatment possible.

Rather than being purely adversarial, in many situations mandated procedural safeguards can also be therapeutic. They can teach a child that the system operates in a fair and objective manner and that the child's and parents' views are valued. This can produce cooperation that benefits all concerned parties. This was one of the goals of the individual education plan (IEP) process mandated by federal and state special education laws (see, for example, the Education for the Handicapped Act, 20 U.S.C. § 1400 *et seq.*). The IEP process is intended to be a cooperative one in which children, parents, teachers, and other professionals have a say in what services the school provides. If there is a disagreement, elaborate hearing procedures are set up by which the child, parents, and school officials can assert their rights. In part, this is a reaction to school districts that were unwilling or unable to deal with certain types of children. On the other hand, it also reflects a positive view of treatment as a cooperative process rather than as a one-way street from the professional to the client.

Summary

There are obviously inherent conflicts between the points of view of attorneys and those of treatment professionals. Differences in basic assumptions lead to hostility and resentment. Children's attorneys often see treatment professionals as insensitive to clients' opinions at best and money or power hungry at worst. Treatment professionals see attorneys as manipulative and arrogant individuals who understand neither the clients' needs nor the pressures of the system that impairs their ability to provide the perfect service to every client. Nevertheless, the best practitioners in both fields have a common interest in the welfare of their clients in general and of children in particular. There should be effective ways to overcome the adverse effects of their differences without eliminating them.

Many social service systems are moving toward coordinating services for children. They are attempting to bring all individuals and agencies who serve children together to resolve the children's problems. One first step toward breaking down barriers would be to include attorneys in this process. Attorneys for children would assist in planning systems so that they include necessary procedures to protect children's rights. At the same time, service providers can help shape these procedures so that they are consistent with optimal treatment. In working together each group can begin to assimilate the positive aspects of other's worldview and to improve its effectiveness in serving children.

Note

1. At the time of this writing, the Court is considering two other juvenile death penalty cases, one of which involves a 17-year-old who was only a few days short of 18 at the time he committed his crime.

3

Troubled Youth
in the Public Schools

Emotionally Disturbed
or Socially Maladjusted?

C. MICHAEL NELSON
ROBERT B. RUTHERFORD, Jr.

Students who exhibit antisocial, acting-out behavior have been thorns
in the side of the American educational system since its beginning.
Determining the extent to which public schools are responsible for
the education of such youth is an issue many school officials would
prefer to avoid or to respond to with policies that exclude them from
the school setting entirely. P.L. 94-142, the Education of the Handicapped Act of 1975 (EHA), did little to alleviate the confusion concerning this issue; the student population defined for services under the label
seriously emotionally disturbed (SED) specifically excludes "children
who are socially maladjusted, unless it is determined that they are
seriously emotionally disturbed" (U.S. Department of Health, Education and Welfare, 1977, p. 42478). In other words, the federal definition
of the SED excludes from consideration those pupils whose behaviors
indicate social maladjustment rather than an underlying emotional
disturbance.

One of the factors affecting the abilities of policymakers and researchers to clarify this issue is the lack of a generally accepted definition of social maladjustment. The term is based on the concept that

certain youths are socialized in a deviant cultural group; that is, their behavior and attitudes are shaped by a social context that encourages them to act in ways that violate the standards and mores of the mainstream culture. However, it is assumed that these individuals are not emotionally disturbed because their behavior is in accordance with the norms of their immediate reference group. The behavior patterns that are considered "normative" of this deviant culture are termed *delinquent*, and the identification of juveniles as delinquent typically is made by the legal system, indicating that the youth in question has been adjudicated by the courts and found guilty of criminal behavior or a "status offense" (defined as behavior judged to be deviant in a minor, such as alcohol consumption, that would not be illegal if performed by an adult). Delinquent behavior, therefore, is considered to be any act that is illegal when performed by a person under the age of majority (i.e., 18 in most states). The term *antisocial behavior*, which is used to describe behavior patterns indicative of social maladjustment, is less restrictive than juvenile delinquency because it includes behaviors that are norm-violating but not necessarily delinquent. Simcha-Fagan, Langner, Gersten, and Eisenberg (1975; cited in Walker, Shinn, O'Neill, & Ramsey, 1987, p. 7) define antisocial behavior as "the recurrent violation of socially prescribed patterns of action." This definition does not assert that such behavior is normative with regard to an immediate cultural group.

A major issue in defining behavior that is representative of social maladjustment but not of serious emotional disturbance appears to be whether the norms of the reference group are deviant relative to the mainstream culture. Therefore, the standards and values of the youth's peer group are important considerations, as well as whether the individual is a member of a deviant social group, such as a delinquent gang (Miller, 1958). Moreover, several demographic factors appear to be associated with an increased probability that a youth will engage in delinquent behavior, including (a) problems in school; (b) low verbal intelligence; (c) parents who are alcoholic or who have frequent arrests; (d) family reliance on welfare, or poor management of income; (e) homes that are broken, crowded, or chaotic; (f) erratic parental supervision and inadequate discipline; (g) parental and sibling indifference or hostility toward the youth; and (h) substance abuse (Kauffman, 1989). These factors also are strongly correlated with serious emotional disturbance. The demographic similarities, the subjectivity inherent in identifying pupils as SED (Benson, Edwards, Rosell, & White, 1986;

Kauffman, 1987, 1989), and the absence of any valid evidence or thought that justifies differentiating between social maladjustment and SED (Grosenick & Huntze, 1980) render the attempted distinction between these groups meaningless.

The position taken in this chapter is that the exclusion of the socially maladjusted from the federal definition is unfounded: It is not supported by research, scholarly opinion, or good professional practice. Further, there are no instruments or methodology that can be used validly or reliably to diagnose SED differentially from social maladjustment. In our view, the problem of delivering effective services to troubled youth supersedes that of differentially diagnosing an adolescent as emotionally disturbed or socially maladjusted. The time spent in attempts at differential diagnosis seldom results in more effective treatment, and the label resulting from this process may allow school personnel to abrogate responsibility by claiming that socially maladjusted youth do not qualify for "special" educational provisions or program modifications. The specific purposes of this chapter are (a) to describe educational services for pupils who exhibit deviant social behavior, (b) to present current approaches to serving troubled youth in the schools, and (c) to explore problems and issues associated with the exclusion of youth identified as socially maladjusted from special education services in the public schools. These purposes are addressed first through an examination of educational services for troubled youth and the evidence demonstrating that socially maladjusted and SED pupils functionally represent the same population in terms of sociocultural demographics, overt behaviors, and appropriate educational practices to meet their needs. Second, a number of implications of narrowly defined special education eligibility definitions and school policies are discussed. Finally, recommendations for improving educational services to youth exhibiting deviant social behavior are offered.

Practices in Public Schools
and the Juvenile Justice System

Development of
Educational Interventions for Troubled Youth

Educational interventions for troubled youth did not emerge as an approach to treatment in their own right until the early 1950s (Kauffman,

1989). Prior to that time, students who displayed socially deviant behavior were excluded from schools, and educational programs for children and youth identified as emotionally disturbed were generally viewed as adjunctive, at best, to the overall therapeutic process, while medicine and psychiatry determined the course of diagnosis and treatment. An exception is the 600 Schools, developed in the late 1940s by the New York City Board of Education to provide educational treatment for emotionally disturbed and socially maladjusted students (Berkowitz & Rothman, 1960). During the 1950s, special day schools (e.g., the League School, Fenichel, 1966; the Orthogenic School, Bettleheim, 1950) were established to serve children with serious emotional disturbances. In the 1950s and 1960s, highly structured special classroom programs in public schools were developed for pupils with moderate to severe behavioral disorders in the public schools (e.g., Haring & Phillips, 1962; Hewett, 1968). In that same decade, Project Re-ED was developed to serve children with emotional and behavioral problems through a residential program based on an ecological model that emphasized teaching rather than treatment and learning instead of personality change (Hobbs, 1965; Rhodes, 1967).

Educational Services for Troubled Adolescents

Educational services for delinquent, socially maladjusted, and seriously emotionally disturbed adolescents have traditionally lagged behind services for younger troubled children (Nelson & Kauffman, 1977) and children and youth with other special education needs (Long, 1983). Education and treatment programs for delinquent and emotionally disturbed adolescents have developed along separate, although occasionally overlapping, tracks.

Socially maladjusted students have a high probability of being served by both the juvenile justice and educational systems. However, these systems have different eligibility criteria, population definitions, and philosophies or priorities (i.e., security versus education).

Because of the availability of more resources and larger student populations, the continuum of services available for behaviorally disordered students (those identified and labeled as SED) in the public schools generally is more extensive than in the juvenile justice system. This continuum includes (a) placement in regular classrooms with no special provisions (an option provided to students who are not identified as handicapped for educational purposes); (b) regular classroom placement with consultation to the teacher by specialized support staff (for pupils who are "at risk" for special education certification, or those who are certified and placed in mainstream settings for part or all of the day); (c) placement in special education resource rooms for part of the day, where students' academic and/or social skills deficits are addressed; (d) placement in a segregated, self-contained special education class for part or all of the school day; and (e) placement in the segregated public day school. These programs, if available, typically are offered within a public school district. Another placement option frequently used with behaviorally disordered pupils is homebound instruction, in which the student remains out of school and an itinerant teacher provides instruction in the home. We choose not to assign homebound instruction a place in the public school continuum of services because it is not a service that is provided within the schools, nor is homebound instruction usually a systematic intervention. In addition, placement options outside the school district may be offered through two more levels of the service delivery continuum: (f) placement in a residential school program (which may be funded by the public school system or by another agency) and (g) placement in a residential treatment program (which includes a range of medical and therapeutic services). Underlying this continuum are the assumptions that the majority of students with behavioral disorders will be served at the upper (less restrictive) levels, and that placement in lower (more restrictive) levels will be reserved for pupils exhibiting more serious behavioral or emotional disturbances. However, three-fourths of all certified behaviorally disordered students (those labeled as SED) in the public schools are educated in self-contained or more restrictive settings (Walker & Fabre, 1987). In contrast, the U.S. Department of Education (1985) reports that 68% of the overall handicapped population are receiving their education in regular classrooms.

Commonalities in the Education of Emotionally Disturbed and Socially Maladjusted Pupils

Educational interventions for delinquent, socially maladjusted, and emotionally disturbed children and youth converged at several points in the recent past. The alternative education movement of the 1960s, which was initially designed for behaviorally "normal" students, was modified in a number of instances to serve emotionally disturbed students (Mesinger, 1986). At the same time, there was a trend away from incarceration of juvenile delinquents in large correctional institutions to placement in community-based alternative programs (Margolis, 1988). These concurrent trends resulted in a number of delinquent and disturbed youth being placed in the same alternative education programs.

Disturbed and delinquent students also often have been the recipients of the same regular education responses to their deviant behavior. Initially, these students might have received a continuum of public school treatment options including counseling, school psychology or social work services, and, perhaps, referral to community-based education and mental health programs. These students are also likely to have been exposed to such public school disciplinary procedures as detention, corporal punishment, in-school suspension, out-of-school suspension, and exclusion (Rose, 1989). However, before students identified as seriously emotionally disturbed are eligible for these disciplinary options, minimal due-process procedures must be implemented. Currently, some states are recertifying a number of emotionally disturbed students into non-special education categories (e.g., socially maladjusted or conduct disordered) in order to be able to apply disciplinary sanctions more freely and to avoid legal penalties for excluding them from public schools (Center, 1988).

The use of applied behavior analysis technology is another area in which educational interventions for both disturbed and delinquent youth have overlapped. Hewett (1968), Haring and Phillips (1962), Whelan (Whelan & Haring, 1966), Walker (Walker & Buckley, 1972), and Patterson (1975), among others, have designed behavioral intervention programs for behaviorally disordered and disturb youth. Simultaneously, a large behavioral literature was developing in the treatment of delinquency (see Rutherford & Swist, 1976). Achievement Place (Phillips, 1968), a behaviorally oriented treatment program for predelinquent youths, has been developed into a widely disseminated group-home treatment model known as the Teaching Family Model (Phillips, Phillips, Fixsen, & Wolf, 1974). Many components of effective behavioral interventions (e.g., behavioral contracts, token economies, data-based decision making) have been applied with both groups of students.

A fourth point of congruence in programming for emotionally disturbed and socially maladjusted youth is the acknowledgment by a number of professionals that these students have the same educational and treatment needs and that, in fact, the research literature supports the position that delinquency or social maladjustment is a handicapping condition (Rutherford, Nelson, & Wolford, 1985; Wolf, Braukmann, & Ramp, 1987). However, as pointed out in the preceding discussion, students who are considered to be socially maladjusted youth currently are not eligible for special education services under P.L. 94-142.

Definitional Ambiguity

The Education for All Handicapped Children Act specifically defines seriously emotionally disturbed as follows:

(i) A condition exhibiting one or more of the following characteristics over a long period of time and to a marked degree, which adversely affects educational performance: a. An inability to learn which cannot be explained by intellectual, sensory, or health factors; b. An inability to build or maintain satisfactory interpersonal relationships with peers and teachers; c. Inappropriate types of behavior or feelings under normal circumstances; d. A general pervasive mood of unhappiness or depression; or e. A tendency to develop physical symptoms or fears associated with personal or school problems.

(ii) The term includes children who are schizophrenic or autistic. The term does not include children who are socially maladjusted, unless it is determined that they are seriously emotionally disturbed. (U.S. Department of Health, Education and Welfare, 1977, p. 42478)

This definition of emotional disturbance proposed by the federal government and adopted, in similar form, by a number of state education agencies, is based upon Bower's 1957 definition of emotional disturbance. As Bower (1982) himself points out, section i of the federal definition is an exact restatement of his definition except for the word *seriously*. Section ii does not appear in Bower's original definition and, as Bower states, appears to be "a codicil to reassure traditional psychopathologists and budget personnel that schizophrenia and autism are indeed serious emotional disturbance on the one hand, and that just plain bad boys and girls, predelinquents, and sociopaths will not skyrocket the costs on the other hand" (p. 56).

The ambiguity of this definition has led many school district administrators to look for guidance from authorities to help them decide who should and should not qualify for special education under the SED label or its equivalent. An attorney has responded to this need with her own interpretation of the EHA definition (Slenkovitch, 1983, 1984), based on psychiatric diagnoses from the *Diagnostic and Statistical Manual,* third edition (DSM III, American Psychiatric Association, 1980). With regard to the exclusion of the socially maladjusted, Slenkovitch (1984) states unequivocally:

> Students may not be placed in special education by virtue of being socially maladjusted, may not be found to be seriously emotionally disturbed because they are behavior disordered, may not be found to be seriously emotionally disturbed because they are antisocial, may not be found to be seriously emotionally disturbed because they have conduct disorders. The law does not allow it. (p. 293)

Social maladjustment is not an EHA serious emotional disturbance. Slenkovitch further asserts that the DSM III diagnostic categories of Conduct Disorder, Antisocial Personality Disorder, and Oppositional Disorder are exempt from the EHA. Students who have been given one of those diagnoses are not eligible for special education unless they also have been assigned another diagnosis that does qualify. That an attorney is making such proclamations about educational classification and diagnostic issues is merely curious; however, it is alarming that she has influenced many school administrators and several state departments to declare students ineligible for special education services if they do not meet this rigid interpretation of the EHA definition.

Neel and Rutherford (1981) suggest a number of possible explanations for why socially maladjusted youth are excluded from eligibility for special education services under P.L. 94-142, including the views that (a) socially maladjusted students are not truly handicapped; (b) many of them will be better served under programs for other existing handicaps where the social maladjustment is but a secondary condition resulting from another, more readily identifiable, handicap; (c) these students' needs are better served either in the general school population, with its own treatment and discipline options, or through the juvenile justice system; and (d) there is no clear educational definition of the term *socially maladjusted*, and the criteria used to identify these students are vague, arbitrary, and sometimes capricious.

One or Two Populations?

The research literature, professional opinion, and professional practice in the education and treatment of troubled youth support the position that socially maladjusted students are handicapped by their behavior and should be included in special education services for handicapped students. The specific exclusion of socially maladjusted youth in the definition of the seriously emotionally disturbed makes the definition "nonsensical by any conventional logic" (Kauffman, 1980, p. 524).

Research studies indicate that social maladjustment is a significant and durable handicapping condition in many children, adolescents, and adults. Walker et al. (1987) conducted a longitudinal assessment of the development of antisocial behavior of boys in school settings. These investigators found that antisocial students experienced significantly greater school failure and had experienced much greater exposure to special education services and/or placements than other students. Specifically, antisocial students exhibited significantly less academic engaged time in instructional settings, initiated and were involved in significantly more negative interactions with peers, and were rated by their teachers as substantially less content and/or adjusted than other students. Shinn, Ramsey, Walker, Stieber, and O'Neill (1987), in a replication of the Walker et al. (1987) study, also found that antisocial students displayed less academic engaged time during instruction, had higher rates of verbally negative behavior during peer interactions, were perceived by teachers as less socially skilled, and had school records documenting greater numbers of serious discipline problems and greater exposure to special education services than their nonantisocial peers.

Walker et al. (1987) suggest that if antisocial students continue to exhibit these problems over time, they will be at an increased risk for school failure, membership in deviant peer groups, school dropout, and eventual delinquency. "The long-term developmental implications for children who display this behavior pattern are extremely serious" (Walker et al., 1987, p. 15).

Antisocial behaviors present in childhood have been found to be remarkably persistent. Robins (1979) reports that delinquents-to-be do poorly in school, challenge the teacher's authority, are truant, and are unpopular with their peers. In her classic follow-up study of deviant children, Robins (1966) found that juvenile antisocial behavior was the single most powerful predictor of adult psychiatric status. (For a further discussion of the development of antisocial behavior in children, see Dishion, Chapter 7, this volume.)

Studies of the prevalence of handicapping conditions among juvenile delinquents indicate that a high percentage of youthful offenders exhibit learning and behavioral handicaps, and that the prevalence of certain disabilities is much greater among this population than among the general population of children and youth (Murphy, 1986). Morgan (1979) conducted a national survey of state juvenile correctional administrators and found that 42% of youthful offenders were identified as handicapped according to P.L. 94-142 criteria. Rutherford et al. (1985) conducted a national survey of state directors of special education and state directors of correctional education. The prevalence estimates of these administrators indicated that an average of 28% of offenders incarcerated in state correctional facilities in the United States were handicapped. In comparison, the Office of Special Education Programs reported that in 1984-1985, 10.76% of all children enrolled in kindergarten through twelfth grade were handicapped (Murphy, 1986).

Some may argue that the prevalence of handicapping conditions other than SED among incarcerated juvenile offenders demonstrates that all socially maladjusted youth are not behaviorally disordered (emotionally disturbed). Moreover, it can be argued that, because not all incarcerated youths are classified as handicapped under P.L. 94-142, social maladjustment does not constitute a handicapping condition. Our response to these arguments is that, first, the research we have just cited (Robins, 1966, 1979; Shinn et al., 1987; Walker et al., 1987) indicates that the school performance of antisocial pupils places them at significant risk for eventual classification in one of the traditional mildly handicapped categories. Second, there is considerable overlap among the mildly handicapped categories. As Kauffman (1989) observes, many students labeled SED demonstrate learning disabilities and measured intelligence in the mildly retarded range. Third, the classification of students into categories according to their handicapping conditions is influenced by political, social, and judgmental factors. That is, whether a pupil is identified is influenced by what the school or correctional program wishes to do with him and what (if any) special education programs are available. The lack of a clear definition of social maladjustment and identification criteria also contributes to the failure to recognize antisocial pupils as at risk in terms of their special education needs. Fourth, as with other handicapping conditions, social maladjustment exists on a continuum from mild to severe. Distinctions among mild, moderate, and severe degrees of some recognized handicapping conditions (e.g., SED) are very hard to make, and efforts to do so with the socially maladjusted are nonexistent. We are not suggesting that youths who commit a single antisocial act should be identified as handicapped any more than should a student who fails a single test or who exhibits a transient behavior problem. However, we do believe that youths who demonstrate continued patterns of antisocial behavior should be screened and considered at risk in terms of needing special education services. Finally, the exclusionary clause in the federal definition of SED encourages authorities not to declare socially maladjusted youth as handicapped.

Professional opinion also indicates that antisocial, delinquent, and socially maladjusted youth are handicapped. Wolf et al. (1987) contend that delinquency, especially when persistent and serious, is a "social disability" that is profoundly limiting to those who exhibit this condition. These authors suggest that children with serious delinquent behaviors may be predisposed from an early age to engage their environments in antisocial and dysfunctional ways.

Kauffman (1989) points out that it requires a curious turn of logic to conclude that many youthful offenders are not entitled to special education services under P.L. 94-142. If serious emotional and behavioral disorders include both overt and covert antisocial behaviors, then finding incarcerated youths who are not behaviorally disordered is a logical impossibility. He further suggests that all or nearly all incarcerated youth are handicapped, if Arnold and Brungardt's (1983) contention (that higher levels of delinquent conduct indicate higher levels of psychopathology) is correct, and if the assumption that those who commit frequent and serious delinquent acts are more likely to be incarcerated is accurate. Finally, Kauffman suggests that if serious antisocial behaviors are not defined as handicapping conditions under the law, then logically indefensible distinctions are drawn between emotional disturbance and social maladjustment.

Professional opinion also indicates that socially maladjusted and emotionally disturbed students cannot be differentially diagnosed. Bower notes that although the definition of emotional disturbance is based upon his 1957 definition, the exclusion of the socially maladjusted does not make sense because he operationally and conceptually defined the emotionally disturbed by the social maladjustments they exhibited. As Bower (1982) states, "The emotionally disturbed child as defined in the Bower study had to be socially maladjusted in school" (p. 58).

Kerr, Nelson, and Lambert (1987) point out that even if the antisocial and frequently illegal behavior of socially maladjusted youth conforms to the standards of their deviant cultural or peer group, it is difficult to see how they can be logically separated from the population of seriously emotionally disturbed students because their behavior *does* violate the norms of the larger social order and is not considered normative or tolerable by the schools. They suggest that these youth should be considered educationally handicapped because most of them exhibit serious learning problems and most have not responded well to traditional school curricula and practices. These pupils need individualized, functional educational experiences rather than a continuation of the teaching approaches that have led to their alienation from the schools. If school authorities were to accept that socially maladjusted youth are eligible for special education services, the issues of definition, eligibility, curriculum, and service delivery models become problems to solve, not reasons for exclusion (Neel & Rutherford, 1981). If socially maladjusted students are characterized by the antisocial behaviors they exhibit, then specialized instruction must be designed to teach appropriate social skills that other pupils learn informally.

In pointing out that P.L. 94-142 provides no clear criteria for distinguishing emotionally disturbed from socially maladjusted children, Long (1983) suggests that

> the key issue is not whether all troublesome children should be labeled emotionally disturbed, but rather, whether the schools, and in the final analysis society, would not be better served if all children who represent aggressive, disruptive behavior, regardless of how they were labeled, received special attention and help early in their lives. The distinction drawn between emotionally disturbed and socially maladjusted children appears to be not only arbitrary and unrealistic, but detrimental as well. (p. 53)

Professional practice also supports treating seriously emotionally disturbed and socially maladjusted students as the same. Currently over two-thirds of the states do not mention the exclusion of socially maladjusted students in their state definitions of emotional disturbance or behavioral disorders (Mack, 1985). Benson (1981) found that, in a sample of state definitions, none offered any criteria or methodology for excluding socially maladjusted students. Although several states recently have attempted to decertify conduct-disordered or socially maladjusted students from special education services based upon Slenkovitch's (1983) interpretation of the distinctions between serious emotional disturbance and social maladjustment, it is apparent that most states have intentionally not imitated the federal model of an exclusionary clause in their definition of students with behavioral or emotional handicaps.

Problems Associated with
Excluding Socially Maladjusted Pupils

In the preceding section we argued that there is no logical or empirical basis for excluding socially maladjusted students from special education programs and that such youth are, in fact, handicapped. The failure to identify as handicapped those students who exhibit chronic antisocial behavior increases the likelihood that they will continue to be deprived of appropriate services by the educational system. However, we also recognize that the education system alone cannot effectively prevent or treat antisocial behavior.

In advocating for broader inclusion of pupils in special education programs for the behaviorally disordered, we are not suggesting that the problems of socially maladjusted students can be solved merely by placing them in special education programs. However, we do believe that special education programs for students with behavioral disorders provide (or should provide) individualized instruction that addresses their academic and social skills deficits. If pupils are identified and given appropriate services early enough in their school careers, perhaps some will be deterred from behavior patterns leading to chronic social maladjustment and lifelong dependence on social welfare, mental health, and correctional services.

We are skeptical that the educational system in general has met the needs of socially maladjusted youth. However, we do believe that schools could have an important role in addressing the complex problem of identifying and treating social maladjustment, and that currently they do not. (For a discussion of schools' contribution to troublesome behavior, see Everhart, Chapter 13, this volume.) The following discussion focuses on the practices of public education agencies that restrict their ability to perform socially important functions.

First, the public schools have not been able to deal effectively with disruptive and delinquent behavior in school settings. Testimony regarding this failure has been widespread in both the media and the professional literature. As Kauffman (1989) observes, assault and victimization of teachers and children, theft, extortion, vandalism, drug and alcohol abuse, and even sexual acting-out behavior can occur daily in and around schools. The school's typical response to problem behavior (detention, corporal punishment, and exclusion) "is woefully inadequate, and does little more than maintain a semblance of order and prevent total abandonment of its traditional programs" (Kauffman, 1989, p. 314). Although school programs that offer a high degree of structure, academic remediation and social skills instruction have produced improvements in attendance and academic progress while reducing delinquent behavior and the need for exclusionary discipline (Safer, 1982), research does not support the long-term effects of such programs. Kauffman (1989) indicates that one factor may be that such interventions usually are supported by state or federal grants, and that programs are discontinued when funding ends.

Second, efforts to identify, diagnose, or differentiate various categories of pupils in terms of who is and who is not eligible for special education services on the basis of such elusive and unreliable criteria as SED versus social maladjustment, conduct disorder, and the like, are misplaced. It is true that not all students should qualify for services that are expensive and in short supply. The right of each student to be educated in the least restrictive environment also must be recognized; that is, educators should determine that the regular education program cannot meet pupils' needs before more restrictive class placements are considered. However, the practice of sorting students into one group that receives services and another group that does not is indefensible. It is now recognized that students who exhibit problematic behavior in the school setting are at risk in terms of potentially needing special education and related services (Kauffman, 1989; Kerr & Nelson, 1989; Walker & Fabre, 1987). The needs of at-risk pupils should be addressed in less restrictive settings through prereferral interventions as a prior condition to determining their eligibility for special education programs. Unfortunately, such practices are rare in the majority of school districts, the "Regular Education Initiative" notwithstanding (Braaten, Kauffman, Braaten, Polsgrove, & Nelson, 1988). As a result, the majority of students exhibiting undesirable behavior receive no services, or inadequate services, in regular education programs. If they are unlucky enough to reside in a state or school district in which they have been labeled as antisocial but not handicapped, they may be suspended, expelled, or shunted into a variety of "alternative" placements. After years of failure and exclusion, some drop out, or are pushed out, of school. Others find their way into institutions and programs for delinquents by virtue of their behavior in the community. In either case, schools fail to recognize or meet the special education needs of students with antisocial behavior patterns.

Third, even special education programs have not demonstrated the ability to prevent or treat delinquent behavior successfully. Pupils with academic and social problems are especially prone to fail at the task of independent adult living. The substantial overrepresentation of educationally handicapped youth in juvenile and adult correctional education programs (Murphy, 1986; Rutherford et al., 1985) bears witness to the tendency for school failure to be associated with social failure, particularly when combined with the "bad demographics" cited earlier (e.g., lower-class culture, broken homes, parental irresponsibility and neglect). These statistics may be used as evidence of the intractability of antisocial behavior patterns (e.g., Walker et al., 1987; Wolf et al., 1987), or to support the contention that the schools are failing to meet the needs of many youth (e.g., Edgar, 1987). As Kauffman (1989) asserts: "Public schools fail many of these students. Many students experience constant academic failure, are functionally illiterate when they end their schooling, do not acquire the skills that will allow for gainful employment, are social misfits, and drop out of school before the age of 16" (p. 314).

We believe that both perspectives are valid. Schools were not designed as institutions to meet the needs of the socially maladjusted; rather, they were intended to prepare young persons for the basic responsibilities of citizenship through formal academic instruction and to inculcate in them accepted social values and behaviors through the cultural milieu of the school environment. It is a truism that schools represent and reward middle-class behaviors and values. While these are important ingredients for success in our mainstream culture, pupils who enter school from minority cultures are very much on the outside. Insensitivity to their differences and failure to respond to their needs only increase their separation from the mainstream. Little wonder, then, that many of these pupils cling to lower-class focal concerns in order to establish their identities.

Fourth, the lack of transition services and cooperative arrangements with other social service agencies perpetuates the tendency of schools to work in isolation. Edgar and his colleagues have analyzed the problems of interagency collaboration with regard to the transition of juvenile offenders between schools and correctional programs (Edgar, Webb, & Maddox, 1987; Webb, Maddox, & Edgar, 1985). They observe that human services programs have developed haphazardly, with different eligibility criteria, entrance and exit criteria, and that types of services may be available only in specific locations, requiring that clients travel to the service provider in order to receive benefits.

Recommendations

As the previous discussion indicates, many authorities observe numerous shortcomings in the public schools' response to antisocial behavior and to pupils who need interventions directed at their maladaptive behavior patterns. Therefore, it is tempting to recommend wholesale changes in the educational system, similar to the cries raised a decade ago to revolutionize schooling (see Nelson, 1977). However, calls for radical reform of the American educational system historically have fallen on deaf ears, and we think it is unlikely that such reform could be accomplished, or even seriously considered, in the present public climate. Our recommendations, therefore, will address changes that take into consideration the realities of current resources and directions in schools as well as in community services. The scope of our suggestions encompasses changes in the internal workings of schools to meet the needs of troubled youth and changes in the way schools articulate with human service agencies in the community.

Improve Services to Troubled Youth in Schools

The appalling lack of special education and related services to pupils who are handicapped by their behavior is sufficient evidence that the educational system is falling short of its charge to provide "free and appropriate" services to students who potentially qualify for special education under the existing SED definition. But we would be remiss to recommend that more students be certified and served under the existing definition, given its many inadequacies. Instead of attempting to identify and place more pupils in special education programs for the emotionally or behaviorally handicapped (i.e., focusing on the outcome of these procedures), the process of identifying and serving students in need itself should be changed. We recommend two major operational changes. First, schools should adopt systematic procedures for screening and identifying pupils who are at risk for emotional or behavioral difficulties early in their school careers. Of course, procedures to identify at-risk students must be accompanied by appropriate intervention if such activities are to be meaningful. The developing technology of prereferral interventions through teacher consultation offers strategies for mobilizing the resources of the regular education system to meet the needs of pupils before more intrusive and stigmatizing special education interventions must be considered. Johnson, Pugach, and Hammitte (1988) observe that special education consultation models have not been widely adopted because such models are incompatible with the use of available school resources. Therefore, the development of teacher assistance teams, composed of school staff identified with the general education program, may be a more effective strategy (see Fuchs & Fuchs, 1988).

The second operational change we recommend is to revise the federal definition of SED. This definition has been widely criticized by the professional community, as we have noted above. Moreover, the Council for Children with Behavioral Disorders (1987), the professional organization of special educators serving the SED population, has called for a change in both the federal definition and the label SED. The specific changes we suggest include eliminating the exclusion of the socially maladjusted and changing the definition's emphasis on interference with academic performance as a primary criterion. A more accurate conceptualization of the nature of behavioral disorders recognizes it as a condition that interferes with the development and maintenance of appropriate social relationships, regardless of whether academic progress is impaired. It should be noted, however, that the subjectivity inherent in defining behavior that is considered deviant from the norm cannot be eliminated. As Kauffman (1989) emphasizes, the definition of behavior as disordered is inescapably judgmental, regardless of how objectively the behaviors in question are measured.

Establish Standards for the
Treatment of Behavioral Disorders in Schools

The lack of clear standards for educational services to pupils who are handicapped by their behavior has in no small way contributed to the absence of programs in many school districts, as well as to the abundance of programs that are haphazard, ineffective, and even harmful to students' ability to profit from their educational experiences. Such standards should include not only a definition of behavioral disorders, but also policies and procedures for operationalizing this definition in terms of screening and identification, prereferral intervention services, comprehensive assessment procedures, eligibility and due-process criteria, and a set of "best practices" regarding the continuum of services for behaviorally disordered pupils, appropriate instructional and behavior management procedures, teacher competencies, and criteria for moving students to less restrictive educational settings and for their decertification as handicapped. The state of Iowa has developed comprehensive guidelines for such programs (Wood, Smith, & Grimes, 1985; Sodac et al., 1988). Others states, such as Ohio and Oregon, have published technical assistance manuals to facilitate professional decision making for behaviorally handicapped students. On the other hand, at least one state (Nevada) has enacted legislation to decertify pupils classified as SED on the basis of an informal checklist purporting to discriminate between the emotionally disturbed and the conduct disordered (i.e., socially maladjusted). Similar efforts are under way in other states, motivated by the exclusionary clause in P.L. 94-142, and, perhaps, by a reluctance to accept responsibility for pupils with antisocial behavior. A set of broadly disseminated standards would clarify acceptable practices and make gross deviations from accountable procedures less likely.

These standards should provide specific expectations for program developers and practitioners not only in terms of pupil/staff ratios, caseloads, identification procedures, admission and release criteria, and the like, but also in terms of the kinds of goals and objectives that are appropriate for behaviorally disordered pupils' individual education plans (IEPs), the range of related services that should be provided, the responsibilities of parents and schools for providing or procuring these services, and specific tasks required of the regular education system. We, like many of our fellow teacher educators, often are dismayed to see IEPs of behaviorally disordered students that contain no goals or objectives pertaining to social behaviors and skills, to find teachers who do not construct lesson plans based on students' IEPs, and to observe that related services are not considered in planning for individual pupils. The goal of a common set of standards is not uniformity among programs for behaviorally handicapped students so much as accountability for administrators as well as guidelines for the implementers of such programs.

**Develop Better Articulation
of Educational and Community Services**

As we have attempted to document, the needs of youngsters with behavioral disabilities often outstrip what schools are able to provide in terms of both the types and the scope of services available. This especially is the case with pupils whose antisocial behavior patterns extend into their communities. P.L. 99-457 (the 1986 amendments to the EHA) strongly encourages schools to establish programs for handicapped children ages 3 to 5, and stresses the provision of transition services to youths moving from public schools to adult situations; the multidisciplinary and multiagency collaboration required for transition planning is the type that should be incorporated into services for behaviorally disordered children of all ages. We advocate that multidisciplinary IEPs be developed for pupils identified as behaviorally handicapped—multidisciplinary in the sense that each child's full range of needs is addressed, and that the services orchestrated extend beyond school walls. Furthermore, we recommend that school and community resources be coordinated to identify and provide early intervention to families at risk—that, is, families in which there is a high probability that at least one child will develop behavioral difficulties in the school or the community. As Wolf et al. (1987) indicate, antisocial youths are likely to require "extended supportive environments" in order to meet the demands of living in our complex society. Data from programs that focus on helping parents develop more effective child-rearing practices with preschool children at risk for behavioral disorders demonstrate the wisdom of early family interventions (Johnson, 1988). By providing intensive support services to families when their children are still young, it seems likely that the need for more expensive services extending into adulthood might be avoided.

In conclusion, we believe that the problem of troubled youth in the schools cannot be addressed in a piecemeal fashion, through services that are fragmented by the service bureaucracies of human service agencies. Moreover, this problem will never be addressed if the professional community continues to engage in hairsplitting debates about whether students are emotionally disturbed and eligible for special services or socially maladjusted and therefore not entitled to special education. Differences among agencies in terms of definitions of their service populations and their eligibility criteria have been a major factor in the failure to provide effective and cost-efficient services to their clients; attempting to make such distinctions *within* an agency (the public schools) is an invitation to even greater failure. In our opinion, refusal to provide appropriate services to any pupil is an indictment of the educational system, just as the inability to solve the problem of antisocial behavior is an indictment of our society. The needs of troubled youth and their families across settings and time must be addressed through multidisciplinary planning and intervention. It may well be some time before our country is ready to take up this challenge. However, we believe that the benefits, in terms of lowering youths' risk of long-term social failure, as well as lowering the social and economic costs of delinquency (Wolf et al., 1987), are worth the efforts required to bring about such change.

References

American Psychiatric Association. (1980). *Diagnostic and statistical manual of mental disorders* (3rd ed.). Washington, DC: Author.

Arnold, W. R., & Brungardt, T. M. (1983). *Juvenile misconduct and delinquency.* Boston: Houghton Mifflin.

Benson, D. (1981). *A study of state definitions and identification criteria for students with emotional or behavioral disorders.* Denver: Colorado Department of Education.

Benson, D., Edwards, L., Rosell, J., & White, M. (1986). Inclusion of socially maladjusted children and youth in the legal definition of the behaviorally disordered population: A debate. *Behavioral Disorders, 11*, 213-222.

Berkowitz, P. H., & Rothman, E. P. (1960). *The disturbed child.* New York: New York University Press.

Bettleheim, B. (1950). *Love is not enough.* New York: Macmillan.

Bower, E. M. (1982). Defining emotional disturbances: Public policy and research. *Psychology in the Schools, 19*, 55-60.

Braaten, S. R., Kauffman, J. M., Braaten, B., Polsgrove, L., & Nelson, C. M. (1988). The Regular Education Initiative: Patent medicine for behavioral disorders. *Exceptional Children, 55*, 21-27.

Center, D. B. (1988). *Curriculum and teaching strategies for students with behavioral disorders.* Englewood Cliffs, NJ: Prentice-Hall.

Council for Children with Behavioral Disorders. (1987). *Position paper on definition and identification of students with behavioral disorders.* Reston, VA: Author.

Edgar, E. B. (1987). Secondary programs in special education: Are many of them justifiable? *Exceptional Children, 53*, 555-561.

Edgar, E. B., Webb, S. L., & Maddox, M. (1987). Issues in transition: Transfer of youth from correctional facilities to public schools. In C. M. Nelson, R. B. Rutherford, & B. I. Wolford (Eds.), *Special education in the criminal justice system* (pp. 251-272). Columbus, OH: Merrill.

Fenichel, C. (1966). Psychoeducational approaches for seriously emotionally disturbed children in the classroom. In P. Knoblock (Ed.), *Intervention approaches in educating emotionally disturbed children.* Syracuse, NY: Syracuse University Press.

Fuchs, D., & Fuchs, L. S. (1988). Mainstream assistance teams to accommodate difficult-to-teach students in general education. In J. L. Graden, J. E. Zins, & M. J. Curtis (Eds.), *Alternative educational delivery systems: Enhancing instructional options for all students* (pp. 49-70). Washington, DC: National Association of School Psychologists.

Grosenick, J. K., & Huntze, S. L. (1980). *National needs analysis in behavior disorders: Severe behavior disorders.* Columbia: University of Missouri.

Haring, N. G., & Phillips, E. L. (1962). *Educating emotionally disturbed children.* New York: McGraw-Hill.

Hewett, F. M. (1968). *The emotionally disturbed child in the classroom.* Boston: Allyn & Bacon.

Hobbs, N. (1965). How the Re-ED plan developed. In N. J. Long, W. C. Morse, & R. G. Newman (Eds.), *Conflict in the classroom* (pp. 286-294). Belmont, CA: Wadsworth.

Johnson, D. L. (1988). Primary prevention of behavior problems in young children: The Houston parent-child development center. In R. H. Price, E. L. Cowen, R. P. Lorion, & J. Ramos-McKay (Eds.), *Fourteen ounces of prevention: A casebook for practitioners.* Washington, DC: American Psychological Association.

Johnson, L. J., Pugach, M. C., & Hammitte, D. J. (1988). Barriers to effective special education consultation. *Remedial and Special Education, 9*(6), 41-47.

Kauffman, J. M. (1980). Where special education for emotionally disturbed children is going: A personal view. *Exceptional Children, 48*, 522-527.

Kauffman, J. M. (1987). Social policy issues in special education and related services for emotionally disturbed children and youth. In N. Haring (Ed.), *Measuring and managing behavior disorders* (pp. x-xx). Seattle: University of Washington Press.

Kauffman, J. M. (1989). *Characteristics of behavior disorders of children and youth* (4th ed.). Columbus, OH: Merrill.

Kerr, M. M., & Nelson, C. M. (1989). *Strategies for managing behavior problems in the classroom* (2nd ed.). Columbus, OH: Merrill.

Kerr, M. M., Nelson, C. M., & Lambert, D. L. (1987). *Helping adolescents with learning and behavior problems.* Columbus, OH: Merrill.

Long, K. A. (1983). Emotionally disturbed children as the underdetected and underserved public school population: Reasons and recommendations. *Behavioral Disorders, 9*, 46-54.

Mack, J. H. (1985). *An analysis of state definitions of severely emotionally disturbed children* (Policy Options Report). Reston, VA: Council for Exceptional Children.

Margolis, R. J. (1988). *Out of harm's way: The emancipation of juvenile justice.* New York: Edna McConnell Clark Foundation.

Mesinger, J. F. (1986). Alternative education for behaviorally disordered youths: A promise yet unfulfilled. *Behavioral Disorders, 11*, 98-108.

Miller, W. B. (1958). Lower class culture as a generating milieu of gang delinquency. *Journal of Social Issues, 14*, 5-19.

Morgan, D. J. (1979). Prevalence and types of handicapping conditions found in juvenile correctional institutions: A national survey. *Journal of Special Education, 13*, 283-295.

Murphy, D. M. (1986). The prevalence of handicapping conditions among juvenile delinquents. *Remedial and Special Education, 7*(3), 7-17.

Neel, R. S., & Rutherford, R. B. (1981). Exclusion of the socially maladjusted from services under PL 94-142. In F. H. Wood (Ed.), *Perspectives for a new decade: Education's responsibility for seriously emotionally disturbed and behaviorally disordered youth* (pp. 79-84). Reston, VA: Council for Exceptional Children.

Nelson, C. M. (1977). Alternative education for the mildly and moderately handicapped. In R. D. Kneedler & S. G. Tarver (Eds.), *Changing perspectives in special education* (pp. 185-207). Columbus, OH: Merrill.

Nelson, C. M. (1988). Social skills training for handicapped students. *Teaching Exceptional Children, 20*(4), 19-23.

Nelson, C. M., & Kauffman, J. M. (1977). Educational programming for secondary school age delinquent and maladjusted pupils. *Behavioral Disorders, 2*, 102-113.

Patterson, G. R. (1975). The aggressive child: Victim or architect of a coercive system? In L. A. Hamerlynck, L. C. Handy, & E. G. Mash (Eds.), *Behavior modification and families* (pp. 267-316). New York: Brunner/Mazel.

Phillips, E. L. (1968). Achievement Place: Token reinforcement procedures in a home-style rehabilitation setting for "pre-delinquent" boys. *Journal of Applied Behavior Analysis, 1*, 214-223.

Phillips, E. L., Phillips, E. A., Fixsen, D. L., & Wolf, M. M. (1974). *The teaching-family handbook.* Lawrence: University of Kansas Printing Service.

Rhodes, W. C. (1967). The disturbing child: A problem of ecological management. *Exceptional Children, 37*, 309-314.

Robins, L. N. (1966). *Deviant children grown up.* Baltimore: Williams & Wilkins.

Robins, L. N. (1979). Follow-up studies. In H. C. Quay & J. S. Werry (Eds.), *Psychopathological disorders of childhood* (2nd ed., pp. 483-513). New York: John Wiley.

Rose, T. L. (1989). Corporal punishment with mildly handicapped students: Five years later. *Remedial and Special Education, 10*(1), 43-52.

Rutherford, R. B., Nelson, C. M., & Wolford, B. I. (1985). Special education in the most restrictive environment: Correctional special education. *Journal of Special Education, 19*, 59-71.

Rutherford, R. B., & Swist, C. (1976). *Behavior modification and therapy with juvenile delinquents: A comprehensive bibliography.* CEC Information Center for Exceptional Children. (ERIC Document Reproduction Service No. RTE 07-3354)

Safer, D. J. (1982). Varieties and levels of intervention with disruptive adolescents. In D. J. Safer (Ed.), *School programs for disruptive adolescents* (pp. 43-65). Baltimore: University Park Press.

Shinn, M. R., Ramsey, E., Walker, H. M., Stieber, S., & O'Neill, R. (1987). Antisocial behavior in school settings: Initial differences in an at risk and normal population. *Journal of Special Education, 21*, 69-84.

Simcha-Fagan, O., Langner, T., Gersten, J., & Eisenberg, J. (1975). *Violent and antisocial behavior: A longitudinal study of urban youth* (OCD-CB-480). Unpublished manuscript, Office of Child Development.

Slenkovitch, J. E. (1983). *P.L. 94-142 as applied to DSM III diagnoses: An analysis of DSM III diagnoses vis-à-vis special education law.* Cupertino, CA: Kinghorn.

Slenkovitch, J. E. (1984). *Understanding special education law* (Vol. 1). Cupertino, CA: Kinghorn.

Sodac, D. G., McGinnis, E., Smith, C. R., Wood, F. H., Dykstra, D. J., & Brees, N. (Eds.). (1988). *The Iowa program standards for interventions in behavioral disorders.* Des Moines, IA: Department of Public Instruction.

U.S. Department of Education, Office of Special Education and Rehabilitation Services. (1985). *Seventh annual report to Congress on the implementation of the Education of the Handicapped Act*. Washington, DC: Government Printing Office.

U.S. Department of Health, Education and Welfare, Office of Education. (1977, August 23). Education of handicapped children: Implementation of Part B of the Education of the Handicapped Act. *Federal Register, 42*(163).

Walker, H. M., & Buckley, N. (1972). *Token reinforcement techniques: Classroom applications for the hard to reach child*. Eugene, OR: E-B.

Walker, H. M., & Fabre, T. R. (1987). Assessment of behavior disorders in the school setting: Issues, problems, and strategies revisited. In N. Haring (Ed.), *Measuring and managing behavior disorders* (pp. 198-243). Seattle: University of Washington Press.

Walker, H. M., Shinn, M. R., O'Neill, R. E., & Ramsey, E. (1987). A longitudinal assessment of the development of antisocial behavior in boys: Rationale, methodology, and first year results. *Remedial and Special Education, 8*(4), 7-16.

Webb, S. L., Maddox, M., & Edgar, E. B. (1985). *The juvenile corrections interagency transition model*. Seattle: University of Washington, Experimental Education Unit.

Whelan, R. J., & Haring, N. G. (1966). Modification and maintenance of behavior through systematic application of consequences. *Exceptional Children, 32*, 281-289.

Wolf, M. M., Braukmann, C. J., & Ramp, K. A. (1987). Serious delinquent behavior as part of a significantly handicapping condition: Cures and supportive environments. *Journal of Applied Behavior Analysis, 20*, 347-359.

Wood, F. H., Smith, C. R., & Grimes, J. (Eds.). (1985). *The Iowa assessment model in behavioral disorders: A training manual*. Des Moines, IA: Department of Public Instruction.

4

Special Education Students at Risk

A Comparative Study of Delinquency

CAROLYN MOLDEN FINK

Joe, a 15-year-old, is struggling in school and may drop out when he turns 16. His school history is one of failure and frustration. He receives special education services, and achievement tests indicate that he lags behind his peers in reading and math skill. It is difficult to determine whether his difficulties in school are due to his learning problems or his behavior problems. His attendance is irregular, and when he comes to class he boasts of recent scrapes with the law.

Joe, a troubled teenager, might be identified by one or more of the following labels: disabled, at risk, or delinquent. Further, he might qualify for an array of mental health, community, juvenile justice, and/or education services. Joe and other students like him are often difficult to reach and may face the uncertain future experienced by school dropouts with limited skills.

How should schools respond to students like Joe? Research on the link between disabilities and delinquency may provide some direction. If, for example, learning disabled or mentally retarded students are at greater risk for delinquency than are non-special education students,

AUTHOR'S NOTE: The study reported in this chapter was completed in collaboration with Dr. Denise Gottfredson. Preliminary results were presented at the November meeting of the American Society of Criminology in Chicago. My thanks to Dr. Gottfredson and ASC discussant Dr. Joan McCord for their critical reading of a preliminary draft of this chapter.

61

then special education may have a crucial role to play. If disabled students do not differ from their nondisabled peers on known risk factors for delinquency, then special education students should at least be considered in general delinquency prevention programming. However, currently very little information exists on the association of risk factors for delinquency and special education students.

Premises

Before an examination of existing evidence for an association between disabilities and delinquency is presented, three premises upon which this work is based will be discussed. The first premise is that categories of disabilities—including learning disabilities (LD), mental retardation (MR), and emotional disturbance (ED), as defined by the Education for All Handicapped Children Act (P.L. 94-142, 1975)—distinguish disabled students from the nondisabled population. Disabilities most often mentioned in connection with juvenile delinquency are LD, MR, and ED (Murphy, 1986) and problems with the definitions of these disabilities have been a concern for educators and researchers. There is some evidence of overlap in characteristics of those defined as LD, MR, and ED. For example, some students labeled LD and MR exhibit behavior problems (Bender, 1987; Epstein, Bursuck, & Cullinan, 1985; Hallahan & Kauffman, 1977), and ED and MR students have learning problems similar to youth labeled LD (Hallahan & Kauffman, 1977; Kauffman, Cullinan, & Epstein, 1987). In general, however, the academic performance of these mildly disabled students does distinguish them from their nondisabled peers (Ysseldyke, Thurlow, & Christenson, 1988). In spite of definitional problems, in this chapter the terms *handicapped, disabled*, and *special education students* will be used interchangeably.

The second premise is that self-report data can be a viable method of assessing behavior of special education students. Researchers of disabilities and delinquency rely on survey or interview data in which students report on their own behavior. Self-report data have also been utilized extensively and have proven valid in criminological research for assessing criminal behavior (Hindelang, Hirschi, & Weis, 1979). In fact, self-reports may yield a more accurate picture of delinquent behavior than official records, considering that much delinquency goes undetected. Still, obtaining self-report data from disabled students presents particular concerns for response accuracy. In one large study of LD and delinquency, researchers addressed this issue and found no evidence for a response bias in their interviewing of LD and non-LD youth about their delinquent behavior (Keilitz & Dunivant, 1986). Careful administration of surveys with assistance to those needing help and assessment of statistical reliability are important indicators of accurate results.

Finally, the third premise is that theoretical models can direct the study and interpretation of results regarding disabilities and delinquency. Most of the data collected on disabilities and delinquency are descriptive. Figuring the percentage of disabled youth among delinquent groups is one way to characterize the problems of disabled delinquents. More compelling, however, are questions related to why youth with disabilities are overrepresented in the criminal justice system and what factors are involved in the process leading to overrepresentation. Though causal inferences are premature, reference to several models can direct inquiry in this area.

Theoretical Models

Several theoretical models have been developed to help explain the interaction between disabilities and delinquency: *Susceptibility* theory suggests that handicaps or deficits such as low self-esteem, need for immediate gratification, and social imperceptions lead directly to juvenile delinquency (JD) (Murray, 1976) (see Figure 4.1). The *school failure* explanation for the association of disability and delinquency posits that school failure, often experienced by special education students, leads to lowered attachment to school and subsequent delinquency (Hirschi, 1969; Murray, 1976) (see Figure 4.2). A third hypothesis, that of *differential treatment*, suggests that systems such as schools, juvenile justice, and corrections respond differently and more punitively toward disabled youth (Keilitz & Dunivant, 1987; Lane, 1980) (see Figure 4.3).

Prevalence of Disabilities and Delinquency

During the past 20 years, researchers have attempted to measure overlap between samples of delinquents and disabled teenagers (Murphy, 1986). In 1976, Murray reviewed research in an effort to investigate the

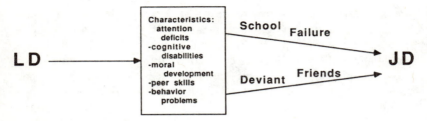

Figure 4.1. Susceptibility Theory

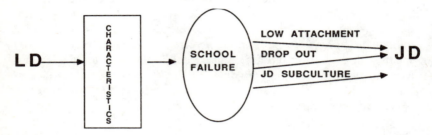

Figure 4.2. School Failure Theory

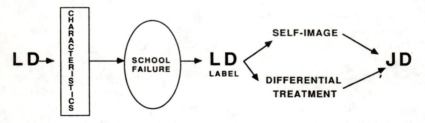

Figure 4.3. Differential Treatment Theory

association between LD and delinquency and found very little causal evidence linking the two populations. The data he did find were beset by problems of definition, design, and presentation. Some problems in research conducted before 1976 still exist in more recent studies, but the picture of the LD delinquent is becoming clearer.

The prevalence of disabilities among delinquent groups varies with definitions used. In one survey of state departments of education and corrections, estimated percentages of handicapped offenders including LD and other disabilities ranged from 0 to 100% of total incarcerated population (Rutherford, Nelson, & Wolford, 1985). A meta-analysis of 22 studies of the prevalence of LD among delinquents and 21 studies of the prevalence of MR among delinquents yielded average prevalence figures of 35.6% and 12.6%. (See Casey & Keilitz, Chapter 5, this volume.) Several studies have compared disabled and nondisabled youth on measures suggested by theoretical models linking disabilities and delinquency: delinquent behavior, personal and social abilities, social bonding, and/or school performance.

Self-reports of delinquent behavior and official data of police contacts for disabled and nondisabled students are obviously of interest to researchers. In one large study, part of the LD/JD project (Keilitz & Dunivant, 1986, 1987), researchers interviewed 1,943 teenagers, half of whom were court-adjudicated delinquent and half of whom were not. Of the whole sample, 26% of the youth tested as LD. Results of this cross-sectional study of students indicate that LD was significantly and directly related to official reports of delinquency. Further, the relationship of self-report delinquency to LD was found to be statistically significant when effects of age, social status, school status, and school attitude were controlled for. In addition, in a sample followed for two years, LD was found to be associated with increases over time in illegal activities.

Other researchers have provided confirming and contradictory findings. Gregory (1986) examined differences among LD, hearing-impaired, speech-disordered, and nondisabled tenth and twelfth graders who completed a nationwide questionnaire. Analysis of results indicated that disabled students reported significantly more police contacts than did nondisabled students. Conversely, other researchers administered a survey to 39 LD and 47 non-LD tenth and eleventh graders and found no differences between LD and non-LD on type and amount of self-report delinquent behavior (Pickar & Tori, 1986).

Personal social factors related to delinquency have also been examined. Analysis of survey results indicated disabled students responded with lower self-adjustment, self-assessment, and work orientation than did their nondisabled peers (Gregory, 1986). Pickar and Tori (1986), after finding no differences on delinquent behavior, found significant differences between LD and non-LD students on two measures of self-concept: (a) intellectual and school status, and (b) popularity. In addition, special education teachers, in responding to a survey, reported that special education students, especially ED students, where were often victimized in school (Lang & Kahn, 1986).

Social bonding is a construct used often in delinquency research, but not in reference specifically to disabled students. Social bonding is relevant to study of special education students, who may differ from non-special education students in their attachment to school. Special education students may be less involved in school activities, more discouraged, and more willing to engage in delinquent behavior at the risk of school punishment. School status and popularity, two measures on which LD and non-LD differ (Pickar & Tori, 1986), could be considered indicators of attachment to school. Evaluation of the ACLD (Association of Children with Learning Disabilities) remediation program (Keilitz & Dunivant, 1986) also lends support to the notion of increased attachments to school lessening the likelihood of delinquency. Delinquents identified by the LD/JD project (N = 150) were offered remediation by a trained LD specialist for varying amounts of time over a two-year period. Researchers found that changes in delinquency were not significantly related to changes in academic achievement, but rather to a change in school attitude that was attributed to a new attachment to the LD specialists.

School failure and low academic achievement of special education students is documented in special education literature and corroborated in research on disabilities and delinquency. Pasternak and Lyon (1982) found that all delinquents tested were underachieving, but disabled delinquents scored lower than nondisabled delinquents. Similarly, in a nationwide survey, disabled tenth and twelfth graders scored much lower on academic achievement tests than regular education students (Gregory, 1986).

Overrepresentation of disabled youngsters among delinquent populations and research on factors that place them at risk for delinquency gives rise to concern about special education students as they move through school. To explore the link between disabilities and delinquency further, the study reported here compares disabled and non-disabled schoolchildren on a number of outcome measures, including self-report and official delinquency and factors associated with delinquency such as problem behavior, personal and social development, social bonding, and school experiences.

Methodology

Sample

As a part of the School Action Effectiveness Study (SAES) (G. D. Gottfredson, 1982; G. D. Gottfredson, D. C. Gottfredson, & Cook, 1983) data on sixth- through twelfth-grade students were collected in an urban school district in the spring of 1982. Data were collected for all students in each of nine secondary schools (four high schools and five middle schools). The response rates for the survey ranged from .69 to .91 and averaged .82. The current study is a secondary analysis on the 3,313 students who participated in the survey administration, 1,174 of whom were LD and 82 of whom were MR. The sample of ED students (n = 9) was too small to be included in this study.

Students were identified as in need of special education by the school district using P.L. 94-142 definitions. School officials identified 3% of the survey sample as MR and 4% as LD. These figures are slightly higher than national averages for disabilities among the school-aged population (U.S. Department of Education, 1988).

Measures

Outcome measures used for this study come from a student survey and from school and court records. The survey, developed for the SAES, is based on extensive research of delinquency and school environments conducted at the Johns Hopkins University. Reliability and validity states for the measures based on a large sample of secondary school youths are reported in a technical manual (G. D. Gottfredson, 1985). Reliability states computed for this study sample were comparable to those reported in the technical manual, and reliabilities generally did not differ for special education and non-special education students.[1] A brief description of the student survey measures and measures taken from school and police records appears in the Appendix to this chapter.

Results

Analyses of covariance (ANCOVA) were performed for the outcome measures using student disability as the independent variable. Covariates for these analyses—race (coded 1 = Black, 0 = other), sex, and age—were obtained from records and found to be significantly related to special education status. Scheffé tests were performed post hoc to examine further the significant main effects. Unadjusted means and standard deviations are reported in Tables 4.1-4.4 along with significance tests based on the ANCOVAs.

Problem Behavior

Data presented in Table 4.1 indicate areas in which disabled students behaved differently from nondisabled students. LD students reported significantly more serious delinquent behavior ($p < .05$) and were referred to the office more often for disciplinary infractions than were non-special education youth ($p < .01$). LD students were also sent to the office significantly more often than MR students ($p < .05$). Among the disciplinary infractions, LD students were punished more frequently than MR and regular education students for misbehavior related to class work (e.g., not completing work, not being prepared for class). Both LD and MR students reported being punished more often in school than did nondisabled students. No significant differences were found among the groups for drug involvement, total delinquency (including drug involvement), and contacts with the police.

Personal and Social Development

Table 4.2 presents differences between special education and non-special education students in personal and social development. LD and MR students reported significantly higher internal loci of control, lower self-concepts, and lower interpersonal competency than did nonhandicapped students ($p < .01$). MR students' reports of rebellious autonomy were higher (though not significantly) than those of youth not identified for special education.

Social Bonding

Table 4.3 shows differences between disabled and nondisabled students on measures of social bonding. LD and MR students both reported significantly more feelings of alienation from the school community, less belief in conventional rules, and less liking for school than did nondisabled students ($p < .01$). These results are consistent in suggesting weak bonding to school and nonconformity to norms for disabled

Table 4.1. Means and Standard Deviations for Problem Behavior of Handicapped and Nonhandicapped Students

		Handicapped Status									
	None			LD			MR				
Outcome Measure	M	SD	N	M	SD	N	M	SD	N		
Self-Reported Serious Delinquency	.07	.14	2,570	.13*	.17	96	.10	.16	55		
Self-Reported Drug Involvement	.20	.26	2,576	.17	.25	95	.17	.23	58		
Total Self-Reported Delinquency	.12	.15	2,567	.16	.16	96	.13	.14	55		
School Punishments	.23	.26	2,656	.35**	.28	101	.34**	.27	64		
Number of Court Contacts	.02	.19	2,936	.03	.23	117	.01	.11	82		
Number of Disciplinary Infractions	.03	.19	2,937	.09**	.39	117	.07[a]	.56	82		

NOTE: Means reported are unadjusted for covariates. Significance tests are from ANCOVAs that use as covariates race, sex, and age. Main effects by handicapped status were significant at $p < .01$ except for Total Delinquency, Drug Involvement, and Court Contacts.

a. LD and EMH means differ significantly at $p < .05$ level.

*Means for this group significantly different from none at $p < .05$ level.

**Means for this group significantly different from none at $p < .01$ level.

Table 4.2. Means and Standard Deviations for Personal and Social Development of Handicapped and Nonhandicapped Students

| | | | | | Handicapped Status | | | | |
| | None | | | LD | | | MR | | |
Outcome Measure	M	SD	N	M	SD	N	M	SD	N
Internal Control	.50	.24	2,427	.61*	.21	85	.61**	.23	56
Rebellious Autonomy	.58	.34	2,354	.57	.30	78	.64	.32	54
Self-Concept	.79	.16	2,293	.69**	.20	80	.66**	.17	49
Interpersonal Competency	.82	.19	2,446	.71**	.26	84	.71**	.26	56

NOTE: Means reported are unadjusted for covariates. Significance tests are from ANCOVAs that use as covariates race, sex, and age. Main effects by handicapped status were significant at $p < .01$ except for Rebellious Autonomy.
*Means for this group significantly different from none at $p < .05$ level.
**Means for this group significantly different from none at $p < .01$ level.

students. MR students reported significantly less attachment to parents than did non-special education students. Means for the LD students for parental attachment were also lower, but did not differ significantly from those of nondisabled students.

Special education students did not report more skipping of school or classes than non-special education students, but data from school records indicated significantly more absences for special education students. In addition, disabled students had significantly more unexcused absences ($p < .05$) than their peers in regular education.

School Experiences

Data on school experiences are presented in Table 4.4. Special education students failed English or math and scored lower on the standardized achievement test than did non-special education students. LD and MR students' test scores put them in the bottom 16% of agemates nationwide in reading and total battery scores.

Disabled students reported practical skills comparable with those of nondisabled students, and MR students reported being more involved in school activities than the other groups. MR students reported receiving significantly more prizes and rewards in school than regular education students ($p < .01$) and more, but not significantly more, than LD students.

LD and MR students reported feeling afraid within and around the school community and reported being more often victimized than nondisabled students. MR students reported significantly more negative peer influences than the other groups ($p < .01$). Means for the LD students for negative peer influence approached significance in the same direction. Table 4.4 shows that LD and MR students are different from nondisabled students in their perceptions of and performance in school.

Summary

Analyses indicate significant differences between LD and nondisabled students on serious delinquent behavior and on in-school referrals for troublesome behavior. Both MR and LD students differed from non-special education students on measures of school punishment, personal and social development, social bonding, and school performance. In particular, special education students reported significantly higher internal loci of control, lower self-concepts, and lower interper-

Table 4.3. Means and Standard Deviations for Social Bonding of Handicapped and Nonhandicapped Students

				Handicapped Status							
	None			LD			MR				
Outcome Measure	M	SD	N	M	SD	N	M	SD	N		
Attachment to School	.75	.23	2,674	.65*	.24	101	.66**	.24	58		
Attachment to Parents	.66	.25	2,848	.60	.27	114	.53**	.30	76		
Belief in Rules	.70	.23	2,472	.59**	.27	85	.58**	.26	58		
Alienation	.33	.25	2,438	.46**	.26	84	.44**	.26	53		
School Nonattendance	.24	.35	2,873	.21	.33	114	.22	.34	77		
Number of Days Absent	5.55	6.01	2,330	7.66*	8.15	88	8.93**	9.93	69		

NOTE: Means reported are unadjusted for covariates. Significance tests are from ANCOVAs that use as covariates race, sex, and age. Main effects by handicapped status were significant at *p* < .01 except for School Nonattendance.
*Means for this group significantly different from none at *p* < .05 level.
**Means for this group significantly different from none at *p* < .01 level.

Table 4.4. Means and Standard Deviations for School Experiences of Handicapped and Nonhandicapped Students

				Handicapped Status					
Outcome Measure	None			LD			MR		
	M	SD	N	M	SD	N	M	SD	N
Percentage of Passing									
English or Math Grades	.64	.48	2,311	.38**	.49	87	.34**	.48	61
Academic Achievement	34.9	24.0	2,865	16.7**	14.8	108	10.1**	8.7	60
Practical Knowledge	1.38	.42	2,465	1.26	.48	83	1.31	.42	53
Involvement in School									
Activities	.26	.19	2,691	.26	.22	101	.32*	.23	63
School Rewards	.28	.34	2,656	.35	.34	102	.50**	.40	65
Fear	.23	.27	2,613	.33**	.28	101	.47**	.30	61
Victimization	.13	.18	2,635	.20*	.23	99	.20**[a]	.24	63
Negative Peer Influence	.19	.18	2,789	.25	.21	114	.27**[a]	.19	65

NOTE: Means reported are unadjusted for covariates. Significance tests are from ANCOVAs that use as covariates race, sex, and age. Main effects by handicapped status were significant at $p < .01$ except for Practical Knowledge.

a. LD and EMH means differ significantly at $p < .05$ level.

*Means for this group significantly different from none at $p < .05$ level.

**Means for this group significantly different from none at $p < .01$ level.

sonal competency than their counterparts in regular education. They reported being less attached to school, less conforming to rules, and more alienated, and were more often absent from school. In addition, their school experience consisted of more failing grades, poorer test performances, more fear, and more victimization than did that of non-special education students. MR students differed from LD students in their reporting of more school involvement, more negative peer influence, and less parental attachment.

Discussion

The data presented here suggest that special education students are more at risk for delinquency than are non-special education students. The mechanisms that have been suggested include susceptibility, social bonding, and school failure. With regard to susceptibility, social awkwardness, low self-esteem, and lack of social skills have been documented with LD students and may cause them to act inappropriately (Bender, 1987; Chapman, 1988; Licht, 1983). In the present study, special education students reported less interpersonal competency; their lack of social skills does distinguish them from regular education students. Some researchers suggest that LD students have immature moral reasoning development; they are more concerned with peer acceptance than with the consequences of their actions (Bryan, Werner, & Pearl, 1982; Derr, 1986). In the present survey, LD and MR students reported more negative peer influence than did nondisabled students, the difference being significant only for MR students. Having a profile of personal characteristics that includes weak social skills, nonconformity to rules, and vulnerability to negative peer influence places disabled students at greater risk for delinquency than nondisabled youth.

In two areas special education students' responses did not indicate higher risks for delinquency than non-special education students. LD students are not reflective in their behavior (Mercer, 1987), and impulsivity is thought to lead to behavior problems in school and in the community (Quay, 1965). Analysis of results on the Rebellious Autonomy scale did not yield any differences between special education and regular education students in attitudes that might reflect impulsivity. Another characteristic often attributed to disabled students is learned helplessness, yet learned helplessness and internal control among LD students have been studied with mixed results (Bender, 1987; Licht,

1983). Lack of internal control that might cause students to feel helpless and discouraged in school was not found for disabled youth in this study. LD students reported a higher level of internal control than nondisabled students. Two possible explanations exist for these findings. Reliability data for Rebellious Autonomy and Internal Control scales were low for the LD sample, suggesting instability in responses for the LD students. It may be that LD students did not understand the questions (contrary to the second premise of this chapter) or that the questions in the scale did not represent the desired characteristic of rebelliousness or internal control for LD students. It may also be that LD students are actually less impulsive and show more internal control than nondisabled students and are less at risk for delinquency with regard to these characteristics.

Results of analyses on social bonding scales are strong and consistent in the direction of special education students' feeling less a part of school and missing more school days than those not identified as special education students. Disbelief in rules, alienation, and nonattendance may be related to dropout rates and delinquent behavior of adolescent youth (Hirschi, 1969). LD and MR students' responses on a variety of items indicated a low attachment to school. This lower school attachment might explain why special education students are more likely than their nondisabled peers to leave school before graduating, with perhaps a greater negative effect on their lives (Levin, Zigmond, & Birch, 1985; Zigmond & Thornton, 1985).

The results of this study can be interpreted with regard to the school failure model. These results are consistent with research that found that academic performances of mildly disabled LD, ED, and MR students did not vary among groups, but was significantly different from performances of nondisabled students (Ysseldyke et al., 1988). Information analyzed for this study showed that LD and MR students were failing classes and lagging behind in school abilities. MR students did report being more involved and gaining school rewards, perhaps ameliorating some of the effects of their academic failure.

Both LD and MR students reported significantly higher levels of fear and victimization at school than did nondisabled youth. This is consistent with special education teachers' perceptions of the victimization of their students (Lang & Kahn, 1986). Victimization is not only related to delinquency (G. D. Gottfredson, 1989; M. R. Gottfredson, 1984); it puts special education students at risk for harm.

Conclusions

Research on the association between disabilities and delinquency continues. The study presented here was conducted in an urban school system in a southern state. Replication of these findings across different populations and geographical regions would clarify findings on suspected links between disabilities and delinquency. Extending the study to include ED students, dropouts, and graduates would broaden the findings. Research on prevention programs that include special education students is needed.

This study does not show the relative effects of the mechanisms hypothesized to cause delinquency. Neither does it deal with the differential treatment theory that links the prevalence of handicapped youth as delinquents to differential treatment by school or the juvenile justice system. A future study could use level of service—part of the school day a student receives special education service—as a measure of school treatment to test part of the differential treatment model.

Differential treatment, in this case special education placement, may also be related to the issue of labeling (Bak, Cooper, Dobroth, & Siperstein, 1987). This study does not test whether special education status is only a label placed on students who display characteristics that put them at risk for delinquent behavior. Research on the effects of labeling students as disabled is equivocal in terms of affecting students' self-appraisals and teacher expectations (Coleman, 1983; Robison & Medway, 1985). Useful in this regard would be a longitudinal study that controlled for prelabel characteristics and looked at the remaining association between LD and MR status and delinquency. Perhaps less definitive would be a cross-sectional study in which characteristics related to special education labeling (e.g., academic deficits, behavior problems) are controlled, and differences between special education and non-special education student behaviors are examined. If characteristics accounted for any or all of the difference, then the argument would be that special education status is not a "cause" of delinquency, but it may be a useful label for the school system to use in attempting to serve at-risk students better.

From the current research base, it is clear that special education students are a population to be reckoned with in terms of delinquency. Schools should be prepared to deal with disabled delinquents and to respond appropriately to their behavior in light of the recent Supreme Court decision regarding expulsion of special education students (*Honig v. Doe,* 108 S. Ct. 592, 1988).

Of particular importance to school officials is how to react to findings regarding fear and alienation of special education youth. Mildly disabled students have two school settings in which to become attached: the regular school environment and their special education classes. Case study researchers found that LD students varied in their attachment to regular education and special education environments, but described an LD student who did not form social bonds in either special education classes or the mainstream (Miller, Zigmond, & Leinhardt, 1988). It was this student who, like the student introduced at the beginning of this chapter, disliked school, had poor attendance, and was in trouble in the community. Schools need to analyze the involvement of disabled students and find out what might contribute to alienation and fear of special education students in schools.

Problems of disaffected youth, especially when compounded by disabilities, are not easily solved. Attention to areas explored in this study—deficit areas, school attachment, and school failure—by parties involved with disabled youth may be able to keep such students off the streets and out of trouble.

Appendix: Measures

Problem Behavior

- *Disciplinary Infractions:* The number of times the student was sent to the office for disciplinary action during the 1981-1982 school year. Types of infractions include attendance (tardiness, skipping class), academic (not completing work, being unprepared for class), and behavior (fighting, stealing).
- *Self-Reported Delinquency* (total): A combination of the items from Serious Delinquency and Drug Involvement scales, with the addition of two questions regarding selling drugs and hitting another student.

For descriptions of the Self-Reported Serious Delinquency, Self-Reported Drug Involvement, School Punishments, and Court Contacts scales, see the Appendix to Gottfredson, Chapter 12, this volume.

Personal and Social Development

- *Internal Control:* A 10-item scale designed to measure the construct of locus of control. A student who thinks that events are beyond his or her control, or external to him or her, would answer positively to an item such as "There is little use in trying to guess what a teacher will ask in a test." A student with internal locus of control expects that his or her efforts make a difference and would answer positively to an item such as "When I make plans I am almost certain I can make them work."

- *Rebellious Autonomy:* Contains three items that reflect a rebellious attitude that might reflect impulsivity or lack of concern for authority and might anticipate trouble with school authority. Examples of items include "Whether or not I spend time on homework is my own business" and "I don't like anybody telling me what to do."

- *Interpersonal Competency:* Contains five items that ask the student to assess how interpersonally skilled he or she is. An example item from this scale is "If I want to, I can explain things well."

For a description of the Positive Self-Concept scale, see the Appendix to Gottfredson, Chapter 12, this volume.

Social Bonding

The measures included under this category are intended to measure constructs central to the social control theory (Hirschi, 1969) of delinquency causation.

- *Attachment to Parents:* Incorporates several items asking students to report how close they feel to their parents and how much they like their parents.

- *Alienation:* Intended to measure the individual's sense of belonging in the school. The scale consists of six items, including "I feel like I belong in this school" and "I feel no one really cares much about what happens to me."

For descriptions of Attachment to School, Belief in Rules, School Nonattendance, and Number of Days Absent scales, see Appendix to Gottfredson, Chapter 12, this volume.

School Experiences

- *Grades:* A binary variable indicating whether or not a student received a failing grade in either English or math for spring semester of the school year in which the study was conducted. The data come from school records.

- *Academic Achievement:* The average national percentile score on the total battery of the California Test of Basic Skills (CTBS) administered in the spring of the year in which the study was conducted. The data come from school records.

- *Practical Knowledge:* Designed to assess students' self-appraisal with regard to seven competencies. The competencies range from knowing how to find out about and apply for jobs to balancing a checkbook.

- *Involvement in School Activities:* Students are asked to indicate if they have spent time on any of 10 in-school and 2 out-of-school activities within the current school term.

- *Fear:* A 13-item scale asking students to report if they stay away from any of a list of places in and around school, and if they feel safe or if they fear someone will hurt them at school.

- *Victimization:* Derived from a series of seven questions asking the students if they have been victims of theft, physical attack, or threats at school over the last month.

For descriptions of School Rewards and Negative Peer Influence scales, see the Appendix to Gottfredson, Chapter 12, this volume.

Note

1. Notable exceptions are School Punishments (for LD and MR), Alienation (LD), Internal Control (LD), and Self-Concept (MR).

References

Bak, J. J., Cooper, E. M., Dobroth, K. M., & Siperstein, G. N. (1987). Special class placements as labels: Effects on children's attitudes toward learning handicapped peers. *Exceptional Children, 54*, 151-155.

Bender, W. N. (1987). Secondary personality and behavioral problems in adolescents with learning disabilities. *Journal of Learning Disabilities, 20*, 280-285.

Bryan, T., Werner, M., & Pearl, R. (1982). Learning disabled students' conformity responses to prosocial and antisocial situations. *Learning Disability Quarterly, 5*, 344-351.

Chapman, J. W. (1988). Learning disabled children's self-concept. *Review of Educational Research, 58*, 347-371.

Coleman, J. M. (1983). Handicapped labels and instructional segregation: Influences on children's self-concepts versus the perceptions of others. *Learning Disability Quarterly, 6*(1), 3-11.

Derr, A. M. (1986). How learning disabled adolescent boys make moral judgments. *Journal of Learning Disabilities, 18*, 160-163.

Epstein, M. H., Bursuck, W., & Cullinan, D. (1985). Patterns of behavior problems among the learning disabled: Boys aged 12-18, girls aged 6-11, and girls aged 12-18. *Learning Disability Quarterly, 8*, 123-130.

Gottfredson, G. D. (Ed.). (1982). *School action effectiveness study: First interim report* (Report No. 325). Baltimore: Johns Hopkins University, Center for Social Organization of Schools. (ERIC Document Reproduction Service No. ED 222 835)

Gottfredson, G. D. (1985). *Effective school battery: User's manual.* Odessa, FL: Psychological Assessment Resources.

Gottfredson, G. D. (1989). The experience of violent and serious victimization. In N. A. Weiner & M. E. Wolfgang (Eds.), *Pathways to criminal violence* (pp. 202-234). Newbury Park, CA: Sage.

Gottfredson, G. D., Gottfredson, D. C., & Cook, M. S. (1983). *The school action effectiveness study: Second interim report* (Report No. 342). Baltimore: Johns Hopkins University, Center for Social Organization of Schools. (ERIC Document Reproduction Service No. ED 237 892)

Gottfredson, M. R. (1984). *Victims of crime: The dimension of risk* (Home Office Research Study No. 81). London: Her Majesty's Stationary Office.

Gregory, J. F. (1986). *A secondary analysis of HSB data related to special education.* (ERIC Document Reproduction Service No. ED 276 219)

Hallahan, D. P., & Kauffman, J. M. (1977). Labels, categories, behaviors: ED, LD, and EMR reconsidered. *Journal of Special Education, 11*, 139-149.

Hindelang, M. J., Hirschi, T., & Weis, J. G. (1979). Correlates of delinquency: The illusion of a discrepancy between self-report and official measures. *American Sociological Review, 44*, 995-1014.

Hirschi, T. (1969). *Causes of delinquency.* Berkeley: University of California Press.

Kauffman, J. M., Cullinan, D., & Epstein, M. H. (1987). Characteristics of students placed in special programs for the seriously emotionally disturbed. *Behavioral Disorders, 12*, 175-184.

Keilitz, I., & Dunivant, N. (1986). The relationship between learning disability and juvenile delinquency: Current state of knowledge. *Remedial and Special Education, 7*(3), 18-26.

Keilitz, I., & Dunivant, N. (1987). The learning disabled offender. In C. M. Nelson, R. B. Rutherford, Jr., & B. I. Wolford (Eds.), *Special education in the criminal justice system* (pp. 120-140). Columbus, OH: Merrill.

Lane, B. A. (1980). The relationship of learning disabilities to juvenile delinquency: Current status. *Journal of Learning Disabilities, 13*, 425-434.

Lang, R. E., & Kahn, J. V. (1986). Teacher estimates of handicapped student crime victimization and delinquency. *Journal of Special Education, 20*, 358-364.

Levin, E. K., Zigmond, N., & Birch, J. W. (1985). A follow-up study of 52 learning disabled adolescents. *Journal of Learning Disabilities, 18*, 2-7.

Licht, B. G. (1983). Cognitive-motivational factors that contribute to the achievement of learning-disabled children. *Journal of Learning Disabilities, 16*, 483-490.

Mercer, C. D. (1987). *Students with learning disabilities* (3rd ed.). Columbus, OH: Merrill.

Miller, S. E., Zigmond, N., & Leinhardt, G. (1988, April). *Experiential features of secondary schooling for high risk LD students: Part 2. Social integration.* Paper presented at the annual meeting of the American Education Research Association, Washington, DC.

Murphy, D. M. (1986). The prevalence of handicapping conditions among juvenile delinquents. *Remedial and Special Education, 7*(3), 7-17.

Murray, C. A. (1976). *The link between learning disabilities and juvenile delinquency: Current theory and knowledge* (Publication No. 027-000-00479-2). Washington, DC: Government Printing Office.

Pasternak, R., & Lyon, R. (1982). Clinical and empirical identification of learning disabled juvenile delinquents. *Journal of Correctional Education, 33*(2), 7-13.

Pickar, D. B., & Tori, C. D. (1986). The learning disabled adolescent: Eriksonian psychosocial development, self-concept, and delinquent behavior. *Journal of Youth and Adolescence, 15*, 429-440.

Quay, H. C. (1965). Psychopathic personality as pathological stimulation seeking. *American Journal of Psychiatry, 122*, 180-183.

Robison, M. A., & Medway, F. J. (1985). Teachers' expectations and attributions for student achievement: Effects of label, performance patterns, and special education intervention. *American Educational Research Journal, 22*, 561-573.

Rutherford, R. B., Jr., Nelson, C. M., & Wolford, B. I. (1985). Special education in the most restrictive environment: Correctional/special education. *Journal of Special Education, 19*, 59-71.

U.S. Department of Education. (1988). *Tenth annual report to Congress on the implementation of the Education for the Handicapped Act.* Washington, DC: Author.

Ysseldyke, J. E., Thurlow, M. L., & Christenson S. L. (1988, April). *Examination of categorical practice in special education: Is it supported by research?* Paper presented at the annual meeting of the American Educational Research Association, New Orleans.

Zigmond, N., & Thornton, H. (1985). Follow-up of postsecondary age learning disabled graduates and drop-outs. *Learning Disabilities Research, 1*(1), 50-55.

5

Estimating the Prevalence of Learning Disabled and Mentally Retarded Juvenile Offenders

A Meta-Analysis

PAMELA CASEY
INGO KEILITZ

Conducting research on mentally disabled and handicapped juvenile offenders is hampered by the lack of consensus among public officials, practitioners, and researchers on the magnitude of the problem. State departments of corrections and education surveyed by Rutherford, Nelson, and Wolford (1985) reported prevalence estimates of handicapping conditions among young offenders in juvenile correctional facilities ranging from 4% to nearly 100%, with a mean of 28%. Administrators of state juvenile correctional facilities surveyed by Morgan (1979) reported a range of estimates of handicaps among juvenile offenders from 0 to 100%, with a mean of 42%. Studies based upon direct observation or examination of records of selected samples of offenders also have produced a broad range of estimates (Murphy, 1986) matching

AUTHORS' NOTE: The research reported in this chapter was funded by a grant (no. G008530203) from the U.S. Department of Education, Office of Special Education and Rehabilitative Services. The views expressed and conclusions drawn in this chapter are those of the authors and do not necessarily reflect positions held by the U.S. Department of Education.

the wide variability of the official estimates reported by Rutherford et al. and Morgan.

As noted by a number of researchers (e.g., Murphy, 1986; Murray, 1976), the problems in determining the prevalence of criminal defendants and offenders with mental disabilities and handicapping conditions are *definitional* (studies employ varying definitions of mental disabilities and handicapping conditions), *diagnostic* (studies use testing instruments that are inappropriate), *procedural* (subjective diagnoses are constructed by the same individuals who ascertain the extent of the disabilities or handicapping conditions), *analytical* (studies are inappropriately designed or use inappropriate statistical tests), and *presentational* (studies fail to provide sufficient information for interpretation of the results). Official estimates of prevalence rates may be confounded by political considerations (Rutherford et al., 1985). Some administrators may be overly inclusive in their definitions of mental disabilities and handicapping conditions, thereby assuring an adequate number to impress funding authorities. Others may deliberately deflate prevalence estimates to ward off charges that their programs are inadequate to meet the needs of identified disabled or handicapped defendants and offenders. A comparison of two surveys of state officials, revealing prevalence estimates ranging from 0 to 100% among states as well as differences as great as 75% among official reports from the same state, suggest that political considerations may be controlling official estimates (Murphy, 1986).

Despite these problems, improvements in our capacity to estimate the prevalence of mental disabilities and handicapping conditions among juvenile offenders and to communicate the dimensions of the problem seem critical to the development of responsible public policy and to the building of effective programs that disabled or handicapped juvenile offenders are legally entitled to receive.[1] Accurate estimates of the prevalence of delinquent youth are necessary for understanding the epidemiology of delinquency and, ultimately, its causes (Farrington, 1987). By determining the prevalence of juveniles who are mentally retarded, learning disabled, or emotionally disturbed at different stages of the legal system (e.g., arrest, detention, adjudication, disposition), and by correlating these prevalence estimates with demographic and social variables, it becomes possible to consider the etiology of their delinquent behavior and identify strategies for effective treatment. Thus prevalence estimates are critical for making policy decisions and for guiding research efforts.

As noted above, however, although many studies have examined the prevalence of mentally disabled and handicapped juveniles in the legal system, consistent and reliable estimates are not available. In response to this problem, the Institute on Mental Disability and the Law of the National Center for State Courts sought to combine in a systematic fashion the disparate information currently available about the prevalence of mentally disabled and handicapped juvenile offenders to produce prevalence estimates that could be used by policymakers, administrators, practitioners, and researchers.[2]

We took the approach of reviewing existing studies rather than conducting a new study because of the extraordinary resources that would be necessary to collect primary data for a national, comprehensive study of the prevalence of youthful offenders with disabilities or handicaps. In addition to the fiscal concerns, we considered three other drawbacks to initiating a new study, discussed by Light and Pillemer (1984, p. ix): the loss of potentially valuable information that already exists, postponement of a decision about prevalence until the new study is completed, and the creation of one more study on prevalence that does not help resolve the conflicting information that currently exists. Because of these drawbacks, we agreed with Light and Pillemer's conclusion that "even with difficult problems, it is worth trying to combine and reconcile conflicting outcomes." The following sections describe in some detail the technique we used for systematically summarizing and synthesizing the literature in order to reconcile conflicting information regarding prevalence estimates.

Aggregation of Studies of Prevalence

Our study of the prevalence of mentally disabled and handicapped offenders was based on the methods commonly associated with meta-analysis, an approach for integrating research findings across studies that was first introduced by Glass and his colleagues (e.g., Glass, 1976; Rosenthal, 1984). We followed the major steps involved in conducting a meta-analysis (compilation of a bibliography, coding of studies on selected variables, and so on), but we did not compute an effect size estimate[3] because most of the studies examining the prevalence of handicapped offenders did not include control or comparison groups. We thus calculated a weighted average prevalence estimate instead of an effect size. That is, each study was rated on a series of variables related to its internal and external validity, and this information then was taken into consideration in calculating the average prevalence rate across studies.

Our original intention was to provide average prevalence estimates for the most frequently occurring disabling or handicapping conditions such as learning disability, mental retardation, emotional disturbance, and speech impairment. However, the number and quality of studies of several of these conditions precluded the calculation of such estimates. A weighted prevalence estimate based on only one study and an average prevalence rate based on a few poorly rated studies are too unreliable to be useful. Therefore, though we will discuss other disabling or handicapping conditions in describing the earlier steps of the technique, our focus will be primarily on the prevalence of juveniles with learning disabilities or mental retardation. Both of these conditions were addressed by a number of different studies.

The research consisted of five steps: (a) literature search and compilation of a bibliography on the topic of disabled and handicapped offenders; (b) selection, review, and description of empirical prevalence studies in this bibliography; (c) rating of the studies; (d) estimation of the prevalence of mentally retarded and learning disabled juvenile offenders; and (e) identification of possible relationships that explain the wide range of prevalence estimates cited in the literature. Each of these steps is described below.

Literature Search and Compilation of Bibliography

We first identified all pertinent literature on the topic of disabled and handicapped young offenders. Only articles that noted *both* handicapped conditions (or their remediation) and the criminal justice system in their titles were included. Articles published before 1975, the effective date of the Education for All Handicapped Children Act (P.L. 94-142), were not included in the bibliography.

Articles were obtained from several electronic and manual indexing services, including the Educational Resources Information Center (ERIC), Psychology Information (PSYCInfo), Legal Resource Index, State Publications Index, and the Criminal Justice Periodical Index. In total, 16 services were searched for relevant articles. Terms that qualified an article for inclusion in the bibliography included, but were not limited to, the following: *handicaps, learning disabilities, disability, emotional disturbance, mental retardation, behavior disorders, brain damage, neurological deficits, special education, rehabilitation, courts, corrections, delinquency, juvenile delinquent, and juvenile courts.* Generally speaking, the searches excluded literature that focused on physical diseases in delinquent groups, except when those diseases were identified by these general descriptors (e.g., Yeudall, Fromm-Auch, & Davies, 1982).

Letters were written to state special education and corrections departments in an effort to obtain unpublished studies relevant to the topic of mentally disabled and handicapped young offenders. A few of the studies received from these state agencies or from cross-references to other articles did not mention both handicapping conditions and the criminal justice system in their titles, but were, nonetheless, considered relevant and included. These searches resulted in a bibliography of 310 articles.[4]

Selection, Review, and Description of Prevalence Studies

Selection of articles. The first task of this second step involved identification of articles from the bibliography that included quantitative studies of the prevalence of mental disabilities and handicapping conditions among juvenile offenders. Each article selected from the bibliography met four criteria:

(1) Juveniles observed, tested, or studied made official "contact" with one or more components of the justice system (e.g., police or other law enforcement agencies, the courts, or correctional agencies).

(2) The study included at least *some* individuals between the ages of 2 and 22 at the time of the study.

(3) The mental disabilities and handicapping conditions assessed approximate those outlined in Section 504 of the Rehabilitation Act of 1973 and the Education for All Handicapped Children Act of 1975.

(4) Reported prevalence estimates were based on direct observation or assessment of the juveniles.

Reports of surveys of administrators and state officials (e.g., Morgan, 1979; Rutherford et al., 1985), narrative reviews of quantitative studies (e.g., Murphy, 1986; Murray, 1976), and studies reporting anecdotal evidence (Mauser, 1974; Poremba, 1975) were eliminated from further consideration during this second step. A few of the excluded studies met all four criteria noted above but failed either to report prevalence estimates or to provide sufficient information to allow the computation of such estimates (e.g., Bachara & Zaba, 1978; Reilly, Wheeler, & Etlinger, 1985; Zinkus & Gottlieb, 1978). A total of 31 articles met all four criteria and formed the data base for the study.

Review and description of selected articles. Each of the 31 articles was described in terms of the following categories of information:

(1) the type of mental disabilities or handicapping conditions studied and the reported prevalence rates

(2) the conceptual and/or operational definition of the disabilities or handicapping conditions investigated

(3) the definition of delinquency or the extent of the juvenile's contact with the justice system

(4) the sample (e.g., size, geographic location, demographics) and the sampling procedures upon which the prevalence estimates were based

(5) the characteristics of any comparison or control groups if included in the study

(6) the nature of the instruments or other assessment devices that were used for identifying, classifying, or diagnosing the mental disabilities or handicapping conditions

(7) the training, experience, and credentials of the individuals who conducted the assessments

(8) the testing procedures and the testing environment

(9) any additional findings related specifically to the prevalence of mental disabilities or handicapping conditions among juvenile offenders (e.g., prevalence estimates for specific demographic groups)

Each of the 31 articles was reviewed at least twice.[5]

Many of the articles reported prevalence rates for more than one handicapping condition (e.g., learning disabilities and mental retardation) and a few reported prevalence rates for more than one sample (e.g., juveniles on probation and juveniles in institutions). *Studies* establishing prevalence rates were thus distinguished from the *articles* in which the studies were reported. That is, each article contributed one or more studies to the analysis. The number of studies, which formed the data base for the analysis, corresponds to the number of prevalence rates represented for all handicapping conditions across the 31 articles.[6]

Table 5.1 describes the overall data base for the analysis, grouping 58 studies by handicapping condition. Roughly three-quarters of the studies reported prevalence rates for either learning disabilities or

Table 5.1. Studies Estimating the Prevalence of Handicapping Conditions
Among Juvenile Offenders

Handicapping Condition	Number of Studies
Learning disability	22
Mental retardation	21
Emotional disturbance	3
Speech impairment	1
Neurological impairment	3
Behavioral disorders	2
Learning disability/emotional disturbance	2
Mental retardation/emotional disturbance	1
Psychiatric disorder	2
Unspecified handicaps	1
Total	58

mental retardation. Only 26% investigated other handicapping conditions. Except where noted, these eight categories are referred to as "other handicapping conditions" throughout the remainder of this chapter.

Reported prevalence rates for learning disabilities range from 1.7% to 77% across 22 studies; for mental retardation the range is from 2% to 30% across 21 studies; and for other handicapping conditions the range is from 0 to 84% across 15 studies.[7] The difficulty of using such a broad range of estimates for meaningful policy and program development is self-evident.

Rating the Studies

Qualitative differences among studies were taken into consideration by rating each study on criteria related to eight different categories: sample size, sampling methods, and the gender and ethnicity of the study's sample—which pertain to the study's external validity—and the study's definition of handicapping conditions, use of primary or archival data, assessment devices, assessment methods, and the evaluators' credentials—which focus on the study's internal validity.

Some of the categories required the rating of objective information such as the size and demographic makeup of the sample. Other categories required more subjective determinations. For example, the appropriateness of the assessment devices required a subjective rating of the study along a descending dimension defined by the following values:

(2) The handicapping condition was identified by standard instruments (diagnostic tests, classifications, and so forth), perhaps appropriately modified, that are widely recognized and used with individuals suspected of having the mental disabilities or handicapping conditions (i.e., the instruments are "good tests"—reliable and valid).

(1) Only limited evidence exists that the instruments used are standard tests widely recognized and used with individuals suspected of having the handicapping condition.

(0) Information about the instruments is insufficient for rating.

(−1) Either no evidence exists that the instruments used to identify the presence of the handicapping condition are standard tests or the instruments are clearly unorthodox.

Generally speaking, studies that used standard tests (e.g., Wechsler Intelligence Scale for Children—Revised or the Wide Range Achievement Test) were given a rating of 2, studies that used group intelligence tests were given a rating of 1, and studies in which the authors developed their own scales for assessing handicapping conditions were given a rating of −1. Some studies employed several different tests and, therefore, conceivably could be represented by more than one code. For example, a study could be rated 2 because it used a standardized individual intelligence test, and 1 because it used, in part, a group intelligence test. Such studies were discussed on a case-by-case basis to determine the most appropriate rating.

Table 5.2 presents the ratings for each of the studies estimating learning disabilities or mental retardation among juvenile offenders. Individual ratings were totaled across all eight categories for each of the studies. The total rating score determined a study's "weight" in computing the average prevalence estimate.

Estimates of Prevalence

Once rated, a weight of 1 to 4 was given to each study based on the quartile of total ratings scores in which the individual study fell. The weights corresponded to the number of times a study's reported prevalence was counted in calculating the average prevalence estimates. For example, a study assigned a total rating in the third quartile of the total ratings scores was counted three times in calculating the overall estimate of prevalence.

Based on the previous three steps, the weighted average prevalence estimate of learning disabled juvenile offenders is 35.6% and the

Table 5.2. Ratings for Each Study Estimating the Prevalence of Learning Disabilities or Mental Retardation Among Juvenile Offenders

First Author (Date)	Sample Size[a]	Sampling Methods[b]	Gender/ Ethnicity[c]	Data Source[d]	Instruments[e]	Definitions[f]	Assessment Methods[g]	Evaluators[h]	Total
Learning Disabilities									
Mauser (1986)	2	2	2	1	1	3.0	1	0	12.0
Lenz (1980)	2	0	0	1	1	1.5	0	0	5.5
Bullock (1979)	3	0	2	-1	2	.5	1	2	9.5
Pasternack (1982)	1	2	2	1	2	3.0	2	2	15.0
Prout (1981)	3	0	1	-1	0	1.5	1	1	6.5
Cheek (1983/1984)	2	2	0	-1	0	0.0	1	2	6.0
Kardash (1983)	3	1	0	-1	0	1.0	1	2	7.0
U.S. General Accounting Office (1977)	2	2	1	1	2	3.0	2	2	15.0
Whitaker (1981)	1	0	0	1	2	2.0	1	1	8.0
Broder (1981)	4	1	0	1	2	3.0	2	2	15.0
Zinkus (1979)	2	0	0	1	2	2.5	1	0	8.5
Smykla and Willis (1981)	1	2	-1	1	2	3.0	0	0	8.0
WESCENMO, Inc. (1979)	3	-1	1	1	2	2.0	2	2	12.0
Robbins (1983a)	1	-1	0	1	2	2.0	2	2	9.0
Smykla (1981b)	1	1	0	1	2	3.0	0	0	8.0
Robbins (1983b)	1	0	0	1	2	2.0	2	2	10.0
Smykla (1981c)	1	1	0	1	2	3.0	0	0	8.0
Goulas (1982)	1	2	1	1	2	3.0	1	2	13.0
Love (1975)	2	-1	1	1	2	1.0	1	2	9.0
Swanstrom (1978)	2	-1	0	0	1	3.0	0	1	6.0
Wilgosh (1982)	2	-1	1	1	2	2.0	0	1	8.0
Sawicki (1979)	2	2	0	1	0	2.0	1	1	9.0

Mental retardation

Prout (1981)	3	0	1	-1	0	2.0	0	1	1	7.0
Kardash (1983)	3	1	0	-1	0	1.0	0	1	2	7.0
Cull (1975a)	4	0	0	-1	1	2.5	1	-1	2	7.5
Cheek (1983/1984)	2	2	0	-1	0	1.0	0	1	2	7.0
McManus (1981)	2	-1	2	1	1	1.5	1	1	2	9.5
Missouri Association for Retarded Citizens (1976b)	4	-1	2	1	1	2.0	1	1	0	10.0
Prescott (1982)	4	1	2	-1	1	3.0	1	0	0	10.0
Missouri Association for Retarded Citizens (1976a)	4	0	2	1	2	2.5	2	1	0	12.5
WESCENMO, Inc. (1979)	3	-1	1	1	2	2.0	2	2	2	12.0
Day (1982)	3	0	2	-1	2	3.0	2	0	1	10.0
Dennis (1975)	3	1	-1	1	1	2.5	1	0	0	7.5
Smykla (1981c)	1	1	0	1	2	3.0	2	0	0	8.0
Mesinger (1976)	4	1	2	-1	1	2.5	1	0	0	9.5
Mauser (1986)	2	2	2	1	1	2.5	1	1	0	11.5
Cull (1975b)	3	1	0	-1	1	2.5	1	1	2	9.5
Goulas (1982)	1	2	1	1	2	3.0	2	1	2	13.0
Sawicki (1979)	2	2	0	1	0	.5	0	1	1	7.5
Smykla (1981b)	1	1	0	1	2	3.0	2	0	0	8.0
Smykla (1981a)	1	2	-1	1	2	3.0	2	0	0	8.0
Bullock (1979)	3	0	2	-1	2	.5	2	1	2	9.5
Pasternack (1982)	1	2	2	2	2	2.0	2	2	1	13.0

a. Rated as follows: 0 = less than 21; 1 = 21 to 50; 2 = 51 to 150; 3 = 151 to 500; 4 = more than 500.

b. Ratings based on two variables: selection procedure and presence of bias in the sample. Ratings for both variables summed to obtain a study's ratings for the category. Selection procedure rated as follows: 0 = no information on selection; 1 = sample selected for convenience, selected using a mixed strategy of sampling (e.g., random selection from a convenience sample) or consisted of all juveniles from one or more facilities; 2 = utilized random sampling. Presence of possible bias in the sample

(continued)

Table 5.2 Continued

rated as follows: −2 = bias toward higher incidence of handicapping conditions (e.g., sample drawn from facility for mentally retarded offenders); −1 = possible bias but directionality unknown; 0 = no indication of bias.

c. Ratings based on two variables: gender and ethnicity. Ratings for both variables summed to obtain a study's rating for the category. Gender rated as follows: −1 = sample included only males or females; 0 = gender was not reported; 1 = sample included both males and females. Ethnicity rated as follows: −1 = sample included only Whites or minorities; 0 = ethnicity was not reported; 1 = sample included both Whites and minorities.

d. Rated as follows: −1 = subjects identified as handicapped based on prior records only; 0 = information on data source insufficient for making a judgment; 1 = subjects identified as handicapped based on original data from tests and/or direct observations.

e. Rated as follows: −1 = no evidence of the use of appropriate standard instruments for identifying the handicap; 0 = information on the instruments was insufficient for making a judgment; 1 = limited evidence of the use of appropriate standard instruments; 2 = used valid and reliable instruments for identifying handicapping condition.

f. Ratings based on three variables: the quantity of information provided for identifying the handicapping condition, the definition's agreement with standard definitions of handicapping conditions, and the definition's level of detail. Ratings for the three variables were summed to obtain a study's rating for the category. Quantity of information rated as follows: 0 = information insufficient for identifying the handicap; .5 = identifying information provided by inference/reference only; 1 = information sufficient for identifying the handicap. Agreement rated as follows: 0 = no information or no agreement with federal, state, or professional groups' definitions of handicapping conditions; .5 = partial agreement with standard definitions; 1 = strict adherence to standard definitions. Level of detail rated as follows: 0 = insufficient detail to replicate even partially (e.g., no tests or criteria mentioned); .5 = sufficient detail to replicate partially; 1 = sufficient detail to replicate completely.

g. Rated as follows: −1 = some evidence of inappropriate testing procedures; 0 = information on assessment methods insufficient for making a judgment; 1 = limited evidence that tests were administered correctly; 2 = strong evidence that tests were administered correctly.

h. Rated as follows: −1 = some evidence evaluators did not have appropriate training/experience; 0 = information on evaluators insufficient for making a judgment; 1 = limited evidence that evaluators have appropriate credentials; 2 = strong evidence that evaluators have appropriate credentials.

Table 5.3 Reported Prevalence, Ratings Score, Weight, and Weighted Prevalence Estimate of Learning Disabled Among Juvenile Offenders

Authors (Date)	Reported Prevalence Estimate	Ratings Score	Weight
Lenz et al. (1980)	6.0	5.5	1
Cheek (1983/1984)	13.5	6.0	1
Swanstrom et al. (1978)	59.7	6.0	1
Prout (1981)	13.0	6.5	1
Kardash & Rutherford (1983)	20.0	7.0	1
Whitaker (1981)	27.0	8.0	2
Smykla & Willis (1981a)	37.0	8.0	2
Smykla & Willis (1981b)	40.0	8.0	2
Smykla & Willis (1981c)	53.0	8.0	2
Wilgosh & Paitich (1982)	62.0	8.0	2
Zinkus & Gottlieb (1979)	36.7	8.5	2
Robbins et al. (1983a)	40.0	9.0	3
Love & Bachara (1975)	57.0	9.0	3
Sawicki & Schaeffer (1979)	77.0	9.0	3
Bullock & Reilly (1979)	9.0	9.5	3
Robbins et al. (1983b)	48.0	10.0	3
Mauser & Cannella (1986)	1.7	12.0	4
WESCENMO, Inc. (1979)	37.0	12.0	4
Goulas (1982)	56.0	13.0	4
Pasternack & Lyon (1982)	12.5	15.0	4
U.S. General Accounting Office (1977)	26.0	15.0	4
Broder et al. (1981)	36.5	15.0	4
Weighted prevalence estimate[a]	35.6%		

a. Weighted prevalence estimate = Σ (reported prevalence estimate × weight)/Σ weight.

weighted average prevalence estimate of mentally retarded juvenile offenders is 12.6%. Tables 5.3 and 5.4 present each study's reported prevalence,[8] total ratings score, and weight.

Relationships Between Prevalence and Other Factors

What accounts for the variability of reported estimates of prevalence of disabilities and handicapping conditions among juvenile offenders? Some researchers attribute it, in part, to the range of definitions, diagnostic instruments, assessment procedures, and research designs used by the different studies (e.g., Murphy, 1986; Murray, 1976). Explor-

Table 5.4. Reported Prevalence, Ratings Score, Weight, and Weighted Prevalence Estimate of Mentally Retarded Among Juvenile Offenders

Authors (Date)	Reported Prevalence Estimate	Ratings Score	Weight
Prout (1981)	2.0	7.0	1
Kardash & Rutherford (1983)	3.0	7.0	1
Cheek (1983/1984)	3.8	7.0	1
Cull et al. (1975a)	3.3	7.5	2
Dennis (1975)	13.0	7.5	2
Sawicki & Schaeffer (1979)	16.0	7.5	2
Smykla & Willis (1981c)	13.0	8.0	2
Smykla & Willis (1981b)	20.0	8.0	2
Smykla & Willis (1981a)	23.0	8.0	2
McManus et al. (1981)	4.2	9.5	3
Mesinger (1976)	14.6	9.5	3
Cull et al. (1975b)	15.3	9.5	3
Bullock & Reilly (1979)	25.0	9.5	3
Missouri Association for Retarded Citizens (1976a)	4.2	10.0	3
Prescott & Van Houten (1982)	6.0	10.0	3
Day & Joyce (1982)	7.4	10.0	3
Mauser & Cannella (1986)	15.0	11.5	3
WESCENMO, Inc. (1979)	6.3	12.0	4
Missouri Association for Retarded Citizens (1976b)	6.3	12.5	4
Goulas (1982)	16.0	13.0	4
Pasternack & Lyon (1982)	30.0	13.0	4
Weighted prevalence estimate[a]	12.6%		

a. Weighted prevalence estimate = Σ (reported prevalence estimate $\times$ weight)/Σ weight.

atory analyses were conducted to investigate the extent of the relationship between the variables rated to obtain the weighted prevalence estimates (definitions, instruments, assessment methods, evaluators, and sampling methods) and reported prevalence rates for learning disabilities and mental retardation. Another variable—furthest penetration into the legal system—that was not used in calculating the average prevalence estimates was considered in these analyses. This variable accounts for how far a juvenile in the study had progressed through the legal system—that is, intake, formal hearing (e.g., adjudication, in need of supervision), diverted into program, or resident of treatment or

Table 5.5. Correlations Between Selected Variables and Reported Prevalence Estimates

Variable	Learning Disabilities (N = 22)[a]	Mental Retardation (N = 21)[b]
Definition of the handicapping condition	.24	.06
Instruments	.20	.51*
Evaluators	.02	−.18
Assessment methods	−.18	.13
Sampling methods	−.22	.53*
Penetration into legal system	−.53*	−.30

a. Data were unavailable for two cases on the variable "penetration into legal system."
b. Data were unavilable for one case on the variable "penetration into legal system."
*$p < .01$.

correctional facilities. The results shown in Table 5.5 suggest directions for future studies.

Furthest penetration into the legal system is the only variable to correlate moderately with the reported prevalence rates of learning disabilities. It accounts for approximately 28% of the variance and has an inverse relationship with learning disabilities, indicating that as juveniles progress through the system, fewer are identified as learning disabled.[9] This may reflect attempts by the juvenile justice system to divert handicapped juveniles from the system at early stages in the adjudication process.

For mental retardation, both sampling methods and instruments correlate moderately with the reported prevalence rates of mental retardation. Sampling methods account for approximately 28% of the variance, and instruments account for approximately 26%. Both of these variables relate to a study's sensitivity in identifying juveniles with the handicapping condition. Thus better sampling procedures and more sensitive diagnostic instruments probably result in more identifications of mentally retarded offenders.

Conspicuous are the small correlations between the definition of the handicapping condition and reported prevalence rates for both learning disabilities and mental retardation. As noted above, problems encountered in trying to standardize definitions of the various handicapping conditions (particularly learning disabilities) are noted by many researchers in the field. A possible explanation for the small correlations is that major discrepancies between definitions gradually have been eliminated by federal and state guidelines.

Conclusions

During 1984, a total of 1,040 publicly operated state and local juvenile detention, correctional, and shelter facilities registered more than one million admissions and discharges. On a single day in February 1985, these facilities held 49,322 residents, of which 93% were accused of, or had been adjudicated delinquent for, acts that would be criminal offenses if committed by others; most of the remaining were "status offenders" such as runaways, truants, and curfew violators (Bureau of Justice Statistics, 1986). The empirical and logical manipulations of our study permit us to estimate that 17,559 (35.6%) of these juveniles would be considered learning disabled and that 6,214 (12.6%) would be considered mentally retarded.

The public, elected and appointed officials, and those directly involved in the management of juvenile offenders may well believe that offenders, regardless of their disabilities or handicaps, least deserve tax dollars (U.S. Department of Justice, 1984). Without a consensus among advocates on the magnitude of the problem, it seems unlikely that disabled or handicapped juvenile offenders will be able to compete for their proper share of increasingly limited public service dollars (Keilitz & Van Duizend, 1984). Unambiguous estimates of the prevalence of mental disabilities and handicaps among juvenile offenders at various stages of the justice system are, in our view, the crucial first step toward development of responsible public policy and effective programs.

The analysis reported in this chapter is an attempt to move public policy toward a consensus on the magnitude of the problem in terms of prevalence estimates. The research provides a clear, albeit tentative answer to the question of the prevalence of learning disabled and mentally retarded juvenile offenders. It provides a framework for replication and adjustment of prevalence estimates, and it proposes the tools and manipulations for making those adjustments. A more conservative adjustment, for example, may include studies of prevalence with weights of 3 or 4, excluding poorly designed studies. (The weighted prevalence estimates based on this method are 35.2% for learning disabilities and 12.7% for mental retardation.) The purposes of such estimates (including whether the risks of Type I or Type II errors are greater) may dictate the methods of adjustment. Finally, the framework easily accommodates the results of additional prevalence studies as they become available.

Those who wish to influence responsible public policy and encourage the development of sound programs for juvenile offenders with mental disabilities and handicaps can embrace at least two approaches characterized by differing viewpoints and tools. The first relies on ideology, doctrinal analysis, chronology of legal entitlements of disabled and handicapped juvenile offenders (e.g., the Developmental Disabilities Assistance and Bill of Rights Act or the Education for All Handicapped Children Act), and anecdote to press for reform. Embraced by legal scholars, this approach begins with the question, What *ought* to be? and applies the tools of reason and logic to universal principles of personal autonomy, privacy, and so forth to answer it. To a large extent, this approach has dominated the field of mental disability and the law (Keilitz, in press). The second approach, in contrast, begins with the question, What *is*? and proceeds to build reform efforts on the *empirical* exploration of that question. At least one commentator has argued that we are at our best an "experimenting society" that is tested by experience and guided by results (Campbell, 1969). In accordance with this approach, social reform follows a course beginning with the determination of the dimensions of a social problem, which leads to innovation, experimentation, followed by demonstration of promise and solutions, widespread implementation, and, ultimately, the institutionalization of reform. The research described in this chapter is consistent with this approach.

Notes

1. For example, the Rehabilitation Act of 1973, P.L. 93-112, 87 Stat. 355 (codified in scattered sections of 29 U.S.C. §§ 701 to 794); the Education for All Handicapped Children Act of 1975, P.L. 94-142, 89 Stat. 773 (codified at 20 U.S.C. §§ 1232, 1405, 1406, 1411-20, 1453 [1982]); the Developmental Disabilities Assistance and Bill of Rights Act of 1975 (amended 1978), P.L. 94-103, 89 Stat. 486 (codified at 42 U.S.C. §§ 6000-81 [1976 & Supp. V. 1981]).

2. The research was conducted as part of the institute's initiative to bring cases involving mental health administration. The research is consistent with the first step of the institute's program of research: (a) problem identification and analysis, (b) program description and analysis, (c) establishment of linkages and relationships, (d) demonstration of promising solutions, and (e) implementation and institutionalization.

3. Light and Pillemer (1983) define effect size as "the difference between the treatment and control group means divided by the control group standard deviation" (p. 37).

4. The bibliography, including key descriptors and indexing services used, may be obtained from the authors (Mental Disability Law Center, National Center for State Courts, 300 Newport Avenue, Williamsburg, VA 23187-8798).

5. Detailed descriptions, including complete citations, of the 31 articles may be obtained from the authors (see address, note 4).

6. The studies by Mesinger (1976) and Steiger (1984) reported prevalence rates for more than one handicapping condition, but the handicapping conditions were not mutually exclusive. Some juveniles could have been counted as having more than one handicapping condition, creating an inflated estimate of the number of handicapped juvenile offenders. The handicapping condition with the highest reported prevalence rate counted as the only study for each of these articles. Cheek (1983/1984) reported prevalence rates based on files from a state juvenile institution and files from the Local Education Agencies (LEA). Only the prevalence rates based on the file from the juvenile institution were used because too little information was available on the LEA files.

7. The ranges of reported prevalence estimates for the other handicapping conditions were as follows: 20-24% for behavior disorder, 0-36% for emotional disturbance, 0-84% for neurological impairment, 20-67.6% for psychiatric disturbance, 3% for speech impairment, 13.5-46% for the dual diagnosis of both learning disabled and emotionally disturbed, 5.8% for the dual diagnosis of both mental retardation and emotional disturbance, and 16% for unspecified handicaps.

8. For the purposes of this research, a few of the prevalence figures were recalculated for technical reasons, for example, to take into consideration missing cases. Therefore, there may be some differences between the prevalence figures reported in the tables and the prevalence figures reported in the research articles. Any discrepancies are explained in full in the final report of the project *The Prevalence of Mental Disabilities and Handicapping Conditions Among Juvenile Offenders*, available from the authors (see address, note 4).

9. Nine of the studies on learning disabilities sampled juveniles who had received formal hearings (e.g., adjudication or in need of supervision) or participated in diversion programs. The weighted prevalence estimate for these juveniles is 42.4%. The estimate for incarcerated juveniles (based on 10 studies) is 22.3%.

References

Bachara, G. H., & Zaba, J. N. (1978). Learning disabilities and juvenile delinquency. *Journal of Learning Disabilities, 11*, 58-62.

Broder, P. K., Dunivant, N., Smith, E. C., & Sutton, L. P. (1981). Further observations on the link between learning disabilities and juvenile delinquency. *Journal of Educational Psychology, 73*, 838-850.

Bullock, L. M., & Reilly, T. F. (1979). A descriptive profile of the adjudicated adolescent: A status report. In R. B. Rutherford & A. G. Prieto (Eds.), *Severe behavior disorders of children and youth* (Vol. 2, pp. 153-161). Reston, VA: Council for Children with Behavioral Disorders.

Bureau of Justice Statistics. (1986, October). Children in custody. *Bulletin*, pp. 1-6.

Campbell, D. T. (1969). Reforms as experiments. *American Psychologist, 24*, 409-429.

Cheek, M. C. (1984). The educational and sociological status of handicapped and non-handicapped incarcerated female adolescents (Doctoral dissertation, University of Maryland, 1983). *Dissertation Abstracts International, 45*(3-A), 954-955.

Cull, W. H., Reuthebuck, G. L., & Pape, N. (1975). *Mentally retarded offenders in adult and juvenile correctional institutions.* Frankfort: Kentucky Legislative Research Commission.

Day, E., & Joyce, K. (1982). Mentally retarded youth in Cuyahoga County Juvenile Court: Juvenile court work research group. In M. B. Santamour & P. S. Watson (Eds.), *The retarded offender* (pp. 141-165). New York: Praeger.

Dennis, F. (1975). Mental retardation and corrections: A research perspective. In M. Santamour (Ed.), *The mentally retarded citizens and the criminal justice system: Problems and programs* (pp. 34-53). Newport, RI: James L. Maher Center.

Farrington, D. P. (1987). Epidemiology. In H. C. Quay (Ed.), *Handbook of juvenile delinquency* (pp. 33-61). New York: John Wiley.

Glass, G. V (1976). Primary, secondary, and meta-analysis of research. *Educational Researcher, 5*, 3-8.

Goulas, F. M. (1982). A diagnostic study of the prevalence of learning disabilities detected in randomly selected referrals to Jefferson County probation services: Jefferson County, Texas (Doctoral dissertation, McNeese State University, 1982). *Dissertation Abstracts International, 43*(6-A), 1926.

Kardash, C. A., & Rutherford, R. B. (1983). Meeting the special education needs of adolescents in the Arizona Department of Corrections. *Journal of Correctional Education, 34*(3), 97-98.

Keilitz, I. (in press). Legal issues in mental health care: Current perspectives. In D. A. Rochefort (Ed.), *Handbook on mental health policy in the United States.* Westport, CT: Greenwood.

Keilitz, I., & Van Duizend, R. (1984). *Youth and the justice system: Can we intervene earlier?* (Prepared statement for the hearing before the Select Committee on Children, Youth, and Families, House of Representatives, 98th Congress, pp. 169-179). Washington, DC: Government Printing Office.

Lenz, B. K., Warner, M. M., Alley, G. R., & Deshler, D. D. (1980). *A comparison of youths who have committed delinquent acts with learning disabled, low-achieving, and normally-achieving adolescents* (Research Report No. 29). Lawrence: University of Kansas, Institute for Research in Learning Disabilities. (ERIC Document Reproduction Service No. ED 217 641)

Light, R. J., & Pillemer, D. B. (1983). Numbers and narrative: Combining their strengths in research reviews. In R. J. Light (Ed.), *Evaluation studies review annual* (Vol. 8, pp. 33-58). Beverly Hills, CA: Sage.

Light, R. J., & Pillemer, D. B. (1984). *Summing up: The science of reviewing research.* Cambridge, MA: Harvard University Press.

Love, W. C., & Bachara, G. H. (1975). A diagnostic team approach for juvenile delinquents with learning disabilities. *Juvenile Justice, 26*(1), 27-30.

Mauser, A. J. (1974). Learning disabilities and delinquent youth. *Academic Therapy, 9*, 389-402.

Mauser, A. J., & Cannella, F. (1986). *Handicapped youthful offenders project: Final report.* (Available from August J. Mauser, Department of Special Education, University of South Florida, Tampa, FL)

McManus, M., Alessi, N., Grapentine, W. L., & Brickman, A. (1981). *A report to the State of Michigan: A psychiatric study of serious juvenile offenders in the state training school system.* Ann Arbor: University of Michigan Medical Center, Children's Psychiatric Service.

Mesinger, J. F. (1976). Juvenile delinquents: A relatively untapped population for special education professionals. *Behavioral Disorders, 2,* 22-28.

Missouri Association for Retarded Citizens, Inc. (1976). *The mentally retarded offender in Missouri with recommendations for a state-wide system of services.* Jefferson City: Author.

Morgan, D. J. (1979). Prevalence and types of handicapping conditions found in juvenile correctional institutions: A national survey. *Journal of Special Education, 13,* 283-295.

Murphy, D. (1986). The prevalence of handicapping conditions among juvenile delinquents. *Remedial and Special Education, 7*(3), 7-17.

Murray, C. A. (1976). *The link between learning disabilities and juvenile delinquency: Current theory and knowledge* (Publication No. 027-000-00479-2; Grant No. 76JN-99-0009). Washington, DC: Government Printing Office.

Pasternack, R., & Lyon, R. (1982). Clinical and empirical identification of learning disabled juvenile delinquents. *Journal of Correctional Education, 33*(2), 7-13.

Poremba, C. D. (1975). Learning disabilities, youth and delinquency: Programs for intervention. In H. R. Myklebust (Ed.), *Progress in learning disabilities* (Vol. 3, pp. 132-149). New York: Grune & Stratton.

Prescott, M., & Van Houten, E. (1982). The retarded juvenile offender in New Jersey: A report on research in correctional facilities and mental retardation facilities. In M. B. Santamour & P. S. Watson (Eds.), *The retarded offender* (pp. 166-175). New York: Praeger.

Prout, H. T. (1981). The incidence of suspected exceptional educational needs among youth in juvenile correctional facilities. *Journal of Correctional Education, 32*(4), 22-24.

Reilly, T. F., Wheeler, L. J., & Etlinger, L. E. (1985). Intelligence versus academic achievement: A comparison of juvenile delinquents and special education classifications. *Criminal Justice and Behavior, 12*(2), 193-208.

Robbins, D. M., Beck, J. C., Pries, R., Jacobs, D., & Smith, C. (1983). Learning disability and neuropsychological impairment in adjudicated unincarcerated male delinquents. *Journal of the American Academy of Child Psychiatry, 22,* 40-46.

Rosenthal, R. (1984). *Meta-analytic procedures for social research.* Beverly Hills, CA: Sage.

Rutherford, R. B., Nelson, C. M., & Wolford, B. I. (1985). Special education in the most restrictive environment: Correctional/special education. *Journal of Special Education, 19,* 59-71.

Sawicki, D., & Schaeffer, B. (1979). An affirmative approach to the LD/JD link. *Juvenile and Family Court Journal, 30,* 11-16.

Smykla, J. O., & Willis, T. W. (1981). The incidence of learning disabilities and mental retardation in youth under the jurisdiction of the juvenile court. *Journal of Criminal Justice, 9*(3), 219-225.

Steiger, J. C. (1984). *Mentally disturbed youths within the division of juvenile rehabilitation residential population.* Olympia, WA: Division of Juvenile Rehabilitation.

Swanstrom, W. J., Randle, C. W., & Offord, K. (1978). *The frequency of learning disability: A comparison between juvenile delinquent and seventh grade school populations.* Unpublished manuscript, Dodge-Fillmore-Olmsted Counties Community Corrections System Learning Disabilities Research Project, Rochester, MN.

U.S. General Accounting Office. (1977). *Learning disabilities: The link to delinquency should be determined, but schools should do more now.* Washington, DC: Author.

U.S. Department of Justice. (1984). *Sourcebook on the mentally disordered prisoner.* Washington, DC: Author.

WESCENMO, Inc. (1979). *Survey of inmates eligible for services according to Public Law 94-142 and recommendations for the creation of a division wide special education system.* Sedalia, MO: Author.

Whitaker, D. W., Jr. (1981). The learning disability-juvenile delinquency link (Doctoral dissertation, Case Western Reserve University, 1981). *Dissertation Abstracts International, 42,* 1070A.

Wilgosh, L., & Paitich, D. (1982). Delinquency and learning disabilities: More evidence. *Journal of Learning Disabilities, 15*(5), 278-279.

Yeudall, L. T., Fromm-Auch, D., & Davies, P. (1982). Neuropsychological impairment of persistent delinquency. *Journal of Nervous and Mental Disease, 170,* 257-265.

Zinkus, P. W., & Gottlieb, M. I. (1978). Learning disabilities and juvenile delinquency. *Clinical Pediatrics, 17,* 775-780.

Zinkus, P. W., & Gottlieb, M. I. (1979). Patterns of perceptual deficits in academically deficient juvenile delinquents. *Psychology in the Schools, 16,* 19-27.

PART II

Social Ecological Perspectives

6

Ecology and Disordered Behavior

An Overview of Perspectives and Assumptions

EDISON J. TRICKETT
SUSAN F. ZLOTLOW

In recent years, the concept of ecology has emerged as a perspective on human behavior (Barker, 1968; Bronfenbrenner, 1979; Hobfall, 1988; Kelly, 1968; Moos, 1974, 1979). While different ecological approaches are currently being developed, all focus on an examination of the relationship between individuals or groups of individuals and their social contexts. Thus behavior is viewed as a transaction between person and setting (see Altman & Rogoff, 1987, for an elaboration of the transactional point of view). Adopting this perspective involves developing frameworks for (a) understanding the nature of the social context, (b) understanding the individual *in context*, and (c) designing interventions that focus on individual-setting transactions rather than on individuals only.

The purpose of the present chapter is to present a brief overview of some of the dominant ecological perspectives and their implications for disordered behavior in adolescents. Because of space constraints, the overview will of necessity forego many of the more subtle differences among the perspectives. However, references will be provided for the interested reader. We begin with a discussion of how researchers in ecological and community psychology have conceptualized social contexts of relevance to adolescents. This is followed by a section on the person in context, beginning with the influential perspective of Bronfenbrenner (1979) and including some specific person-setting interaction assumptions from Kelly and his colleagues (Kelly, 1971; Kelly & Hess, 1987; Trickett, Kelly, & Vincent, 1985). We conclude with a brief discussion of how an ecological perspective affects the design and evaluation of interventions involving adolescents and the settings of importance to them.

The Social Context: An Active and Organized Influence on Adolescent Behavior

Virtually all ecological perspectives on behavior view the social context or environment as the object of study and intervention. Rather than being portrayed as a projective screen onto which individuals impose idiosyncratic meaning, or being seen as a relatively undifferentiated force with which individuals must contend, the ecological environment consists of specific processes, norms, and structures that exert active influence on the individual. For purposes of example, three contrasting perspectives on the ecological environment are reviewed. They include (a) the ecological metaphor developed by Kelly, (b) the social ecology perspective developed by Moos, and (c) the behavior setting approach to ecological psychology developed by Barker. Each has been used extensively in work with settings of relevance to adolescents.

Kelly's Ecological Metaphor: The Ecological Processes of Adaptation, Cycling of Resources, Interdependence, and Succession

The origins of Kelly's ecological metaphor lie in field biology, where entire biological communities represent the object of study and level of analysis. Kelly and his colleagues (Kelly, 1968, 1971, 1986, 1989; Kelly & Associates, 1979; Trickett, 1984; Trickett et al., 1985: Trickett & Mitchell, in press) have elaborated on four processes that, taken together, describe the ecological environment: adaptation, cycling of resources, interdependence, and succession.

The adaptation principle. The adaptation principle is the broadest principle, referring in general to the adaptive requirements of the environment within which the adolescent must function. Here, the demand characteristics of a setting impose options and constraints on individuals through structures, norms, policies, and attitudes of both peers and individuals in positions of authority. Deviance, then, is defined not as a quality of the individual but by the fit between the general adaptive demands of the setting and the adaptive capabilities of individuals. The development of special programs, on the other hand, focuses on creating appropriate environments in terms of the adaptive requirements they place on individuals.

The cycling of resources principle. Cycling of resources refers to the manner in which resources necessary for the maintenance and development of the ecological environment are defined and distributed throughout the setting. A resource perspective on the social context implies a search for the strengths found in the setting. Resources come in many varieties (see Hobfall, 1988), including technology, interpersonal competence, linkages with external groups and organizations, and the traditions of the setting that provide a context for decision making. Resources are not confined to formal roles in any system, for, within each system, both formal and informal resources are necessary for the system members to complete their tasks. In service settings, for example, although people are often assigned resource roles such as dispensing materials, providing counseling, or engaging in management tasks, these functions may also be filled informally by individuals occupying other formal roles, such as secretaries, aides, or cafeteria workers. Cycling of resources, then, focuses on how resources in the ecological context are defined, distributed throughout the setting, and developed.

The interdependence principle. The interdependence principle focuses on how the component parts of the ecological environment are connected. The implication for understanding is that change introduced in any subsystem or component has ramifications for other parts of the system. Often, for example, a policy change intended to improve a certain aspect of the environment can unexpectedly create adverse consequences elsewhere in the system. For example, requiring that students maintain a certain grade point average to qualify for participation in athletics may change not only the nature of the athletic teams fielded, but also the pressures experienced by students and teachers in the classroom. The interdependence principle, then, promotes an assessment of how people, policies, and programs fit together to form a coherent whole made up of interrelated parts.

The succession principle. The succession principle deals with how the ecological environment evolves over time. The historical perspective implied in the principle helps in understanding how the system came to its present equilibrium. Inquiry into how policies or programs have evolved provides a framework for thinking about how to approach the development of new initiatives. It further provides an appreciation of the complexities that prior programs have had to overcome. The succession principle also has a future orientation, however, that addresses the kind of environment to which the setting aspires to be. Understanding hopes is as important a part of the ecological context as understanding problems that currently exist.

The ecological metaphor has served to direct inquiry and intervention in a variety of contexts (see Kelly, 1966; Mills & Kelly, 1972), but its most frequent application has been in schools, particularly high schools. Interventions in public schools are described in Kelly and Hess (1987), Trickett et al. (1985), and Trickett and Birman (1989). A more general conceptual statement on intervention is found in Kelly (1989). Its basic premise, however, is to view the ecological context through an emphasis on understanding how various ecological processes operate in any particular social setting.

Moos's Social Ecological Approach:
Ecological Contexts Have Personalities

For the past 20 years, Moos has been evolving a perspective on social ecology that differs considerably from Kelly's ecological metaphor. Based on a concern with optimizing positive impact of environments on individuals, Moos has centered his approach on the development of instruments designed to assess the social climate or "personality" of numerous social settings. These include correctional institutions for adolescents (Moos, 1975), high school and junior high school classrooms (Trickett & Moos, 1973), and halfway houses (Moos, 1975).

Rather than conceptualize the ecological environment in terms of ecological processes, Moos has delineated three domains of experience that characterize a wide range of settings: (a) the relationship domain, (b) the goal-orientation domain, and (c) the system maintenance and change domain. The relationship domain focuses on the quality of interpersonal relationships among and between individuals occupying different roles in the setting. Thus, in classrooms, relationships between students and teachers and among students are assessed in terms of how supportive they are. The goal-orientation domain includes those aspects of the social climate that relate to the goals for which the environment was created. For example, in high school classrooms competition for grades and task orientation around learning constitute the goal-orientation dimensions. In psychiatric wards, however, emphasis placed on developing personal insight is a goal-orientation dimension, because learning to understand oneself is a goal of psychiatric wards, whereas learning academic material is the classroom goal. The system maintenance and change domain highlights the authority structure, rules, and degree to which innovation is fostered in the setting. Thus Moos's social ecological perspective focuses on relationships, goals, and the authority structure of social settings.

The ways in which these different domains are emphasized in different settings constitute the general "environmental press" (Murray, 1938) or emphasis placed by the environment on certain behaviors. When programs are started, when new institutions begin, when innovative efforts at designing interventions are contemplated, they often include the notion that if a certain kind of atmosphere can be created, the program can achieve its goals. The social climate may emphasize rules of accountability, the development of connecting interpersonal relationships, or specific processes to achieve program goals. All of these imply that it is desirable to create a certain kind of social climate to carry out the program.

The concept of social climate is operationalized through a series of social climate scales. These scales assess the social climate through the perceptions of members in it. Thus the social climate of high school classrooms can be assessed from the perspectives of students and teachers; the social climate of correctional institutions, from the perspectives of inmates, guards, and supervisory personnel. Both research and intervention studies have been conducted with these instruments, and much of this is summarized in three books by Moos (1974, 1975, 1979) on educational settings, correctional settings, and psychiatric settings. With respect to basic research, different kinds of social climates have been shown to exist in different types of schools and to produce different kinds of outcomes for adolescents, and are determined by a complex set of factors that include not only the importance of individuals but organizational and demographic factors as well.

With respect to intervention studies, several articles have reported the use of the scales in a survey feedback approach to aid in changing the social climate of the setting. Here, both "real" (how the setting is currently perceived) and "ideal" (how people would like the setting to be) versions of the social climate scales are given. The discrepancies between real and ideal climate are then used to stimulate discussion about where change efforts should be directed (for more extensive discussions, see Barrett & Trickett, 1979; Moos, 1974).

The social ecological approach to understanding the ecological environment, then, differentiates it into three different domains that are assessed through the perceptions of individuals in it. It focuses on the climate or "personality" of the setting, and has produced voluminous research showing that the ecological context is patterned, produces significant effects on individuals, and can be changed through planned assessment and intervention.

Barker's Behavior Setting Theory: The Ecological Environment as a Series of Behavior Settings

While Kelly's approach focuses on ecological processes and Moos's on social climate, the third example of an ecological approach, that of Roger Barker, focuses on the definition and categorization of the places where behavior in natural settings occurs. Central to Barker's approach is the notion of the behavior setting, a space-bound and time-delimited entity that coerces or pulls for certain kinds of behaviors with little regard for individual differences. That is, it is the behavior setting that "causes" the behavior, more than the importance of the individuals in the setting.

The setting promotes certain behaviors not only through social norms about appropriate behavior, but by the way the setting is physically arranged. Thus the arrangement of chairs in a classroom, with students sitting facing the teacher, supports or is isomorphic with the behavior one generally sees in classrooms (e.g., teachers talking with/to students who in turn talk with the teacher). While there are, of course, variations among classrooms, the basic premise is that to understand behavior, it is most important to know *where* someone is rather than *who* someone is. While perhaps overstated, Barker's emphasis on place has served as a useful contrast to the individualistic bias that has characterized the dominant paradigms of psychology and special education (see Leone, 1989; Sarason, 1981).

Barker's methodology is to break down the ecological environment into its discrete behavior settings. Thus a school may be described in terms of its classrooms, lunch periods, extracurricular activities, and athletic events. Indeed, this approach has been used to describe a wide range of settings, from schools (Barker & Gump, 1964), to rehabilitation settings for the physically disabled (Willems & Halstead, 1978), to churches (Wicker, 1969), to entire communities (Barker, 1978). Such a procedure allows one to assess what, specifically, the ecological environment offers individuals in it. Are there, for example, specific settings in the environment where troubled youth can have informal contact with adults? Is a behavior setting available for the airing of program conflict? A behavior setting analysis allows a close look at how the intentions, goals, and issues faced by institutions or programs for youth map onto its ongoing workings. This in turn sets the stage for creating or designing settings to accomplish necessary tasks.

Large organizations can be broken down into discrete behavior settings, and behavior settings within a larger organization or community can be aggregated according to type. Price and Blashfield (1975), for example, did such an analysis of the behavior settings found in contrasting communities. They discovered such groupings as those related to business, leisure-time activities, and recreational settings for youth. This type of aggregate analysis helps one understand the overall opportunity structure of the ecological environment for supporting certain populations (e.g., behavior settings for the remediation of troubled youth) and promoting certain environmental goals (e.g., supervised recreational settings for youth). Thus behavior setting analysis can be used to assess institutions or communities and can be analyzed in terms of specific settings or aggregates of types of settings. In either instance it highlights what is and is not viable for the development or remediation of youth.

In addition to the value of behavior setting analysis as a descriptive taxonomy, Barker and his colleagues (see particularly Wicker, 1987) have developed theory in terms of how behavior settings are regulated and how they affect the experience of individuals. Called "staffing theory," in its most simplified form it focuses on how the ratio of individuals to available behavior settings affects individual options, experience of marginality, and satisfaction with and involvement in the social context (see Price, 1976). For example, Barker and Gump (1964) conducted a behavior setting analysis of schools of different sizes, ranging from roughly 100 students to well over 1,000. They found, of course, that larger schools had a greater number of behavior settings available to students, but that in terms of the ratio of students to behavior settings, smaller schools had more behavior settings per student. To keep these settings going in the smaller schools, students were pulled to participate in more activities. Thus more students were involved in a wider range of activities than was true for students in the larger schools, where more specialization of skills and talents was required to "make the team" or "play the lead in the school play." This, in turn, meant that proportionally more students were marginal to the ongoing life of the larger schools than they were in smaller ones. This kind of dynamic formulation of staffing theory has recently been extended by Wicker (1987) to include more subtle aspects of how settings arise and how individual differences can affect participation in a setting. The basic thrust, however, remains the same: Ecological psychology from this perspective focuses on behavior settings and how they promote and constrain individual behavior.

Summary

The development of concepts for understanding the social context is a prerequisite of the development of an ecological perspective. The bottom line, however, involves the kinds of effects such contexts have on individuals and the processes that mediate these effects. An increasing amount of evidence on the impact of various ecological contexts and factors such as unemployment or economic swings in the country is accumulating. Data suggest that such ecological effects are far reaching. With respect to schools, for example, Rutter (1983), in a summary statement on the impact of school environments on individual behavior, asserts that schools per se have been shown to affect the psychological development and behavior of students in a variety of areas, from self-esteem to rates of truancy. (For research on ecology and troubled youth in particular, see Conrad & Schevers, 1983; Leone, Luttig, Zlotlow, & Trickett, in press.)

Ecological Perspectives on Individual Behavior: Individual Behavior Is Embedded in Social Contexts

The first section of the chapter briefly outlined three ecological perspectives on the nature of the social context. Here, an ecological perspective on individual behavior is outlined. When viewed ecologically, behavior is seen as transactional; that is, to understand individual behavior and its meaning, one must understand not only individual qualities but how the individual is embedded in varying social contexts, for these contexts exert both direct and indirect influence on individuals.

One of the most comprehensive perspectives on the ecology of individual behavior is found in Bronfenbrenner's (1979) book *The Ecology of Human Development*. Here, Bronfenbrenner describes the ecological environment of the individual as reflecting the influence of forces operating at multiple levels of analysis over time. Following an outline of his perspective, three additional tenets from Kelly's ecological metaphor are offered to concretize implications of Bronfenbrenner's perspective.

Bronfenbrenner's Ecology of Human Development

Bronfenbrenner (1979) begins with the following definition: "The ecology of human development involves the scientific study of the progressive mutual accommodation between an active, growing human being and the changing properties of the immediate settings in which the developing person lives, as this process is affected by relations between those settings, and by the larger contexts in which the settings are embedded" (p. 21). He continues: "The ecological environment is conceived topologically as a nested set of arrangements of concentric structures, each contained within the next. These structures are referred to as the micro-, meso-, exo-, and macrosystems" (p. 22). Each of these levels of the social context carries implications for understanding individual behavior.

The microsystem. The microsystem involves the relationship between an individual and a given immediate setting with definable boundaries. Microsystems of particular interest for troubled adolescents may include the adolescent as he or she interacts with family, special education programs, the correctional institution, or peer-dominated contexts of a formal or informal nature. Here, research focuses on how the individual and the specific context interact. Bronfenbrenner stresses the importance of how the setting is experienced by the individual in understanding individual behavior and asserts "the impossibility of understanding that behavior solely from the objective properties of an environment without reference to its meaning for the people in the setting" (p. 24).

Not surprisingly, little research on troubled youth has focused on youth in context, preferring an individual approach to assessment and intervention (Frank & Davidson, 1983). In a critique of research on correctional populations, for example, Reppucci and Clingempeel (1978) highlight the need for environmental studies that focus on person-environment interactions across a variety of microsystems of relevance to correctional populations both inside and outside the correctional facility. With respect to schools, Hamilton (1983) cites three characteristics of ecological research consistent with Bronfenbrenner's microsystem concept: (a) attention to the interaction of person and environment; (b) viewing the teaching and learning process as one involving continuous interaction and interchange, thus emphasizing the *process* of education rather than the *product*; and (c) viewing the perceptions and attitudes of system members (students, teachers, administrators, and so on) as valuable information about the functioning of the system. In sum, microsystem analyses focus on the behavior of the individual in a specific setting and emphasize the importance of how the setting is experienced by the individual.

The mesosystem. Whereas the microsystem involves the person in a specific setting, "a mesosystem comprises the interrelation among two or more settings in which the developing person actively participates. . . . A mesosystem is thus a system of microsystems" (p. 25). Several kinds of interrelations are specified as examples of mesosystem relationships that can affect individual behavior. The most frequent instance involves multisetting participation. Multisetting participation occurs when an individual participates in more than one setting, such as home and school, each of which can affect how the individual experiences and behaves in the other. Bronfenbrenner cites the process of going from one microsystem to another as an ecological transition, emphasizing that the individual is moving across social contexts that may provide him or her with quite contrasting microsystem ecologies.

As is the case with microsystem research, the call for such work far exceeds the work itself. Loeber and Dishion (1983), for example, discuss the importance of assessing multiple contexts in understanding delinquency. In reviewing past literature, they suggest that a cluster of contexts or microsystems relate to delinquency in males, including parental ability to set limits and supervise, conduct problems in the community, and conduct and academic problems in school. Further evidence of the value of a mesosystem analysis of individual behavior comes from Brook, Whiteman, and Gordon (1983), who examined three domains of adolescent life in relation to drug use—individual personality, peer relationships, and family functioning. They found that all these domains, independently and in combination, predicted drug use. In a more clinical vein, Moos and Fuhr (1982) used social climate scales involving home, school, and work environment to assist an adolescent girl and her family in understanding how various settings of importance were interacting to cause problems for the adolescent. Such work suggests the importance of assessing how the settings within the mesosystem interact to influence adolescent behavior.

The exosystem. While the mesosystem involves two or more settings in which the child actively participates, the exosystem "refers to one or more settings that did not directly involve the developing person as an active participant, but in which events occur that affect, or are affected by, what happens in the setting containing the developing person" (p. 25). This definition is clarified by Bronfenbrenner in explaining that "to demonstrate the operation of the exosystem as a context influencing development it is necessary to establish a causal sequence involving at least two steps: the first connecting events in the external settings to processes occurring in the developing person's microsystem and the second linking the microsystem processes to developmental changes in the person within that setting" (p. 237).

The logic behind exosystem influences is nicely illustrated in Bronfenbrenner's discussion of the effects of television on children. Most research on the effects of television on children and youth assess its direct effects, such as the arousal of certain behavior potentials, notably violence and aggression. An exosystem analysis, however, might focus on a more indirect though just as powerful an effect; namely, that television exerts its influence not directly but through the way in which it affects the youth's family microsystem. "The primary danger of the television screen lies not so much in the behavior it produces as the behavior it prevents—the talks, the games, the family festivities and arguments through which much of the child's learning takes place and his character is formed" (Bronfenbrenner, 1974, p. 170). One can extrapolate this example of an exosystem influence to various issues of potential relevance to troubled adolescents, such as the impact of parental working conditions on parent-child negative interaction at home and its subsequent implications for the youth. The point, once again, is that the experience and behavior of the adolescent is intertwined with what happens in settings that exert no *direct* influence.

The macrosystem. The macrosystem is made up of the consistencies that exist in the broader content and fabric of the society. These patterns, or "regularities," to use Sarason's (1972) term, are assumed to be different in different cultures, and are manifested in each of the three prior levels of analysis of ecological influence (micro-, meso-, and exo-). The study of macrosystem influences allows researchers to examine the processes through which broad cultural values and attitudes are reflected in the social structures that, in turn, affect the experiences of youth. From an ecological perspective, the important point is to trace the larger macrosystem processes through these other systems. Thus correlating changing economic indices with reported incidence of adolescent depression would not fulfill ecological criteria unless the impact of such macro changes was assessed in terms of its influence on one level of the ecological context; for example, the stress placed on families, which in turn was linked to the adolescent outcome of depression.

Though empirical research in this area is scarce, Braginski (1986), in a thoughtful article on the nature of indifference in our society, provides one example of how such macro phenomena may operate. He posits a number of "ingredients" of the broader culture that foster indifference. These include (a) a social system that assigns values to individuals based on their overall worth to the system, (b) the belief that survival of some members of the system rests on the failure of other members of the system, and (c) ownership of tangible or intangible goods or qualities may spare individuals from negative social consequences, such as discrimination, that others will have to suffer. Under this set of societal assumptions, indifference on the part of the disenfranchised becomes a necessary adaptation to social institutions. Once indifference is fostered, further discrimination and negative feedback about worth make it increasingly difficult for youth labeled as problematic to change. (For another example of how broad social influences are reflected in intervention programs for youth, see Frank & Davidson, 1983.)

Three Additional Ecological Assertions

Bronfenbrenner's framework for the ecology of human development is indeed an overarching one that convincingly demonstrates that individual behavior reflects far more subtle and complex influences than can be captured by the term *personality*. The immediate context, the relationships among various contexts, and the broader culture all inform our ecological understanding of the individual. Three other specific implications of an ecological perspective on the individual will now be briefly presented.

Individuals Are Socioculturally Embedded

In Bronfenbrenner's discussion of the microsystem, he asserts the importance of understanding how the individual experiences the setting as opposed to its more objective qualities in predicting behavior. While such experiencing is affected by a wide range of factors, an ecological perspective adopts the following emphasis: The meaning of settings to individuals is embedded in a sociocultural matrix of experiences and beliefs internalized by the individual through transactions with the broader culture over time. By *sociocultural matrix,* we mean the various kinds of cultural attitudes and "messages" transmitted through various ecological systems influencing the adolescent. One aspect of this involves the ways in which labels influence both the experience and behavior of the labeled individual and those who have the power to label. There may, for example, be a tendency on the part of institutions and service providers dealing with troubled youth to talk about, and indeed view, individuals in terms of labels such as *delinquents, learning disabled,* and *drug users.*

The ecological concern with the sociocultural matrix, however, is intended to prevent these labels from decontextualizing our understanding of adolescents. Rather, the notion is to put the specific behaviors of troubled youth in context in an effort to understand the worldview from which the behavior springs. Sipola (1985), for example, has proposed a model of the development of deviant behavior in adolescents that includes an assessment of the community where the adolescent lives, the social network of the adolescent, and the individual's personality and behavior. Specific variables include the impact of social class, housing density, urban versus rural location, availability of resources, social support, psychological distress, delinquency, violent crimes, and drinking. While Sipola's model does not focus on how these different levels of ecological influence may interact to affect the adolescent, it does assert that adolescent behavior is indeed embedded in a sociocultural matrix.

Perhaps the most salient factors of the sociocultural matrix that are still underemphasized in theory and practice involving troubled youth involve social descriptors that, in our culture, carry pervasive implications. Race, socioeconomic status, gender, sexual orientation, and disability represent some of the more salient cultural constructions that carry meaning for individual experience. While much has been written in psychology about race, class, and gender, in particular (e.g., Dohrenwend & Dohrenwend, 1981; Gilligan, 1982; Jones, 1982; Ramirez, 1983), the specific implications of these more general statements are not always clear to us when we are attempting to understand and intervene in the lives of troubled youth.

For example, the various controversies surrounding the validity and social consequences of IQ testing (Cronbach, 1975; Kamin, 1974) highlight the potential role of cultural embeddedness in interpreting the results of standardized tests. This chapter's second author has worked with Native American populations, and has often confronted the apparent discrepancy between the adolescent's average or above-average verbal aptitude and his or her eventual scores on standardized tests. Without considering how the culture of the adolescent fits the content of the tests and the demand characteristics of the testing situation, test scores alone may have been misinterpreted to the detriment of the adolescent. The ecological emphasis on sociocultural embeddedness reminds us that we all, client and professional, come from somewhere, that our own contexts have shaped the worldview through which we interpret our ecological environment.

**Individual Behavior Is Expected to Vary
from Setting to Setting**

A contextualized view of individual behavior focuses not on the traits or qualities of individuals *in vacuo*, but on how individual characteristics interact with the multiple settings in which individuals are involved. These settings are expected to vary in terms of their demand characteristics and to "activate" different aspects of the individual's personality. While some consistency in behavior across settings exists (see Endler & Hunt, 1966; Mischel, 1968), from an ecological perspective one would not assume that an adolescent would behave similarly with family, peers, and institutional staff. Behavior will vary across settings; it is a function of the interaction, not of the person.

Indeed, one of the most influential research programs highlighting this issue occurred about 30 years ago and involved children defined as emotionally disturbed (Rausch, Dittman, & Taylor, 1959; Rausch, Farbman, & Llewellyn, 1960). In this project, emotionally disturbed children in an intervention program were assessed across settings and over time and compared to a control group of children not diagnosed as emotionally disturbed. Of relevance to the present discussion was the general finding that for both groups of children behavior varied considerably from setting to setting. Thus free play outside encouraged the expression of more aggressive behavior than was present in the more structured indoor activities. In general, the emotionally disturbed children were somewhat more consistent in their behavior across settings than were those in the control group. This suggests that one aspect of emotional disturbance may involve the relative lack of ability to differentiate among situations or, from Bronfenbrenner's perspective, to experience different situations as similar. However, even in this group, behavior varied considerably from setting to setting.

The situation specificity of behavior has several implications for understanding troubled youth. First, it serves as a caution against attributing too much predictive power to an assessment that focuses only on the personal qualities of the adolescent. Rather, it suggests the value of a multisetting assessment process that cuts across varied domains of the adolescent's life space. Further, it allows the assessor to focus on the potential strengths, positive coping skills, and social resources of the adolescent. Assessment of youth referred because of problem behavior tends to focus on those contexts where the problem is expressed, not on those aspects of adolescent life where things are going well.

Behavior Adaptive in One Setting
May Be Maladaptive in Others

This final assertion about the ecology of individual behavior focuses on the different demand characteristics of the different settings the adolescent must negotiate. It represents an acknowledgment that transitions from school to work, prison to the outside world, or hospital to family often require the adolescent to face situations with new adaptive requirements. Even on a daily basis, youth exist in a matrix of settings, the requirements of which may differ widely. The relationship between home and school, for example, is often one of conflicting norms, attitudes toward authority, and styles of learning. An understanding of the ways in which settings call for different adolescent responses can clarify the meaning of adolescent behavior in each of the settings.

A corollary of the notion that behavior adaptive in one setting may be maladaptive in others is provided by Trickett (1984): "Individual adaptation to any *particular* setting may vary widely and still be adaptive, depending on the other settings which he or she must negotiate" (p. 251). This point is amplified through the following perhaps extreme, though instructive, example:

> Consider the following example told to me by a teacher in a racially mixed inner-city alternative school. The student body was, at that time, 60% white, 40% black, and the staff 90% white. The school was not strict in terms of rules and regulations; students would often hang out in the halls rather than attending class. Among the "regulars" who hung out was a 19 year-old black student, who drove a new Lincoln to school, dressed and acted as "Superfly," and always carried an obvious roll of bills. During the school day, he would hang out in the halls or outside the building. His situational adaptation was to play it cool, an option made available because of the particular norms of the school. After school was over, and his peers had left, however, he would return to school for tutoring by one of his teachers. It was the teacher's hunch that adapting to school in the normative sense of going to class, etc., was seen as conflicting with his highly valued street image. However, he also knew that he needed to learn to read. His way of adapting was *not* to adjust to the behavioral expectations of the school by going to class, to avoid overt school behavior which conflicts with his peer group or street image, yet find a way to learn those school-related skills he felt was necessary. (Trickett, 1984, pp. 271-272)

In this instance, assessing the meaning of behavior in a single setting (e.g., the school) without an understanding of the other settings in the student's life would have resulted in a woefully incomplete understanding and, perhaps, the development of an intervention that would have implicitly required of the student that he forsake the values and attitudes most salient to him. Here, the flexibility of the school allowed the student to save face and learn to read simultaneously.

Ecology and Interventions for Troubled Youth

Preceding pages have outlined a series of ecological perspectives and assumptions about the social context and individual behavior in it. This final section addresses some implications for the design and evaluation of interventions involving troubled youth. These implications are based on the ecological goal of creating system impact and strengthening the social settings serving youth (for an elaboration of this perspective, see Kelly, 1989; Kelly & Hess, 1987; Trickett & Birman, 1989; Trickett et al., 1985). They include (a) redesigning the social context to improve the functioning of individuals, (b) using interventions as a means of increasing the resources of the settings where the interventions occur, and (c) evaluating the interventions in terms of environmental as well as individual impact.

Ecologically Based Interventions
Involve a Redesigning of the Social Context

The importance of conceptualizing ecological interventions as involving a change in the social context flows from research and theory showing how both the immediate ecological environment and various higher-level systems and their relation to each other influence individual behavior (e.g., Bronfenbrenner, 1979). Ecologically based interventions thus cut across levels of analysis, from interventions in a single setting to more macro-level efforts involving systems and, indeed, national policy (e.g., P.L. 94-142). The spirit of this system change goal is not to become radical system blamers; rather, the intent is to care about and try to improve the settings serving youth through designing interventions that make a positive difference in the setting. The varied ecological perspectives described earlier provide guidelines for the design of such interventions.

For example, the survey feedback approach described in Moos's social ecological approach represents one such technology. This technology was briefly described above, and includes the giving of "real" and "ideal" social climate scales to adolescents and service providers in the same setting. The discrepancy between the real and ideal environments is then used to stimulate discussion about instituting environmental changes. The intervention is then instituted and evaluated after a period of time to see if perception of the real environment has changed in the direction intended by the intervention. Such interventions have been reported in psychiatric inpatient facilities (Pierce, Trickett, & Moos, 1970) and halfway houses (Moos, 1975).

Another example of redesigning the social context is reported by Felner, Ginter, and Primavera (1982). This intervention was intended to ease the transition from junior high school to high school, and was accomplished by redesigning the role of teacher and developing a supportive peer group among entering students. More specifically, students were grouped such that they shared a number of classes rather than dispersing into new groups after each class, and teachers were provided opportunities to get to know small groups of incoming students well. Students involved in the program had higher grades, less absenteeism, and more positive perceptions of the school environment than a matched control group who participated in the regular high school program. (For extensive examples of interventions involving redesign of the social context, see Felner, Jason, Moritsugu, & Farber, 1983; Seidman, 1983.)

Ecologically Based Interventions
Focus on Increasing Local Resources

While the previous topic focuses on the level of analysis at which the intervention is targeted, this topic focuses on the resource goal of ecologically based interventions. Most often when interventions are implemented for troubled youth, the singular focus is on how the program affects the immediate population of concern: the incarcerated youth, the pregnant teenage mother, the group of emotionally disturbed adolescents. Yet programs for such groups are often added to existing settings; they may rise and fall with the vicissitudes of external funding; they may take on a life of their own independent of the ongoing functioning of the setting where they are located. They may leave no trace when they end, or they may significantly help youth *and* the setting as well.

It is this latter impact that draws the attention of ecologically oriented interventionists. The goal is to design interventions in such a way that they become future resources for the setting because they strengthen the setting's resources. This implies a long-term, often subtle, incremental approach to intervention that relies on the development of collaborative and empowering relationships between the intervention team and the host environment. One aspect of this, for example, has been termed "environmental reconnaissance" (Kelly, 1989) and involves the active assessment of who and what in the host environment can be brought into the intervention plan to make it more powerful and enduring.

Because this approach is unusual in the design and implementation of intervention programs, research examples are only now emerging. Kelly and Hess (1987), for example, have reported a series of case studies in public schools that illustrate mental health consultation as a preventive intervention designed to create resources in the schools hosting the consultation. In one, Gonzales (1987) reports on how the school's initial concern with certain adolescents mirrored certain kinds of faculty problems of morale and commitment. This understanding led her to create interventions for teachers that could then trickle down to students. In another, Vincent (1987) designed an intervention for two schools that were merging into one. She drew on the knowledge and skills of indigenous teachers and administrators to create positive ripple effects during the initial merger year (see also Kelly, 1989; Trickett & Birman, 1989; Trickett et al., 1985).

**Evaluating the Success of
Ecological Interventions Includes Assessing
Environmental as Well as Individual Impact**

Previous sections of this chapter have discussed varied implications of an ecological perspective for the assessment of individual behavior: that it not involve a single setting but be assessed across settings; that the appropriateness of the intervention be framed in terms of the sociocultural embeddedness of individuals; that the impact of intervention *on individuals* be assessed across various aspects of the individual's ecology. An ecological perspective, however, also includes an assessment of the impact of the intervention on the setting where it occurs. The setting endures beyond the life of many programs and is indeed created to be an enduring resource for current and future cohorts of troubled youth. Thus it is vitally important that interventions be evaluated in terms of their setting impact as well as their individual impact.

There are several kinds of criteria to use in making such an assessment. They flow from the ecological perspectives previously discussed. One set of criteria may be structural. Are new settings created that endure beyond the life of the program or that come to serve as a resource for the organization more generally? Are structures for increasing the availability of relevant outside resources developed as a consequence of the intervention? Other criteria may involve a change in norms or attitudes. Is deviance, for example, defined in a more culturally sensitive way by institutional staff? Are norms around collaborative problem-solving enhanced? Has a sense of community been encouraged and hopes for future innovations kindled by the intervention? Most globally, have the resources of the setting been conserved and expanded as a consequence of how the intervention was designed and carried out? Within this aspect of the ecological perspective, then, interventions designed to remedy individual problems of troubled youth serve as preventive interventions for settings by increasing the competence of setting members.

Conclusion

The overall ecological orientation discussed in this chapter, while gaining momentum in various areas of psychology and special education (Leone, 1989), is still a relatively unelaborated perspective on conceptualizing human behavior. This chapter is intended to provide the contours of this more global perspective, but it is by no means exhaustive. The implications of ecology in terms of assumptions about the social context, individuals, and intervention suggest a rethinking of how we conceive of and respond to the behavior of troubled youth. It provides an impetus for the development of a context-bound understanding of individuals whose primary difficulties stem from the way they cope with the social context *and* the way the social context copes with them.

References

Altman, I., & Rogoff, B. (1987). World views in psychology: Trait, interactional, organismic, and transactional. In D. Stokols & I. Altman (Eds.), *Handbook of environmental psychology* (pp. 7-40). New York: John Wiley.

Barker, R. G. (1968). *Ecological psychology.* Stanford, CA: Stanford University Press.

Barker, R. G. (Ed.). (1978). *Habitats, environments, and human behavior.* San Francisco: Jossey-Bass.

Barker, R. G., & Gump, P. V. (1964). *Big school, small school: High school size and student behavior.* Stanford, CA: Stanford University Press.

Barrett, D. M., & Trickett, E. J. (1979). Change strategies and perceived environment data: Two conceptual models and their applications. *Journal of Community Psychology, 7,* 305-312.

Braginski, B. (1986). The meaning of indifference. *Journal of Social and Clinical Psychology, 4,* 235-243.

Bronfenbrenner, U. (1974). Developmental research and public policy. In J. Romanyshyn (Ed.), *Social science and social welfare.* New York: Council on Social Work Education.

Bronfenbrenner, U. (1979). *The ecology of human development.* Cambridge, MA: Harvard University Press.

Brook, J. S., Whiteman, M., & Gordon, A. S. (1983). Stages of drug use in adolescence: Personality, peer, and family correlates. *Developmental Psychology, 19*, 269-277.

Conrad, K. J., & Schevers, T. J. (1983). *The effects of PL-94-142 on school services to adolescents with behavior disorders in Illinois.* Paper presented at the 61st Annual Meeting of the International Council for Exceptional Children, Detroit. (ERIC Document Reproduction Service No. 152 536)

Cronbach, L. (1975). Five decades of controversy over mental testing. *American Psychologist, 30*, 1-14.

Dohrenwend, B. S., & Dohrenwend, B. P. (Eds.). (1981). *Life stress and illness.* New York: Watson.

Endler, N., & Hunt, J. M. (1966). Sources of behavioral variance as measured by the S-R Inventory. *Psychological Bulletin, 65*, 336-346.

Felner, R. D., Ginter, M., & Primavera, J. (1982). Primary prevention during school transitions: Social support and environmental structure. *American Journal of Community Psychology, 10*, 277-290.

Felner, R. D., Jason, K., Moritsugu, J., & Farber, S. J. (1983). *Preventive psychology.* New York: Pergamon.

Frank, S., & Davidson, D. S. (1983). Ideologies and intervention strategies in an urban sample of drug-abuse agencies. *American Journal of Community Psychology, 11*, 241-259.

Gilligan, C. (1982). *In a different voice.* Cambridge, MA: Harvard University Press.

Gonzales, L. R. (1987). A community service for a rural high school. In J. G. Kelly & R. E. Hess (Eds.), *The ecology of prevention: Illustrating mental health consultation* (pp. 37-71). New York: Haworth.

Hamilton, S. T. (1983). Socialization for learning: Insights from ecological research in the classroom. *Reading Teacher, 37*, 150-157.

Hobfall, S. E. (1988). *The ecology of stress.* New York: Hemisphere.

Jones, J. (1982). *The paradigm of racism: Cultural biases in psycho-social science.* Unpublished manuscript, American Psychological Association, Washington, DC.

Kamin, L. (1974). *The science and politics of I.Q.* Hillsdale, NJ: Lawrence Erlbaum.

Kelly, J. G. (1966). Ecological constraints on mental health services. *American Psychologist, 21*, 535-539.

Kelly, J. G. (1968). Towards an ecological conception of preventive interventions. In J. G. Carter (Ed.), *Research contributions from psychology to community mental health* (pp. 76-100). New York: Behavioral Publications.

Kelly, J. G. (1971). Qualities for the community psychologist. *American Psychologist, 26*, 897-903.

Kelly, J. G. (1986). Context and process: An ecological view of the interdependence of practice and research. *American Journal of Community Psychology, 14*, 581-589.

Kelly, J. G. (1989). *A guide to conducting prevention research in the community.* New York: Haworth.

Kelly, J. G., & Associates. (1979). *Adolescent boys in high school: A psychological study of coping and adaptation.* Hillsdale, NJ: Lawrence Erlbaum.

Kelly, J. G., & Hess, R. E. (Eds.). (1987). *The ecology of prevention: Illustrating mental health consultation.* New York: Haworth.

Leone, P. (1989). Beyond fixing bad behavior and bad boys: Multiple perspectives on education and treatment of troubled and troubling youth. *Monograph in Behavioral Disorders, 12*, 1-10.

Leone, P., Luttig, P., Zlotlow, S. F., & Trickett, E. J. (in press). Understanding the social ecology of classrooms for adolescents with behavioral disorders: A preliminary study of differences in perceived environments. *Behavioral Disorders.*

Loeber, R., & Dishion, T. J. (1983). Early predictors of male delinquency: A review. *Psychological Bulletin, 94,* 68-99.

Mills, R., & Kelly, J. G. (1972). Cultural adaptation and ecological analysis: Analysis of three Mexican villages. In S. Golann & C. Eisdorfer (Eds.), *Handbook of community mental health.* New York: Appleton-Century-Crofts.

Mischel, W. (1968). *Personality and assessment.* New York: John Wiley.

Moos, R. H. (1974). *Evaluating treatment environments: A social ecological approach.* New York: John Wiley.

Moos, R. H. (1975). *Evaluating correctional and community settings.* New York: John Wiley.

Moos, R. H. (1979). *Evaluating educational environments.* San Francisco: Jossey-Bass.

Moos, R. H., & Fuhr, R. (1982). The clinical use of social ecological concepts: The case of an adolescent girl. *American Journal of Orthopsychiatry, 52,* 111-122.

Murray, H. A. (1938). *Explorations in personality.* New York: Oxford University Press.

Pierce, W. D., Trickett, E. J., & Moos, R. H. (1970). Changing ward atmosphere through staff discussion of the perceived ward environment. *Archives of General Psychiatry, 26,* 35-41.

Price, R. (1976). Behavior setting theory and research. In R. H. Moos (Ed.), *The human context* (pp. 213-247). New York: John Wiley.

Price, R., & Blashfield, R. K. (1975). Explorations in the taxonomy of behavior settings: Analysis of dimensions and classifications of settings. *American Journal of Community Psychology, 3,* 335-351.

Ramirez, M. (1983). *Psychology of the Americas: Mestizo perspectives on personality and mental health.* New York: Pergamon.

Rausch, H. L., Dittman, A. T., & Taylor, T. J. (1959). The interpersonal behavior of children in residential treatment. *Journal of Abnormal and Social Psychology, 58,* 9-26.

Rausch, H. L., Farbman, I., & Llewellyn, C. G. (1960). Person, setting, and change in social interaction. *Human Relations, 13,* 305-333.

Reppucci, N. D., & Clingempeel, W. G. (1978). Methodological issues in research with correctional populations. *Journal of Consulting and Clinical Psychology, 46,* 727-746.

Rutter, M. (1983). Stress, coping and development: Some issues and some questions. *Journal of Child Psychology and Psychiatry, 22,* 323-356.

Sarason, S. B. (1972). *The creation of settings and the future societies.* San Francisco: Jossey-Bass.

Sarason, S. B. (1981). *Psychology misdirected.* New York: Free Press.

Seidman, E. (Ed.). (1983). *Handbook of social intervention.* Beverly Hills, CA: Sage.

Sipola, J. (1985). Community structure and deviant behavior among adolescents. *Youth & Society, 16,* 471-497.

Trickett, E. J. (1984). Towards a distinctive community psychology: An ecological metaphor for training and the conduct of research. *American Journal of Community Psychology, 12,* 261-279.

Trickett, E. J., & Birman, D. (1989). Taking ecology seriously: A community development approach to individually based preventive interventions. In L. Bond & B. Compas

(Eds.), *Primary prevention and promotion in the schools* (pp. 361-390). Newbury Park, CA: Sage.

Trickett, E. J., Kelly, J. G., & Vincent, T. A. (1985). The spirit of ecological inquiry in community research. In E. Susskind & D. Klein (Eds.), *Community research: Methods, paradigms, and applications*. New York: Praeger.

Trickett, E. J., & Mitchell, R. E. (in press). An ecological metaphor for research and intervention in community psychology. In M. S. Gibbs, J. Lackenmeyer, & J. Sigal (Eds.), *Community psychology: Theoretical and empirical approaches*. New York: John Wiley.

Trickett, E. J., & Moos, R. H. (1973). The social environment of junior high and high school classrooms. *Journal of Educational Psychology, 65*, 93-102.

Vincent, T. A. (1987). Two into one: An ecological perspective on school consolidation. In J. G. Kelly & R. E. Hess (Eds.), *The ecology of prevention: Illustrating mental health consultation* (pp. 113-149). New York: Haworth.

Wicker, A. W. (1969). Size of church membership and members' support of church behavior settings. *Journal of Personality and Social Psychology, 13*, 278-288.

Wicker, A. W. (1987). Behavior settings reconsidered: Temporal stages, resources, internal dynamics, context. In D. Stokols & I. Altman (Eds.), *Handbook of environmental psychology* (pp. 613-653). New York: John Wiley.

Willems, E. P., & Halstead, L. S. (1978). An eco-behavioral approach to health status and health care. In R. G. Barker (Ed.), *Habitats, environments, and human behavior* (pp. 169-189). San Francisco: Jossey-Bass.

7

The Peer Context of Troublesome
Child and Adolescent Behavior

THOMAS J. DISHION

A common theme throughout this volume is that children's troublesome behavior can be viewed from a number of different theoretical and analytical perspectives. This chapter represents the position that troublesome child behavior is embedded within a more general social ecology and is best understood as not being within the child (Patterson, Reid, & Dishion, in press). Working within a social interactional perspective (Cairns, 1979; Patterson, 1982; Patterson & Reid, 1984; Patterson et al., in press; Snyder, 1987), children's social and emotional development is seen as embedded within literally thousands of interpersonal transactions per day where certain patterns of action-reaction sequences become generalized across settings and agents (e.g., parents and peers). Most of these patterns of reacting to interpersonal situations are adaptive, automatic, mundane, and not particularly interesting to behavioral scientists. However, some of these patterns are maladaptive. The particular sense in which the term *troublesome* is used within this chapter is to describe maladaptive patterns of child behavior that are *antisocial*. Antisocial behavior produces child conflict and causes personal distress to the youngster, his or her intimates, and society in general. Ultimately,

AUTHOR'S NOTE: Support for this research was provided by Grant No. MH 37940 from the Center for Studies of Antisocial and Violent Behavior, NIMH, U.S. PHS, and Grant No. DA 05304, National Institute of Drug Abuse, U.S. PHS. Carol Kimball is acknowledged for her editorial help and preparation of the tables, and Will Mayer for his preparation of the figures. Patti Chamberlain, Deborah Capaldi, and Kevin Moore are gratefully acknowledged for their suggestions on previous drafts of this chapter.

repetition of this maladaptive pattern invokes the label of *troublesome* from caretaking adults.

The focus of this chapter is to look at the interrelation between antisocial behavior and children's experience with peers. This issue is looked at in two ways: First, to what extent does troublesome child behavior limit the availability of peers with whom a child may develop friendships? Second, to what extent does a limited network of friends undermine children's social adjustment in adolescence and young adulthood? When thinking about these questions, it is tempting to isolate the focus of the study on the child within the peer group, ignoring other realms of influence as they might affect the child's peer experience. Such a narrow focus increases the risk of overemphasizing peers and their role in socialization. In the research reviewed in this chapter, peer reactions and peer group influences will be studied in juxtaposition to parenting practices.

Working Model

Before going into detail about the analyses and results addressing the question of the role of peers in troublesome behavior, it is necessary to outline (see Figure 7.1) my assumptions in thinking and researching questions related to child problem behavior. The model shown in Figure 7.1 represents a consensus among a group of investigators at the Oregon Social Learning Center (OSLC) who have concentrated their professional time on studying parenting processes as they relate to child and antisocial behavior (Chamberlain & Patterson, 1984; Dishion, Patterson, Skinner, & Stoolmiller, 1989; Fagot & Kavanagh, 1988; Patterson & Bank, 1985; Patterson & Forgatch, 1987; Patterson & Reid, 1984; Patterson et al., in press). We use the term *working* to describe the model because the key hypotheses are subject to revision depending on new information. For example, in our earlier research on adolescent delinquency (Patterson & Dishion, 1985), we incorporated the concept of the deviant peer group into our family management model based on the research findings reported by sociological investigators such as Delbert Elliott (Elliott, Huizinga, & Ageton, 1985). This addition has led us into examining the interrelation between family and peer processes that may lead to adolescents' being exposed and vulnerable to the influence of deviant peers.

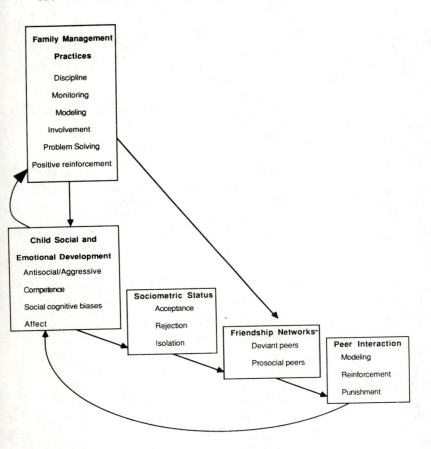

Figure 7.1. An Applied Model of the Influence of Parents and Peers on Child
Social and Emotional Development

The joint focus on the parent and peer systems is also consistent with
what Bronfenbrenner (1986) describes as a mesosystem model. Such a
model is supraordinate to the extent that hypotheses are provided that
relate two spheres of the child's social experience (e.g., parents and
peers). Inspection of Figure 7.1 reveals that the model is family based
and places parenting practices as central in the process of becoming
persistently troublesome. Family management practices have been
identified (discipline, monitoring, positive reinforcement, parent involvement, problem solving, and parent modeling), primarily on the

basis of 20 years of clinical experience using the parent training model with conduct problem children (Patterson, 1982; Patterson et al., in press). The relation between parenting practices and future problem behavior is well established. For example, in a review of longitudinal research reporting the prediction of male delinquency, it was found that disorganized, chaotic, and lax supervision were among the best predictors, even compared to measures of earlier measured behavior problems (Loeber & Dishion, 1983).

Our recent work with the Oregon Youth Study (OYS) also shows a direct and strong association between family management practices and troublesome child behavior (Patterson & Forgatch, 1987; Loeber & Dishion, 1984; Patterson, 1986; Patterson & Bank, 1985; Patterson et al., in press; Patterson & Stouthamer-Loeber, 1984), adolescent delinquency (Patterson, Capaldi, & Bank, 1989; Patterson & Dishion, 1985), and drug use (Dishion & Loeber, 1985; Dishion, Patterson, & Reid, 1988). In this research we have adopted a strategy of intensive measurement of parenting processes, including home observations, daily telephone interviews, and detailed structured interviews with both the child and parents. The general research strategy and findings from these studies will not be detailed here but are summarized within Patterson et al. (in press).

The analysis of the peer context of child and adolescent troublesome behavior in this chapter will be based on data provided by an ongoing longitudinal study on child and adolescent behavior called the Oregon Youth Study. Currently this study includes only boys, which is an obvious limitation of the data set and model. The long-term goal of this research program is to evaluate these hypotheses on samples of girls. The primary reason for beginning with an exclusively male sample is that the incidence of serious delinquent behavior is much higher in males than in females (Elliott et al., 1985). Before the data are presented, some of the details of the OYS research methods will be provided.

The Oregon Youth Study

The Sample and Procedures

The Oregon Youth Study began in 1983 and has employed a cohort-sequential longitudinal design to study the role of family management practices, family contextual variables, and peer influences on the development of antisocial behavior, chronic delinquency, drug (ab)use, and depression (Patterson et al., in press). The OYS sample is made up of two cohorts, of 102 and 104 boys and their families, recruited in 1983-1984 and 1984-1985. The study was conducted in a Northwest community with a population of 150,000 to 200,000, with the three school districts in this area participating in the research project. The data in the following analyses were collected when the boys were 9-10 and 11-12 years old, or in the fourth and sixth grades, respectively.

Boys and their families were recruited from the schools. The 10 elementary schools with the highest density of neighborhood delinquency (i.e., arrest records within school districts) were selected from the 43 public elementary schools within the study community. The sampling order was randomly selected among the 10 schools for each cohort. Some families were considered ineligible for the study for the following reasons: (a) plans to move from the area within the initial assessment period; (b) a foreign language was the primary language. A total of 13% and 7% of Cohorts 1 and 2, respectively, were considered ineligible for one of these two reasons.

From all families eligible to participate in the OYS, 74.4% agreed to participate (Capaldi & Patterson, 1987). Capaldi and Patterson (1987) compared the participant boys with the refusers and found that there were no statistically reliable differences between the boys on the primary clinical scales of the teacher version of the Child Behavior Checklist (Achenbach & Edelbrock, 1986). When compared to national norms (Patterson et al., in press), it was found that families in both cohorts seemed to be of lower socioeconomic status, with a somewhat higher percentage of unemployed parents than would be expected in a representative sample. Both cohorts are predominantly White (99%).

Measurement and Analysis Strategy

Every other year, the boys and their families in the OYS were assessed on a full range of independent and dependent variables. To accomplish this, families were observed in the home (Dishion, Loeber, Stouthamer-Loeber, & Patterson, 1984) and interviewed, school data were collected (school records, teacher ratings), telephone interviews were conducted, and a family problem-solving task (Forgatch, Fetrow, & Lathrop, 1985) was videotaped. The entire battery took approximately 20 hours for two-parent families to complete. A construct development approach was used for data reduction within this study that was heavily guided by an earlier version of the working model of child antisocial behavior shown in Figure 7.1 (Loeber & Schmaling, 1985; Patterson, 1982; Patterson & Bank, 1985; Patterson & Dishion, 1985; Patterson & Stouthamer-Loeber, 1984). Consistent with the ideas of Campbell and Fiske (1959) and Cronbach and Meehl (1955), each construct in the model was operationally defined by a multimethod and agent measurement strategy. The resulting measurement model and basic findings for the first wave of the OYS are described in detail in *Antisocial Boys* (Patterson et al., in press).

Assessing each of the main theoretical constructs with a multimethod and agent approach presents a challenge for standard univariate statistical methods in terms of data reduction and analysis procedures. However, developments in the use of structural equation modeling (Bentler, 1980; Dwyer, 1983; Jöreskog & Sörbom, 1983) have made it possible to define latent constructs with multiple indicator data and to test comprehensive models using an overall chi-square goodness-of-fit test. A clear advantage of using structural equation modeling (SEM) is the ability to test the measurement model (i.e., factor loadings of the indicators on latent constructs) and the structural model (estimated empirical relation among constructs) simultaneously within one analysis. Details of this approach to data analysis can be found in comprehensive reviews (e.g., Bentler, 1980) and in more complete expositions of the statistical model (e.g., Dwyer, 1983; Jöreskog & Sörbom, 1983).

Several models will be discussed in the section that follows, and each is also available in published journals for more detailed review by the readers. We began with a procedure that statistically compares competing explanatory models (Bentler & Bonnett, 1980) and in this way hope eventually to narrow the field of possible alternative hypotheses.

Peers and Troublesomeness

The Link Between Troublesomeness and Peer Rejection

The first question to be addressed is to what extent children's problem behavior and social skill deficits elicit negative reactions from peers, leading to eventual rejection. The concern for rejected children has generated a large body of research on (a) the behavioral adjustment (antisocial/aggressive behavior, social skills deficits, and hyperactivity), (b) the academic competence (e.g., Coie & Dodge, 1988; Coie & Kupersmidt, 1983; Dodge, 1983; French, 1988), and (c) the social cognitive characteristics of the rejected child (e.g., Dodge & Coie, 1987). These studies provide strong support for the hypothesis that the social characteristics of children relate directly to their acceptance among the conventional peer group within the school context.

Until recently, children's development of peer relations has been studied in isolation, without directly studying the influence of families. For most socialization researchers, it makes sense that patterns of adjustment learned within the family will directly translate to patterns of adjustment with peers. In some ways the relation may be rather direct and easily interpretable. For example, children who learn to be aggressive within families will attempt those skills when in the company of peers. Similarly, shy and withdrawn children within the family may repeat this style away from home and simply fail to achieve any reaction from peers, including intimate relationships. Considerable progress has been made in studying the long-term progressions of aggressive and withdrawn patterns over the life course (e.g., Caspi, Elder, & Bern, 1987). Putallaz (1987) has completed research on the correlation between mother-child interaction and child-peer interactions, as well as sociometric status. Observational data, collected within a laboratory setting, indicate that agreeable mother-child interaction correlated ($r = .41$, $df = 41$) with the child's use of a similar style with peers. Children's disagreeable behavior with other children in the laboratory task correlated with their social status in school ($r = -.45$; $df = 20$).

We approached the same question using a slightly different tactic. We were interested in testing the hypothesis that parent discipline interactions in the home were related to the boy's lack of skill and disposition to be antisocial, and consequently being peer rejected. To test this idea, the following constructs were developed on the OYS sample: Parent Discipline, Peer Rejection, Child Antisocial, and Child Academic Skills.

SEM (Jöreskog & Sörbom, 1983) was used to evaluate this hypothesis (Dishion, in press), and the results are shown in Figure 7.2. In these analyses the measure of peer rejection was composed of the judgment of peers at school in a nomination format, including the following items: (a) "kids who you like as friends," (b) "kids who make friends easily," (c) "kids who don't get along with most other kids," and (d) "kids who you don't want to be friends with." The positive nominations were summarized into a measure of peer acceptance and the negative nominations into a measure of peer rejection.

The Parent Discipline construct was defined using home observations of parent-child interaction, consistent with the approach taken by Patterson and Bank (1985). It is important to note that this is a measure of coercive discipline, or the lack thereof. It appears that the concept of discipline is such that it is much easier to measure poor discipline practices than it is to measure discipline skill (Patterson et al., in press).

Parents, teachers, and children served as informants on the child's antisocial behavior across settings. Academic skill was defined using teacher judgments and standardized tests of academic achievement.

The results of the SEM test of the peer rejection hypothesis are shown in Figure 7.2. In summary, the chi-square goodness-of-fit test supported the hypothesized model that the effect of poor parental discipline on peer rejection was mediated by the child's antisocial behavior and academic skills. Note that the simple indirect effect model did not adequately fit the data (chi-square = 39.81, $p < .07$, $df = 28$). In the model, the chi-square goodness-of-fit test was significant, indicating a reliable difference between the model and the observed correlations among the measures. The model was subsequently revised to include an effect path from the child's antisocial behavior to academic skill deficits, which is consistent with the data presented by Patterson et al. (1989), showing the exacerbating effect of children's problem behavior on their academic achievement. This "exacerbated effect" model was also found to fit the data adequately (chi-square = 33.64, $p < .18$, $df = 27$), in support of the hypothesis. This model explained 48% (1-residual variance, zeta) of the variance of peer relations. Adding the direct effect of Parent Discipline practices to Peer Relations did not significantly improve the fit of the exacerbated effect model.

This series of analyses was a useful exercise in conceptualizing a model of peer rejection that explicitly includes parent-child interaction as a causal process. These data are correlational and, of course, do not stand alone as a confirmation of a causal hypothesis. However, both the data presented here and those presented by Putallaz (1987) support the idea that parent-child interaction is the critically important setting where children's behavior problems develop. It is the conventional peers' reaction to the child's troublesomeness that leads to peer rejection. In agreement with this idea, children who were categorically defined as rejected (Coie, Dodge, & Coppotelli, 1982) had been exposed to poorer parental discipline and monitoring practices and came

A) Simple Indirect Effect Model

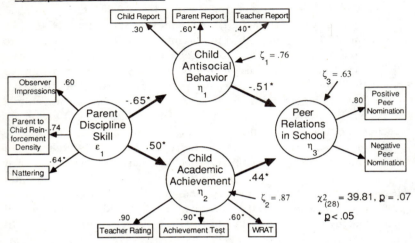

B) Exacerbated Indirect Effect Model

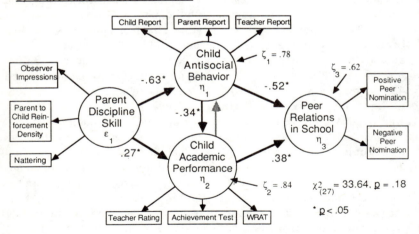

Figure 7.2. A Simple Indirect Effect Model

SOURCE: Dishion (in press).
NOTE: For Figure 7.2A, $\chi^2 = 39.81$, $p = .07$. For Figure 7.2B, $\chi^2 = 33.64$, $p = .18$.
*$p < .05$.

from families reportedly having more stress and lower socioeconomic status (Dishion, in press). These data emphasize the need to consider the full range of ecological settings when studying the troubled child, including the interrelation between children's experience within the family and how this influences their adjustment with peers (Hartup, 1983).

Continuity in Peer Problems

Studies on the continuity of peer sociometric status seem to indicate that children who are rejected continue to be classified by their peers as rejected across time even following transitions from elementary school to middle school (Coie et al., 1982). It is useful also to consider to what extent children unliked by peers continue to have peer difficulties two years later, not only in the eyes of their peers, but also from their own perspectives and from those of their parents and teachers. Using the Coie et al. (1982) system of defining sociometric status, we identified the following groups: (a) Rejected, (b) Neglected, (c) Controversial, (d) Average, and (e) Popular. Rejected children are those who are activity disliked, Neglected children are those who are ignored and unliked, and Controversial children receive a mixture of positive and negative sociometric nominations.

The first question was, To what extent do children with problematic peer relations develop negative global perceptions of peers? At age 12, the boys were asked (through questionnaires) about their attachment to peers, their liking of peers at school and in the neighborhood, and their perception of the extent to which their friends engaged in positive behaviors with them. The mean z score for each of the five groups was examined. Using a MANOVA to test whether the expected multivariate effect would be found, it was revealed that the five sociometric groups did not statistically differ in the child's perception of peer relationships (see Table 7.1). Consistent with the lack of a multivariate effect, the univariate F tests did not show reliable differences among the sociometric groups in the expected direction. In the eyes of the boys, the quality of their peer relationships at age 12 were not related to being unliked by peers at school at age 10.

We also looked at the relation between being rejected at age 10 and more objective measures of peer conflict and impoverished peer networks at age 12 from the view of parents, teachers, and the child. For the parent's report we used items from the Child Behavior Checklist

Table 7.1 Means (average Z scores) and Standard Deviations for Peer Adjustment Indicators at Age 12 by Sociometric Status (10 years)

Child's perception of univariate peer relationkships at age 12[a]	Rejected	Neglected	Controversial	Average	Popular	F Test
Armstrong—Child's Attachment to Peers	-.23 (.98)	.08 (1.42)	.04 (.717)	.04 (1.0)	.26 (.77)	ns
Friend Observation Checklist—friend to child	.37 (1.03)	.23 (1.43)	.02 (.97)	-.16 (.94)	.17 (.95)	p < .07
Social control: kids at school	-.11 (.98)	.35 (1.27)	.09 (.69)	.05 (1.05)	-.11 (.85)	ns
Social control: kids in neighborhood	-.07 (1.05)	-.16 (1.08)	-.17 (1.14)	.06 (.99)	.11 (.91)	ns
Univariate Peer Problem[b]						
Parent CBC	.61 (1.06)	.56 (1.18)	.05 (.91)	-.11 (.87)	-.40 (.92)	p < .05
Teacher CBC	.46 (1.27)	.56 (1.21)	.09 (.94)	.03 (.94)	-.48 (.53)	p < .05
Child PDR Report Peer Problems	-.04 (.76)	.05 (1.05)	.15 (1.19)	.04 (1.05)	.13 (.99)	ns
Parent PDR Peer Problems	.33 (1.35)	-.30 (.65)	-.28 (.84)	.03 (.98)	-.17 (.79)	ns
Parent Ratings Peer Relations	.47 (1.05)	.38 (1.27)	-.15 (1.13)	.05 (.89)	-.23 (.97)	p < .05
N	30	11	14	112	26	

a. Wilks's lambda ns.
b. Wilks's lambda = .79; $p < .002$.

(CBC) (Achenbach & Edelbrock, 1983) assessing poor peer relations (i.e., number of friends, how often he does things with friends, getting along with kids, being teased, not being liked, and preferring to play with younger children). Similar items were used for the score derived from the teacher version of the CBC. In daily telephone calls both the parent(s) and the child were asked about conflicts with peers within the last three days; the number of yes responses were summarized over six telephone interviews. A parent rating instrument was designed to assess peer relations, including the following items: "feels other kids don't like him," "is picked on or teased," "gets into arguments with peers."

As shown in Table 7.1, there was a significant multivariate effect on these five measures of peer adjustment taken at age 12 as a function of sociometric status at age 10 (Wilks's lambda = .79, $p < .002$). In general, the direction of effects is consistent across measures where peer Rejected and Neglected boys experienced more problems with peers at age 12 when compared with other sociometric groups. Rejected and Neglected boys showed similar profiles across the five measures of peer problems, except on the parent telephone report of conflict. Inspection of the means for the parent report of conflict measure reveals that the Rejected group was experiencing more conflict than the other groups, whereas the parents of the Neglected boys reported less; however, these trends were not statistically significant.

These data support the notion that there is a continuity of relationship problems that a good portion of troublesome boys experience over time. However, the continuity is indicated only with more objective measures of peer relational problems. When relying exclusively on the child's global report of liking and attachment to peers, there appears to be no effect for being rejected or neglected. Incidentally, forming a composite score from the objective measures of peer relation problems also showed better predictive validity to other measures of child maladjustment, compared to a construct measuring the child's liking of peers. For example, the Peer Problems construct at age 12 correlated with the child's report of depression ($r = .30$, $df = 200$, $p < .001$), a composite measure of antisocial behavior ($r = .60$, $df = 200$, $p < .001$), deviant peers ($r = .51$, $df = 200$, $p < .001$), self-esteem ($r = -.37$, $df = 200$, $p < .001$), and parent monitoring ($r = -.41$, $df = 200$, $p < .001$).

We think that the troubled child's problems with peers are best understood in conjunction with parenting practices, his or her behavioral adjustment, and his or her social network. Next, some research will be discussed that examines the hypotheses about the joint influence

Table 7.2. Number of Boys with Police Contact by Wave 2 and 3 Within the Five Sociometric Groups

	Police Contact	No Police Contact	Percentage
Rejected	14	16	46.7
Neglected	1	10	9.1
Controversial	4	10	28.6
Average	26	98	21
Popular	3	24	11.1

NOTE: Chi-square (4) = 13.2, $p < .01$.

of parenting practices (i.e., monitoring) and peer relations in the boy's exposure to deviant peer influences, and the effect of these influences on his social adjustment.

Peer Rejection as a Cause of Troublesomeness

Numerous investigators document the long-term adjustment problems of children who experience peer rejection (Cowen, Pederson, Babigian, Izzo, & Trost, 1973; Hartup, 1983; Janes, Hesselbrock, Myers, & Penniman, 1979; Parker & Asher, 1987; Roff, 1961; Roff & Sells, 1970). In their recent review, Parker and Asher (1987) present data showing that rejected children are more at risk for delinquency, truancy, and adolescent adjustment problems. For the OYS boys we looked at the court records of the Rejected, Neglected, Controversial, Average, and Popular boys at age 14-15. These data are presented in Table 7.2, in terms of the percentages of boys having any police contact. Note that peer rejection seems uniquely predictive of later delinquency when compared to being neglected by peers. In fact, Neglected boys at age 10 seemed to have a reduced risk of police contact at age 14-15 (9.1%). The base rate of police contact for the two cohorts of boys was 23.3%. As can be seen, the Rejected boys were at far greater risk (46.7%) for having police contact than were the other sociometric groupings.

One explanation of these findings is that rejected children are more at risk for exposure to deviant peer influences. There is substantial evidence that the deviant peer group provides a social context that encourages problem behavior (e.g., Elliott et al., 1985). Patterson et al. (in press) have referred to this idea as the "shopping hypothesis." The idea describes a process where rejected children tend to select out other rejected children as peer associates, basically because of the limited social network available to them. Because other rejected children are antisocial, the rejected peer group is also the deviant peer group. In agreement with this idea, we found that at age 10 Rejected children were more likely to nominate other Rejected children as friends than were other sociometric groups, despite the trend for all children to prefer the prosocial popular boys. Research by Ladd (1983) also has revealed that Rejected children tend to spend more time with other Rejected children. It appears that this process of selective association begins as early as age 6, in the first grade, where studies have shown higher levels of antisocial behavior when rejected children (males and females) associate with other rejected children, when compared with normal peers (Cillessen, 1989).

Parent monitoring practices also play an important role in the process of the child's drift to a deviant peer group. Steinberg (1986), using a straightforward measurement approach, showed that unsupervised time after school was correlated with children's exposure to deviant peers and susceptibility to peer pressure. In our own research we have found that parent monitoring practices correlated with deviant peer influences in adolescence (Patterson & Dishion, 1985; Snyder, Dishion, & Patterson, 1986). Not until recently have we had the opportunity to test the longitudinal hypothesis that both parent monitoring practices and peer rejection increase the child's risk for becoming a member of a deviant peer group.

In testing the hypothesis, the constructs Peer Relations and Parent Monitoring were assessed at ages 10 and 12 for the OYS boys and their families (see Figure 7.3). Inspection of Figure 7.3 reveals that the measurement of the three constructs (Parent Monitoring, Peer Relations, and Deviant Peers) was approximately equivalent across the two ages. Peer Relations was defined on the basis of peer nominations at age 10 and on teacher ratings of Peer Acceptance and Peer Rejection at age 12. Parent Monitoring was defined on the basis of interviews with the child, telephone interviews with the parents, and global impressions of interviewers at both assessment times. The Deviant Peer construct was based on the child's report of exposure to deviant peers (age 12 only) and on parent and teacher global ratings of the level of deviance of the boy's friends on the Child Behavior Checklist (Achenbach & Edelbrock, 1983). The specifics of the model testing and measurement approaches are described in more detail in Dishion, Patterson, et al. (1989).

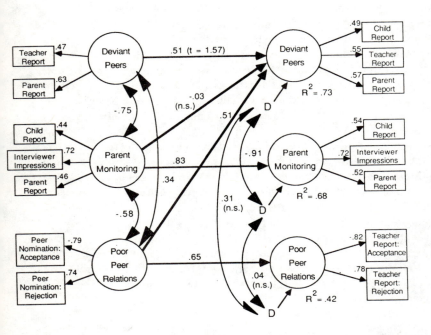

Figure 7.3. Peer Relations and Parent Monitoring in the Drift to Deviant Peers

SOURCE: Dishion et al. (1989)
NOTE: $N = 180$; $\chi^2_{(70)} = 87.64$; $p = .08$; BBN = .886. All parameters $T \geq 2.00$ except where noted.

SEM was used to compare three competing models, following the model testing format recommended by Anderson and Gerbing (1988) and Bentler and Bonnett (1980):

(1) The measurement model simply allows all constructs to correlate with all other constructs in the model. This is a saturated model to the extent that all possible causal paths are unconstrained. The measurement model serves as an atheoretical baseline with which alternative models compete in explanatory value.

(2) The correlated stability model represents the three constructs stable from age 10 to 12 and correlated over time. This is the most parsimonious of

Table 7.3. Summary Statistics for Alternative Process Models

Model	df	Chi-Square Goodness of Fit	p Value
Measurement	66	81.00	.10
Stability model	72	103.22	.01
Lagged effect	70	87.64	.08

longitudinal models in that there are no hypothesized causal (lagged) effects among the three variables, and all three may be determined by a fourth, unspecified, variable.

(3) The lagged effect (theoretical) model (see Figure 7.3) represents the hypothesis of a lagged effect of Poor Peer Relations and Parental Monitoring at age 10 on Deviant Peers at age 12. This model best fits a test of causality in that the causal variables precede the dependent variable in time (2 years) and are tested in competition with the stability of the Deviant Peer construct.

The comparative fit of these three models using the chi-square goodness-of-fit test (summarized in Table 7.3) supported the hypothesis that boys' peer relations increase the risk of exposure to deviant peers by age 12. The results of these analyses indicate that a model that incorporates Deviant Peers at age 10 and Poor Peer Relations at age 10 accounts for 73% of the variance in the age 12 Deviant Peer construct (see Figure 7.3). Parent Monitoring at age 10 did not predict deviant peer exposure at age 12 over the stability of that variable and earlier peer relations problems. These findings do not indicate, however, that parental supervision practices are trivial to understanding a boy's exposure to deviant peers. In fact, the concurrent correlations between Deviant Peers and Parental Monitoring were comparable to those between Poor Peer Relations at ages 10 and 12. However, in the context of the test of a lagged effect of Parental Monitoring on Deviant Peer exposure over a period of two years, earlier peer relations were a moderately superior predictor. These data are certainly consistent with the hypothesis that immediate changes in the parent's supervision of the child would be accompanied by less exposure to deviant peers (Patterson et al., in press). The actual test of this hypothesis awaits an experimental manipulation, which is currently in progress.

These analyses are especially useful for considering the joint influence of parenting practices and the peer acceptance outside the family to adolescent adjustment. Consistent with the ecological emphasis of this section of the volume, children's troublesomeness may be best understood by considering the synergistic influence of their experiences in both the family and peer domains.

The Influence of Troublesome Peers

There are several mechanisms through which the deviant peer group can exacerbate the maladjustment of the troublesome child. First, association with deviant peers was highly correlated with the peer conflict measure, indicating that such friendships may reinforce coercive patterns of interaction and fail to teach these children the important productive social skills necessary for successful intimate relationships (Gottman, 1983; Sullivan, 1953). As seen in the above analyses, problems with peers for Rejected and Neglected children continue, regardless of whether the child develops a network with other troublesome children. One might expect that a simple measure of average length of close friendships for the troublesome child would be less than that for the well-socialized child. A review of the developmental literature by Berdt (1989) indicates that this is an important area for further research.

A second mechanism that deviant peer relationships may have in undermining adolescent adjustment is through reinforcement of deviant behavior. There is considerable research showing the powerful influence of the deviant peer group on adolescent adjustment problems such as juvenile delinquency (Elliott et al., 1985; Patterson & Dishion, 1985) and substance use (Dishion, Crosby, et al., 1989; Dishion & Loeber, 1985; Elliott et al., 1985; Kandel, 1973). These outcomes are more likely associated with having peers who themselves are delinquent or are drug users, and the effect of such peers on various forms of deviance. Clearly, by early adolescence, peers provide a highly influential social milieu in which both prosocial and antisocial interactions might be imitated, reinforced, shaped, practiced, and maintained. As shown in Figure 7.1, it was hypothesized that peer reinforcement processes explain the influence of deviant peers on deviance. Research on children in a school setting (Hartup, Glazer, & Charlesworth, 1967) and adolescents within a juvenile detention center (Buehler & Patterson, 1966) supported this idea.

A significant gap in the current research is the exclusive reliance on the child's self-report to measure the influence of deviant peers. In an attempt to deal with this issue a peer interaction task (PIT) was designed to assess the interpersonal influence processes taking place between adolescents and their friends, as well as adolescents' reports on the characteristics of their friendships. The design of this task was inspired by research reported by Panella and Henggeler (1986) showing that conduct-disordered boys were distinguished from normals and anxious adolescents by virtue of their interactions with their friends and strangers as assessed on a videotaped problem-solving task. In particular, conduct-disordered boys showed fewer of the positive social behaviors that were found to be associated with interactions with friends.

The goal of the peer interaction task in the OYS was to determine the relative reinforcement for antisocial behavior found for antisocial boys and their friends compared to normal friendship dyads. To prepare for using a similar task with the OYS boys, a pilot study was conducted using a small sample ($n = 20$) of adolescent boys from the community, roughly half of whom were known to be involved in delinquent behavior from other clinical studies within our center.

In a telephone interview each boy and his parents were asked the names of the four boys with whom the boy spends the most time. A friend was selected that both the parents and boys identified. The boy and his friend were asked to come to OSLC for a two-hour session, where they both completed the Elliott et al. (1985) self-report measure of delinquency and substance use, were interviewed as to the history of their relationship, completed a Friend Dyadic Adjustment scale providing ratings on the quality of their friendship with their peer, and completed a 25-minute videotaped problem-solving session. The problem-solving session consisted of 25 minutes in which the boys were asked to plan an activity together (something they could do within the next week) and then take turns solving two of the study boy's problems and two of his friend's (5 minutes for each problem). The order of problem solving was randomly determined. To prepare for the problem-solving session, the boys were asked to complete a Problem Checklist, which identified problems with friends or parents that may have occurred in the previous month. Because of the pilot nature of this research, the following data are best considered suggestive and will be followed by similar analyses using the OYS boys.

The results of the pilot study are presented in Table 7.4, providing the correlations between the characteristics of the boy's peer associate's interpersonal behavior and the target boy's self-reported delinquency, substance use, and parent-reported problem behavior on the CBC, parent version, using the Delinquency scale. The interpersonal behavior

Table 7.4   Correlation Between Dyadic Peer Interaction and Adolescent Delinquency and Substance Use ($N = 20$)

Peer Interaction Task Scores (nonsequential)	Target Child Deviance			
	Self-Reported Delinquency	Self-Reported Alcohol Use	Self-Reported Marijuana Use	Parent CBC Delinquency
Proportion anitsocial qualifier				
peer	.43***	.54***	.34*	.30
target boy	.54****	.57***	.30*	.13
Prosocial content rate				
peer	.29	.11	.32*	.26
target boy	.21	.30**	.56****	.42**
Aversive content rate				
peer	.61***	.01	.42**	.20
target boy	.38**	.13	.51***	.53**

*$p < .10$; **$p < .05$; ***$p < .01$; ****$p < .001$.

of the boys was coded from the videotapes using the Peer Process Code (Dishion, Crosby, et al., 1989). This coding system consists of 24 content codes that classify interpersonal behavior among adolescents. The content codes are classified into Prosocial (e.g., Positive Verbal, which includes compliments, approval, praise, and so on) and Aversive (e.g., Negative Verbal, which includes criticism, disapproval, and the like). The target child's and peer's prosocial and aversive behavior within the task were summarized as a rate per minute score. Also included in the format of the Peer Process Code was the Social Qualifier dimension, where, in addition to content, the boy's interpersonal behavior was qualified as being Antisocial, Neutral, or Prosocial. Interpersonal behavior was qualified as Antisocial, including suggestions, approval, or descriptions of illegal or rule-breaking behavior either within the videotaped session (e.g., tearing the camera off the wall, mooning the camera) or outside the session. The summary score used to reflect the level of antisocial talk for the boys and their friends was the Proportion of Antisocial Qualifier score. This score reflects the extent to which deviant behavior is promoted or socialized within the adolescent dyad.

Table 7.4 reveals that the Proportion Antisocial Qualifier score correlated with all indices of adolescent troublesomeness except for the parent's report on the CBC, although this correlation was in the expected direction. Thus both the peer's and the target boy's level of approval and talk about antisocial activity correlated with the total number of delinquent acts reported within the last year as well as reported frequency of alcohol and marijuana use. Note that both the target child's and peer's number of antisocial behaviors within this task correlated equally with the target child's self-reported delinquency. These data provide preliminary support for the hypothesis that adolescent peer friendships, at the very minimum, provide a social ecology in which problem behavior can be modeled and practiced and perhaps even reinforced and strengthened. This supports the sociological findings on the strong influence of deviant peers on delinquency across samples and methods (e.g., Elliott et al., 1985).

The model tested by Dishion, Patterson, et al. (1989) seemed to indicate that it was low peer acceptance from the conventional peer group as well as poor parental supervision practices that increased the risk that boys would belong to a deviant peer group. A corollary of this hypothesis is that the friendships and interpersonal transactions of the deviant peer group should be of lower quality when compared to nonproblem adolescent boys interacting with their peers. The deviant peer group is typically made up of boys who have a history of rejection from the conventional peer group. The data in Table 7.4 partially address this hypothesis and provide some interesting results. As is consistent with the hypothesis, the higher rates of aversive behavior (for either the boy or his friend) within the PIT were associated with higher rates of self-reported delinquency and marijuana use and the parent's report of problem behavior on the CBC. This finding is consistent with Patterson's (1982) conceptualization of the coercion process that begins within the context of family interaction and generalizes to the child's exchanges with significant others outside the home.

The small sample size of these pilot data ($n = 20$) mandates replication and extension of these findings. However, these data have provided initial encouragement for this program of research, and the post hoc hypotheses arising from these analyses will be pursued in the OYS sample. For example, there may be some tendency for relationships within the deviant peer group to be both enmeshed and characterized by abrasive or aversive interpersonal behavior. In many ways the tendency of children described as "troublesome" to form friendships with other troubled children may be adaptive in providing the youngster with an interpersonal context with ample positive reinforcement for their coercive interaction styles. The question remains, and will be addressed in future studies, as to the long-term influence troubled peers exert on each other. It is possible that friendships among antisocial children represent a constructive process, teaching such children the essential skills for developing other satisfying intimate relationships. It may well be the antisocial child who fails to develop any friendships who is most at risk when considering other outcomes more related to psychopathology (e.g., depression).

Summary and Implications

Summary

A working model was discussed that emphasized the synergistic role of parenting practices and peer socialization on child and adolescent troublesome behavior. Also reviewed was a series of studies conducted at OSLC from the Oregon Youth Study sample supporting the idea that children's troublesome behavior places them at risk for rejection by the conventional peer group within the school context. Peer rejection was shown to increase the likelihood that the troublesome child will develop a friendship network composed of deviant peers. Looking only at boys, it appears that the development of deviant friends may have a long-term negative impact by providing (a) a social context where noxious behavior can be practiced and reinforced and (b) a rich source of reinforcement for problem behavior that increases the likelihood of negative adult outcomes (e.g., jail) as well as habits that may further interfere with the adolescent's mastery of critical developmental milestones (e.g., finishing high school, marriage, work skills).

Although within this chapter there is a heavy emphasis on the peer context of troublesome behavior, from a broader perspective, the model is family based. Evidence for the influence of parenting on peer adjustment was provided, specifically, in the role of parent discipline practices on boys' success with peers in school, as well as the effect of parent monitoring practices on the child's drift to a deviant peer group. These analyses indicated that efforts to change peer process and adjustment without addressing parenting practices may be less successful than those that include an intervention aimed at parenting practices. This approach to considering the joint influence of parents and peers conforms with Bronfenbrenner's (1986) suggestion for supraordinate models (i.e., mesosystem models) that make explicit the interrelation between two socialization systems in explaining children's adjustment. This research is to date incomplete in that it has not yet been demonstrated that children's peer context provides additional information in predicting children's long-term outcomes over and above their own behavior and their family context. (For a review of the family's role in the development of troublesome behavior, see Snyder & Huntley, Chapter 10, this volume.)

Moreover, the research on peer interaction processes that add to the socialization of adolescent problem behavior is preliminary and awaits replication and extension from the ongoing Oregon Youth Study. In part, the success of this program of research on troublesome child behavior is seen as an outcome of combining developmental and clinical research programs on troublesome children. Future research is also obviously needed in determining the applicability of these ideas to girls, although, in a general sense, we know that troublesome behavior in girls leads to peer rejection (Coie et al., 1982) and that deviant peer influences are highly correlated to delinquency in adolescent females (Elliott et al., 1985).

In a highly critical and thoughtful discussion, Meehl (1978) has complained of little progress in the confirmation or disconfirmation of psychological theories. Part of the problem, according to Meehl, is the exclusive reliance on statistical inferences based on the null hypothesis test. The problem with this approach to theory testing is that the null hypothesis is almost always an implausible alternative hypothesis, and failure to reject this alternative is not a strong statement toward theory confirmation. Like theories in the physical sciences, psychological models should lend themselves to making specific predictions given specific circumstances (i.e., lead to the derivation of point estimates under experimental conditions) and therefore should be less dependent on statistical testing. Theories that provide accurate and interesting predictions under well-defined experimental conditions, according to Meehl, are the most useful to the social science enterprise.

The implication of this approach for the current research is that a more rigorous test of the findings would be to manipulate the independent variables experimentally and determine if improvements in the child's peer relations follow. Thus the findings in the current research are an initial step toward understanding the major influences on boys' adjustment with peers in middle childhood. The model should also be useful on an individual level, where a child's adjustment at school among peers can be accurately predicted from his or her social behavior and academic skills, and that change in these variables precede improvement in peer relations. The formal testing of such propositions can lead only to increased understanding of the major determinants of peer relations and social behavior and an increasingly complex and accurate social model. In this way, the thoughtful use of both clinical and developmental research in a research program can be seen as dialectical.

The next step in this line of research, currently under way, is to manipulate parent monitoring and peer relation skills experimentally in the form of randomized clinical interventions to determine if improvement results in reduced influence of deviant peers and lower levels of problem behavior. The approach taken now is to evaluate these interventions on a sample of 120 families of at-risk early adolescents. The youngsters are selected as at risk for substance abuse based on a screening interview administered to concerned parents calling to be involved in the intervention research. At this date, the sample population (50% male and 50% female) is at risk on a variety of dimensions, and appears to be quite heterogeneous. For example, 42% of the boys (11-14 years old) were reported by parents on the CBC to be two standard deviations above the mean on the Hyperactivity Scale. The girls, on the other hand, are more at risk on internalizing problems. For example, 50% report clinically significant levels of depression on the Child Depression Research Scale (Birleson, 1981).

References

Achenbach, T. M., & Edelbrock, C. (1983). *Manual for the Child Behavior Checklist and revised Child Behavior Profile.* Burlington: University of Vermont Press.

Achenbach, T. M., & Edelbrock, C. (1986). *Manual for the Teacher's Report Form and Teacher Version of the Child Behavior Profile.* Burlington: University of Vermont Press.

Anderson, J. C., & Gerbing, M. (1988). Structural equation modeling in practice: A review and recommended two step approach. *Psychological Bulletin, 103*, 411-423.

Bentler, P. M. (1980). Multivariate analysis with latent variables. *Annual Review of Psychology, 31*, 419-456.

Bentler, P. M., & Bonnett, D. G. (1980). Significant tests and goodness-of-fit in the analysis of covariance structures. *Psychological Bulletin, 88*, 588-606.

Berdt, T. (1989). Friendships in childhood and adolescence. In W. Damon (Ed.), *Child development today and tomorrow* (pp. 332-348). San Francisco: Jossey-Bass.

Birleson, P. (1981). The validity of depressive disorder in childhood and the development of a self-rating scale: A research report. *Journal of Child Psychiatry and Psychology, 22*, 73-88.

Bronfenbrenner, U. (1986). Ecology of the family as a context for human development. *Developmental Psychology, 22*, 723-742.

Buehler, R. E., & Patterson, G. R. (1966). The reinforcement of behavior in institutional settings. *Behavior Research and Therapy, 4*, 157-167.

Cairns, R. B. (1979). *The analysis of social interaction: Methods, issues, and illustrations.* Hillsdale, NJ: Lawrence Erlbaum.

Campbell, D. T., & Fiske, D. W. (1959). Conversant and discriminant validation of the multitrait and multimethod matrix. *Psychological Bulletin, 56*, 81-105.

Capaldi, D., & Patterson, G. R. (1987). An approach to the problem of recruitment and retention rates for longitudinal research. *Behavioral Assessment, 0191-5401, 1*69-177.

Caspi, A., Elder, G. H., & Bern, T. J. (1987). Moving against the world: Life-course patterns of explosive children. *Developmental Psychology, 23*, 308-313.

Chamberlain, P., & Patterson, G. R. (1984). Aggressive behavior in middle childhood. In D. Schaffer, A. A. Ehrhardt, & L. L. Greenhill (Eds.), *The clinical guide to child psychiatry.* New York: Free Press.

Cillessen, T. (1989, April). *Aggression and liking in same-status versus different-status groups.* Paper presented at the biennial meeting of the Society for Research in Child Development, Kansas City, MO.

Coie, J. D., & Dodge, K. (1988). Multiple sources of data on social behavior and social status in the school: A cross-age comparison. *Child Development, 59*, 815-829.

Coie, J. D., Dodge, K., & Coppotelli, H. (1982). Dimensions of types of social status: A cross-age perspective. *Developmental Psychology, 18*, 557-570.

Coie, J. D., & Kupersmidt, J. B. (1983). A behavioral analysis of emerging social status in boys' groups. *Child Development, 54*, 1400-1416.

Cowen, E. L., Pederson, A., Babigian, H., Izzo, L. D., & Trost, M. A. (1973). Long-term followup of early detected vulnerable children. *Journal of Consulting and Clinical Psychology, 41*(3), 438-446.

Cronbach, L. J., & Meehl, P. E. (1955). Construct validity in psychological tests. *Psychological Bulletin, 52*, 281-302.

Dishion, T. J. (in press). Family ecology. *Child Development.*

Dishion, T. J., Crosby, L., Rusby, J. C., Shane, D., Patterson, G. R., & Baker, J. (1989). *Peer process code: Multidimensional system for observing adolescent peer interaction.* Unpublished training manual. (Available from Oregon Social Learning Center, 207 East 5th Street, Suite 202, Eugene, OR 97401)

Dishion, T. J., & Loeber, R. (1985). Adolescent marijuana and alcohol use: The role of parents and peers revisited. *American Journal of Drug and Alcohol Abuse, 11*(1, 2), 11-25.

Dishion, T. J., & Loeber, R., Stouthamer-Loeber, M., & Patterson, G. R. (1984). Skill deficits and male adolescent delinquency. *Journal of Abnormal Psychology, 12*, 37-54.

Dishion, T. J., Patterson, G. R., & Reid, J. B. (1988). Parent and peer factors associated with drug sampling in early adolescence: Implications for treatments. In E. R. Rahdert & J. Grabowski (Eds.), *Adolescent drug abuse: Analyses of treatment research* (NIDA Research Monograph 66) (pp. 69-93). Washington, DC: Government Printing Office.

Dishion, T. J., Patterson, G. R., Skinner, M. S., & Stoolmiller, M. (1989, April). *A process model for the role of peers in adolescent social adjustment.* Paper presented at the biennial meeting of the Society for Research in Child Development, Kansas City, MO.

Dodge, K. A. (1983). Behavioral antecedents of peer social status. *Child Development, 54,* 1386-1399.

Dodge, K. A., & Coie, J. D. (1987). Social-information-processing factors in reactive and proactive aggression in children's peer groups. *Journal of Personality and Social Psychology, 53,* 1146-1157.

Dwyer, J. H. (1983). *Statistical models for the social and behavioral sciences.* New York: Oxford University Press.

Elliott, D., Huizinga, D., & Ageton, S. (1985). *Explaining delinquency and drug use.* Beverly Hills, CA: Sage.

Fagot, B., & Kavanagh, K. (1988). *Context of attachment.* Unpublished manuscript. (Available from Oregon Social Learning Center, 207 East 5th Street, Suite 202, Eugene, OR 97401)

Forgatch, M. S., Fetrow, B., & Lathrop, M. (1985). *Solving problems in family interaction.* Unpublished training manual. (Available from Oregon Social Learning Center, 207 East 5th Street, Suite 202, Eugene, OR 97401)

French, D. C. (1988). Heterogeneity of peer-rejected boys: Aggressive and nonaggressive subtypes. *Child Development, 59,* 882-886.

Gottman, J. M. (1983). How children become friends. *Monograph of the Society of Research in Child Development, 48*(3, Serial No. 201). (Available on microfilm from University Microfilms International, 300 North Zeeb Road, Ann Arbor, MI 48106)

Hartup, W. W. (1983). Peer relations. In P. H. Mussed (Ed.), *Handbook of child psychology* (Vol. 4). New York: John Wiley.

Hartup, W. W., Glazer, J. A., & Charlesworth, R. (1967). Peer reinforcement and sociometric status. *Child Development, 38,* 1017-1024.

Janes, C. L., Hesselbrock, V. M., Myers, D. G., & Penniman, J. H. (1979). Problem boys in young adulthood: Teacher ratings and 12-year followup. *Journal of Youth and Adolescence, 8,* 453-471.

Jöreskog, K. G., & Sörbom, D. (1983). *LISREL VI: Analysis of linear structural relationships by the method of maximum likelihood* (2nd ed., Versions 5, 6). Chicago: International Educational Services.

Kandel, D. B. (1973). Adolescent marijuana use: Role of parents and peers. *Science, 181,* 1067-1081.

Ladd, G. W. (1983). Social networks of popular, average and rejected children in school settings. *Merrill-Palmer Quarterly, 29,* 283-307.

Loeber, R., & Dishion, T. J. (1983). Early predictors of male delinquency: A review. *Psychological Bulletin, 94,* 68-98.

Loeber, R., & Dishion, T. J. (1984). Boys who fight at home and school: Family conditions influencing cross-setting consistency. *Journal of Consulting and Clinical Psychology, 52,* 759-768.

Loeber, R., & Schmaling, K. B. (1985). Empirical evidence for overt and covert patterns of antisocial conduct problems: A meta-analysis. *Journal of Abnormal Child Psychology, 13,* 337-352.

Meehl, P. E. (1978). Theoretical risks and tabular asterisks: Sir Karl, Sir Ronald and the slow progress of soft psychology. *Journal of Consulting and Clinical Psychology, 46*(4), 806-834.

Panella, A., & Henggeler, S. W. (1986). Peer interactions of conduct-disordered, anxious-withdrawn, and well-adjusted Black adolescents. *Journal of Abnormal Child Psychology, 14*(1), 1-11.

Parker, J. G., & Asher, S. R. (1987). Peer relations and later personal adjustment: Are low-accepted children at risk? *Psychological Bulletin, 102,* 357-389.

Patterson, G. R. (1982). *Coercive family process.* Eugene, OR: Castalia.

Patterson, G. R. (1986). Performance models for antisocial boys. *American Psychologist, 41,* 432-444.

Patterson, G. R., & Bank, L. (1985). Bootstrapping your way through the nomological thicket. *Behavioral Assessment, 8,* 49-73.

Patterson, G. R., Capaldi, D., & Bank, L. (1989). An early starter model for predicting delinquency. In D. Pepler & K. H. Rubin (Eds.), *The development and treatment of childhood aggression.* Hillsdale, NJ: Lawrence Erlbaum.

Patterson, G. R., & Dishion, T. J. (1985). Contributions of families and peers to delinquency. *Criminology, 23,* 63-79.

Patterson, G. R., & Forgatch, M. S. (1987). *Parents and adolescents: I. Living together.* Eugene, OR: Castalia.

Patterson, G. R., & Reid, J. B. (1984). Social interactional processes within the family: The study of moment-by-moment family transactions in which human development is embedded. *Journal of Applied Developmental Psychology, 5,* 237-262.

Patterson, G. R., Reid, J. B., & Dishion, T. J. (in press). *Antisocial boys.* New York: Cambridge University Press.

Patterson, G. R., & Stouthamer-Loeber, M. (1984). The correlation of family management practices and delinquency. *Child Development, 55,* 1299-1307.

Putallaz, M. (1987). Maternal behavior and children's sociometric status. *Child Development, 58,* 324-340.

Roff, M. (1961). Childhood social interactions and young adult bad conduct. *Journal of Abnormal Psychology, 53*(2), 333-337.

Roff, M., & Sells, S. B. (1970). Juvenile delinquency in relation to peer acceptance-rejection and socio-economic status. *Psychology in the Schools, 5,* 3-18.

Snyder, J. (1987, June). *Learning and family interaction.* Paper presented at the Second Annual Summer Institute for the Family Research Consortium, "Understanding Family Life Transitions," Santa Fe, NM.

Snyder, J. J., Dishion, T. J., & Patterson G. R. (1986). Determinants and consequences of associating with deviant peers. *Journal of Early Adolescence, 6,* 29-43.

Steinberg, L. (1986). Latchkey children and susceptibility to peer pressure: An ecological analysis. *Developmental Psychology, 22,* 433-439.

Sullivan, H. S. (1953). *The interpersonal theory of psychiatry.* New York: W. W. Norton.

8

From Classic to Holistic Paradigm

The Troubled or Troubling Child as Environment Creator

WILLIAM C. RHODES

In *Women's Ways of Knowing*, Belenky, Clinchy, Goldberger, and Tarule (1986) conclude from their naturalistic study of the developmental influences involved in women's ways of knowing that "our basic assumptions about truth and reality and the origins of knowledge shape the way we see the world and ourselves as participants in it" (p. 3). In recent years there has been a radical shift from the classic paradigm of science to a new scientific paradigm. This movement, growing out of the revolt in physics by relativity and quantum mechanics, challenges our basic assumptions about reality, truth, and the origins of knowledge guiding the education of our children. The basic assumptions of classic science are, largely, also those of education. The classic assumptions are built around an "object world" existing independently of the child's mental constructs of that world. This classic "physical" reality is founded on external substance existing in outside space, and in external conditions of objects, time, and local causality. The paradigm shift in science requires that our perspectives on education, particularly as related to socially marginalized children, be reexamined at a fundamental level.

Because of classic influence, we educators have stressed *objective* sources of knowing, truth, and reality. We have also taught that the way to gain accurate knowledge is to break down "external" reality into manageable bits and pieces. We have emphasized that this is the only sure way to reliable and valid information. We have warned and cautioned children about mistaking their own wishes, feelings, expectations, and personal intentions for true knowledge. Under the imperious scrutiny of classic science, we have taught children to remove the self as much as possible from objective information about their world. In the educative process, we have eroded children's confidence in inner ways of knowing and have made the "self" suspect in their eyes. This has come from an honest attempt on our part to separate self as observer from what is being observed.

Trouble for the Child

Awed by classic science's seemingly successful mastery over reality, we have called into question children's own inner resources and have taught them to invest themselves in external sources of truth, knowledge, and reality. All children, but particularly the troubled or troubling child who achieves only marginal status in our schools and society, come to see the external environment as dictating or controlling their existence.

Troubled children, particularly, come to believe that there is little or nothing they can do to influence these "external" circumstances. Under our innocent tutelage these children comes to look upon "inner" events as separated from reality and claimable only through either fighting against or totally withdrawing from the reality that they have been taught lies outside themselves. Troubled children have learned to conceive of a split between their psychological world and the real world. They begin to believe that they must rely upon an external world for self-validation, for knowledge, and for reassurance of their own reality. They learn that their own existence lies in the hands of the "other"— other people, other things. All else becomes suspect, and their sense of order and control is attributed to external physical or material powers.

Wholeness

Children's way of seeing the world and themselves as participants in it is at odds with the data of the new scientific paradigm. However, we do not have to take the quantum leap to realize that our classic educational approaches have tended to split children from both themselves and their world, and to encourage fragmented styles of thinking and fragmented experience of "external" reality. The work of Jean Piaget (1950, 1971, 1975, 1981, 1983, 1986) and Lev Vygotsky (1978, 1987) should have alerted us to the weakness in our classic educational assumptions about children's ways of knowing.

The assumptions about truth, reality, and the origins of knowledge that shape the way children see their environment and themselves as participants in it rest upon a particular logical bias. That bias, Boolean logic, is built upon the classic split between subject and object. Boole's (1958) mental laws color all of children's relationships to themselves and their world because we have taught them to think exclusively with Boolean logic. These "laws of thought," codified by the Scottish schoolmaster George Boole, have undergirded all of the classic sciences' search for knowledge since Boole explicated them in 1854.

Developmental Research

Although early developmental researchers Piaget and Vygotsky operated within the classic paradigm, their findings presented an opposite model to the Boolean case. They supported a holistic view of the relationship between the child and his or her world. In a strange way, the challenge to classic thinking in Vygotsky's *Mind in Society* and the shifting paradigm views in the 18th Nobel Conference, titled *Mind in Nature* (Elvee, 1982), can be seen as companion pieces. Vygotsky's child development research reveals the world as a complex of processes in which apparently stable objects, as well as images of them inside the child's head, are undergoing incessant self-directed changes.

In *Mind in Nature*, John Wheeler (1982) suggests that science throw out the term *observer* entirely and substitute the term *participator* because of the active and creative role of the mind in maintaining and furthering the reality process. Wheeler offers the radical view that until the human mind had developed to the point that it could participate in the evolutionary process, there could have been no real world.

Piaget (1986), investigating child mental growth within the framework of the classic scientific paradigm, does not claim that physical entities are probabilities as does the new scientific paradigm. However, he does say that the child *constructs* reality. Using *projection* in the broader psychological usage, as different from the Freudian usage, he studied the mental development of the child's projection of object, time, space, and causality. In his data the child takes about 12 years following birth to attain the mental schemes or mental development to "construct" these concrete projections of the conditions of reality around the central kernel of the self. In other words, this is the length of time it takes a child to obtain a sense of "place" in the world as a distinct "self." By 2 years of age, however, the child has already separated out the "self" as a special, distinctive object, among all of the objects he or she has learned to construct. Since object, or substance, is the first schema system developed, the other schemas of space involved in a sense of place—that is, schemas of time and causality—are constructed out of the child's grasp of "objects."

The Self and Its Structuring Capacity

We educators have not fully realized the significance of Piaget's work in terms of its questioning our assumptions about truth, reality, and the origins of knowledge. Piaget's (1981) data confirm, as he says, that the very relationship between a living being and its environment is characterized by one thing: that the thinking, feeling, and intending self, instead of submitting passively to the environment, modifies that environment by imposing a structure of its own upon it (pp. 6-7). Piaget's extensive studies of child development indicate that any potential information origination "in" the environment is never received by the self in its primordial state, for it is immediately transformed by the child's currently developed mental schemas, which aggressively reach out to shape that nascent environmental information according to the child's own mental images of reality. Thus it is impossible to separate the environment from the child's mental manipulations of it. This is the basis for Piaget's conclusion that the child "constructs" reality out of the mental complex of object, space, time, causality, and the various derivative mental processes and the manipulations that flow from that complex of reality conditions.

Even though Piaget can be grouped only with classic theorists and researchers, his work forms a bridge to the changing paradigm in science. For, in a sense, in his concepts of assimilation and accommodation he also sees the observer as changing what is observed by the very act of observation. However, as a classicist, he does not take the strong position assumed by Heisenberg (1974) in the famous Copenhagen Interpretation, which views waves/particles, or all physical processes, as only a tendency for some "thing" to exist—a quantitative version of "potentia" in Aristotelian philosophy. This new view of science introduced something "ghostlike," something standing halfway between the idea of an event and the actual event, a very strange kind of physical reality standing in the middle between possibility and actuality. Observation, or the act of measurement, makes the possible real; nothing is real until observed (Gribbin, 1987).

All thinkers within the new scientific paradigm, not only consciousness theorists, look upon reality as a complex whole that unifies subject and object into a seamless composite. They obliterate the subject-object split so prevalent in classic thought. Wolf's (1984) thesis follows John Wheeler in designating the new scientific era as "Era III": the scientific era of *meaning*, because it turned away from the goal of prediction and control that characterized the classic paradigm. The new science now turns to a paradigm of *meaning*, the meaning of ourselves in our world. Era III in science seeks understanding rather than control of the self and its universe.

Fragmented Minds, Fragmented Worlds

The modern cognitive followers of Piaget and Vygotsky have strengthened the place of awareness in learning. Their work is responsible for the school's teaching of "thinking skills" today (de Bono, 1983; Feuerstein, 1979, 1980; Lipman, 1984; Sternberg, 1984). The implications of this critical study for verbal conditioning and the more general question of learning without awareness clearly demonstrated that awareness, in relation to other behaviors, is requisite to the development of an adequate theory of human learning.

This is the cognitive bridge to the wholeness paradigm of theoretical physicists such as Wheeler (1982), Bohm (1984), Wolf (1984), and Stapp (1971), who view consciousness awareness as the sine qua non of the very environment that in operant conditioning is considered to be apart from the child and the environment that provides social or physical reinforcers to the "operant response." The new worldview makes awareness the critical variable in the existence of the total universe. Stapp's mathematical analysis of the fundamental quantum phenomena is the basis for the "new" view as contrary to the mechanistic worldview in classic behaviorism. It is not surprising, therefore, that Wolf (1984) should see this as the quantum phenomena basis for a "new" psychology. Wolf says, in fact, "The 'new psychology,' like the 'new physics' alters radically our view of ourselves and our role in the universe" (p. 326). He says that even psychologists and psychiatrists have believed, like other classic scientists, "that there is a fundamental material basis for mental phenomena" (p. 185). He says that these mental disciplines believe that mind is a catchall concept that includes physical processes too complex to be understood. With this fundamental prejudice, he says, classic psychology has backed itself into a corner from which it can never return. Therefore, he claims: "There simply is no hope for such psychology today. Why? Because this sacred tenet of science is plain nonsense. There is not the slightest shred of evidence of a physical world acting independently of human thought" (p. 185).

Fragmented Thinking

Such a revolutionary view of the "new psychology" brings into focus the centrality of the child's thinking process and "thinking skills." It makes cognition and metacognition central to the existence of all reality. This new worldview not only makes thinking processes fundamental to the meaning of the self and its universe, it also has direct relevance for education's recent emphasis on the teaching of fundamental *thinking skills*. It tells us that the excellent work of Feuerstein (1979, 1980), de Bono (1983), Sternberg (1984), and Lipman (1984) has to be reexamined and reconceptualized. For, actually, these very modern versions of thinking skills curricula are limited because they are couched within the framework of the older classic view of psychology.

From the perspective of the shifting paradigm in science, classic educators tend to teach the child to think in fragmented ways, and this style of thinking, in turn, tends to fragment the child's world into incoherent and unintegrated bits and pieces. This is the only way classic science has taught its research observers to gain knowledge of their presumed external world.

Education has followed this model in all of its teaching. It is natural, therefore, that even modern thinking skills curricula also follow the same model, based on classic cognitive psychology. This seems to be true even though Piaget and Vygotsky have presented a more holistic model of the natural course of the development of the child's thought processes. Piaget has said that not only can we not separate self and environment in mental development, we cannot separate the "place-defining" mental schemas of object, space, time, and causality. These constructs develop as a thoroughly interdependent composite in the child's mind. Piaget's (1986) studies of these presumed "external" dimensions of the "physical" environment agree with Einstein's contri-bution that these dimensions are actually "modes of thought" rather than conditions of the environment. Piaget's (1971) study *The Child's Conception of Time* was suggested to him in a conversation with Ein-stein (p. vii), so it would seem expected that there should be correspon-dence between Piaget's developmental theory and Einstein's relativity theory. But Piaget's other studies also show clearly that object, time, space, and causality are all interdependent reality construction pro-cesses in mental development.

David Bohm (1984), a leading theoretical physicist, is particularly critical of our fragmenting style of thinking and our teaching of frag-menting thinking skills. He feels that we treat knowledge as static and fragmentary because our thinking processes themselves, our mental attitudes, have been trained to this form of perception of reality. He says that if we could learn to attend to, and learn to be aware of, thought in its actual flux of becoming, then we would not fall into the habit of treating the content of thought as though it existed in the "external environment" (p. 63).

Awareness and Thinking Skills

Educators should keep in mind the relevance of Bohm's analysis as they teach children how to think, the skill that underlies all knowledge and learning. Our foundation thinking skills curricula are actually basic to all of children's future life and learning. However, no matter how valid, no matter what quality may exist in such current curricula (Feuerstein, 1979, 1980), if they presume a separation between the thought processes and the reality that these processes are thinking about, they can have only negative consequences in a child's existence.

Let us turn again to Bohm's (1988) ideas, drawn from quantum data, of the kinds of consequences that flow from teaching children to think in fragmenting ways. Classic (or Boolean) thinking, Bohm feels, lies behind all of our major problems in our relationship to our world and the relationships among individuals, groups, and even nations. If children could learn to think in a style that would transform their minds to view themselves and their relationship to the world holistically, there would be a new set of possibilities for more harmonious and fruitful relationships to the self and its world.

Disharmony and Distortion

Our thinking process, however, says Bohm (1988), involves a classic science view of the way we perceive and experience reality. It provides an overall mind-set that we pass on to our children and that, he believes, has devastating consequences for the child's relationship to the self and its world. In this overall mind-set, we regard the parts appearing in our thought as primary and independently existent constituents of reality, including ourselves—that is, corresponding to our thoughts that there is some*thing* in reality. The overall classic worldview, in which the whole of existence is considered as made up of such elementary parts, will give strong support to this fragmentary way of thinking. And this, in turn, expresses itself in further thought that sustains and develops such a worldview. Thus we have a circular process that maintains fragmentary thinking, and a fragmentary mind sees fragmented processes in a fragmented world.

And so, Bohm concludes, such ways of thinking, of attainment of knowledge, are evidently and inherently destructive. For example, he says, though all parts of humankind are fundamentally interdependent and interrelated, the primary and overriding significance given to the distinctions among people, families, professions, nations, races, religions, and ideologies prevents human beings from working together for the common good, and even for survival.

Bohm in Summary

To paraphrase Bohm, the classic vision of fragmentary thinking, which we pass on to our children, is giving rise to a reality that is constantly breaking up into disorderly, disharmonious, and destructive partial activities. Therefore, according to Bohm, in teaching thinking processes in the school, we should explore ways to develop a mode of thinking that starts with the most encompassing possible whole and goes down to subwholes in a way *appropriate for the actual nature of things* as the new physics has demonstrated. Such teaching would help to bring about a different reality for children, one that is more creative, harmonious, and orderly.

Later in this chapter, I will expand on the relevance of Bohm's holistic argument for the problem of children's alienation from themselves and their world, and for all the child problems that we now view as either environmentally or physically "caused." I will also discuss praxis that could grow out of this new paradigm, particularly how we might explore ways of teaching children to "think" that might move our present thinking skills teaching away from the classic into the new holistic paradigm.

30 Years That Shook Classic Science

To understand the ideas of the shifting scientific paradigm, and the prescriptions for healing the disharmony and disorder that exists in the individual's growth and development, we must look at the revolution that brought about this fresh view of reality. Although this revolutionary paradigm may have expressed itself most forcibly in physics, its power is much more generalized than physics or even than the whole field of science. It is being expressed in psychology, philosophy, the humanities, and the arts. However, the brief documentation of the revolution offered below will stick primarily to the 30 years that shook physics and the aftermath of this explosion. I am indebted to Heinz Pagels (1984) for the general outline of that momentous 30-year history.

Planck's Reluctant Assessment

Determinism was the only conclusion that could be reasonably drawn from Newtonian physics throughout the long era of its reign. It was only at the beginning of the twentieth century that its control began to wane. Originally, even the father of quantum mechanics, Max Planck, could not accept the implications of his own discovery for the end of the deterministic viewpoint in physics.

Max Planck's momentous discovery came out of his experimentation with black-body radiation. He discovered that if you heat a metal bar in a light-tight room to a high enough temperature, it will emit light that can be measured to produce a "black-body radiation curve." This curve did not fit the classic view of nature as a continuum. Rather, it suggested that the energy exchange in the light-tight room consisted of chunks, or quanta. Such was the beginning of 30 years that shook physics to its foundations.

Einstein's Reality

This was the same year, 1900, that Einstein finally graduated from the Zurich Polytechnic Institute, only by cramming for examinations. In 1902 he took a job with the patent office in Berne. In 1905 he published three momentous papers in the *Annalin der Physik* that radically shifted the course of scientific history. Thus, coming on top of Planck's discovery of the quanta, the new physics of the twentieth century and its exodus from deterministic mechanism began.

Einstein's first paper served to prove the existence of atoms. His second landmark paper dealt with the photoelectric effect, in which a beam of light, shining on a metal surface, causes an electric current to flow when electrons are emitted. Einstein's third article in the *Annalin* was on the special theory of relativity. This was certainly overkill. Einstein would have won a place in history with any one of these three papers. Understanding space and time in physics required that we distinguish our subjective experiences of them from the measurement of them. Einstein said that space was simply what we measure with a measuring rod and time is what we measure with a clock. However, under certain circumstances, both the measuring rod and the clock can be changed in their measurements.

Although Einstein never accepted the fundamental probabilistic thesis of quantum mechanics that forevermore altered the nature of reality, he can be held responsible for determinism's demise. Einstein put the human observer in the center of the measurement process. Naively, we have assumed that two measurers would obtain the same results—not so in relativity theory. Einstein showed how the measurement of space and time changes between two observers moving at a constant velocity relative to one another. He also demonstrated that a moving clock marks time more slowly than one at rest. For example, imagine two friends, one standing on a station platform and the other on a moving train. For the friend on the platform, the wristwatch of the friend on the train actually moves more slowly. If the train were moving near the velocity of light, time changes would slow down close to zero. This is why, in the frequently used example, if we have twins, one in a spaceship above the earth and one remaining on the earth, the twin in space would age more slowly than the one on earth. The one on earth would get older faster if his twin remained in space for a long time.

Einstein's three articles kicked over the traces of determinism and prepared the way for a nondeterministic universe. However, until his death, he did not accept this now generally accepted conclusion.

Particle or Wave

Einstein showed that light, like a fusillade of tiny bullets, could behave in particlelike fashion. This was a startling contradiction of the proven nature of light, which was that it behaved like water waves. This wave nature of light had been documented again and again, and now it was being shown that it consists of particles? How can that be? Here was a puzzling paradox in nature. *Both* waves and particles? *Either* waves or particles? How could this be? Classic science was not a paradigm of either/or, both/and. Classic science came to firm, exclusionary conclusions. Nevertheless, in that heady, confusing, exhilarating period of rapid, startling discovery, waves were shown to behave like particles and particles were demonstrated to behave like waves, depending on the intentions of the observer.

The complete break with classic physics, says Gribbin (1987), came with the realization that not only protons and electrons but all "particles" and all "waves" are in fact a mixture of wave and particle. Quantum theory, in 1925, was a quagmire of theoretical perspectives that included both quantum discontinuities and the arbitrary use of classic theory.

Duality and Nature

By 1925 the scientific world was being presented with a total break from the absolutism of the long-reigning classic view. The age of wave-particle duality and the role of the observer had really begun. It introduced a totally new way for physics to perceive physical reality. This is a view that is actually closer to our own experience, since life is not experienced by us as black or white, either/or. It marked the end of science's either/or way of looking at the world and introduced the new, non-Boolean logic of both/and.

In 1924, Niels Bohr and colleagues had introduced the idea that waves were "probability waves." This was a totally new idea in physics, and it undermined scientific current. It referred to what was somehow already happening, but had not yet been actualized. It talked about a *tendency* to happen without actually becoming a real event. As Heisenberg (1958) states, "It meant a tendency for something. It was a quantitative version of 'potentia' in Aristotelian philosophy. It introduced something standing in the middle between the idea of an event, and the event itself, a strange kind of physical reality just in the middle between possibility and reality" (p. 41).

The Actualizing Observer

Before going further into quantum duality, let us examine this quantum notion as it differs from Piaget's idea of accommodation and assimilation. In assimilation, there is the notion of a real or actual physical event that is transformed in the child's accommodation of, and to, the event coming from the "outside." In quantum theory, on the other hand, there is no real event, only a "potentia" that stands halfway between possibility and reality; a ghost of an event, if you will. It becomes an actualized event only when the child reaches out with inner awareness of its half presence and makes it real. Physicists found themselves dealing with energy that somehow processed information and that had to include the observer.

Consciousness Enters the Universe

von Neumann, a mathematician, looked at the untidy nature of quantum physics and decided to systematize it mathematically. In the process, he identified intelligence or consciousness as the critical element in the dynamic fundamental quantum phenomena or process whereby "potentia" became real or actual. His famous mathematical analysis of quantum theory, *The Mathematical Foundations of Quantum Mechanics*, published in 1932, can be said to show that physics and psychology are two sides of the same coin. At the point that consciousness enters the picture the *possibility* in the wave potential is collapsed into *actuality*. The "wave function," according to von Neumann's view, is not quite a thing but it is more than an idea. It occupies a strange middle ground between idea and reality, where all things are possible but not actual. When consciousness takes the stage, thinking and thing merge into real space and time. The wave function "collapses" into reality. von Neumann's work points to a fusion of ontology, epistemology, and psychology that is only now beginning to emerge. And out of this also emerges a new logic opposed to Boolean logic. This is quantum logic, which has been developed by David Finkelstein. It is the logic of *experience*, not the language of symbols such as words and mathematics. It is at once more real and more immediate than a set of rules that epitomizes verbal and mathematical symbols.

Schrodinger (1958), Wigner (1967), and Stapp (1971) are some of the quantum theorists who are identified with the consciousness or mental interpretation of the strange quantum phenomena. Elvee's *Mind in Nature* (1982) also presents some views on how the mind takes a central place in nature.

Although the 30 years of revolution set the groundwork for the "new physics," and, refluently, the "new psychology," there have still been astounding discoveries in the 1960s, 1970s, and even the 1980s. The work of Bell, d'Espagnat, Aspect, and others challenged and experimentally violated the assumption of local causality, a view that undergirded all of classic science (Gribbin, 1987). Among other consequences of this work is that, as David Bohm has said, we can now conclude that we are all parts of a single system. Literally, everything is connected to everything else. Thus only a holistic approach to the universe is likely to explain phenomena such as human consciousness. Another abstraction that flows from the new scientific paradigm is Wheeler's conception of a "participatory universe" (i.e., we are not observers but participants).

Intelligence and Trouble

Both *intelligence* and *trouble* take on new meaning in the shifting scientific paradigm. Intelligence, or the child's consciousness, self, or mental factor, becomes a key to the existence of reality. Trouble implies disharmony in the wholeness of the self-environmental complex that constitutes the child's existence. The avenue to harmony is children's intelligence or psychological processes, for, in a sense, children's processes of intelligence are the markers of their reality, of their self-environmental complex. Here the term *intelligence* is used in the framework of shifting scientific paradigm, and the new holistic psychology, to include all of the higher mental processes that incorporate thinking, feeling, and doing.

Instruction, as pointed out by Vygotsky, operationally influences children's development. Without instruction, the inherent potential for development of children and their mental processes does not fully unfold. On the other hand, as Feuerstein's (1979, 1980) research within the classic paradigm has shown, it is possible to develop functional thinking skills, reasoning, or intelligence through instruction. Although, in the United States, we usually associate Feuerstein's system of instruction with mental retardation and the enrichment of children's basic intelligence, it is not just cognition that Feuerstein is influencing. He has used his instructional program with all categories of troubling and troubled conditions in children.

The New Instruction

My colleagues and I are engaged in a program of instructional research that uses the holistic paradigm and the new psychology as its rationale. We want to extend children's higher mental powers so that they can participate in the process of reality construction and can become fully aware of their power in doing this.

Environmental Patterning Through Thinking

Many of our activities in what we are calling a "reality modeling curriculum" bear a close resemblance to those used in previously validated cognitive process instruction (de Bono, 1983; Feuerstein, 1980; Lipman, 1984; Sternberg, 1984). That is, like some researchers, we teach the construction and processing of reality through Piagetian-type thinking activities organized around object, space, time, and causality. In the area of objects, for instance, the child learns to use mental schemas and processes to directly experience, manipulate, and solve problems involving "attributed chains." These are chains of similarities and differences in shape, size, volume, color, texture, and so on. In the area of space, the child is coached in manipulating and solving a host of problems involving the modeling of objects and various attitudes, positions, locations, and movement in spatial frames. In the construction of time, the child experiences and manipulates a variety of object-related, movement-related spatial sequences involving past, present, and future.

Self-World Patterning Through Thinking

However, our instructional program departs from the usual "thinking skills" or cognitive process curriculum in that all of these activities are directly referred to, and are extensions of, the thinking self engaged in the modeling of reality. We want children to activate deliberately and be conscious of the full range of feelings, meanings, intentions, and expectations accompanying the cognitive construction of object, space, time, and causality. In some cognitive instruction programs, children are encouraged to "think aloud" and to keep "think books" in which they record their critical development in thought processes. We do the same. However, we go further into the metacognitive realm by coaching children to become thoughtfully aware of the thinking self or "me-object" in the center of all these constructive activities.

Our rationale comes from the complementary psychological views of Piaget (1986) and the physical phenomenal views of the new physics. Piaget shows that the gradual construction of, and mental separation of, the self as a thinking and feeling object among other objects is developed simultaneously with the construction of object, time, space, and causality. The new physics sees the thinking observer as the actualizer and modeler responsible for the realization of his or her own physical world. Therefore, we have designed our instruction to incorporate activities that give children direct experience in using the mind to reflect back upon itself. We want children to know that they are the active thinking agents of these reality-constructing activities. We coach students to think consciously about the "me-object" or self as the hub of these other related thinking and constructing activities. When children are in the process of orienting themselves to dimensions in space, we want them to realize that they are the primary referents or measures of those dimensions.

One of the activities we use is the game Twister. In this game, one child directs another to place hands and feet sequentially in the "upper-right corner" or the "northeast corner" of a large plastic sheet placed on the floor. In performing these directional acts, children absorb very compound learnings. They become able to transpose "upper-right-hand corner" to "most northeast corner," and vice versa. They learn something firsthand about Einstein's relativity, where spatial directions, like time, are always relative to the self experiencing them. Such directions are not preordained conditions in the universe, but are modes of thought that have to be developed in a child's mind before he or she can give meaning to the game. Finally, the children experience themselves as the animate centers of the small world bounded by the Twister sheet. The excitement and myriad other feelings of the game become part of this directional accomplishment. The self reflects back upon itself and knows that it is patterning its representative reality. It knows that it is the agent putting information into its environment to make the game come alive. Confidence is built into the self as it masters the activity. This is one of the ways in which we try to help children realize that they are both givers of structure and givers of meaning in their world.

Self-Centering

We also encourage children to develop their "inner spaces" through their thought processes. Varying some of the experimental activities derived from personnel construct psychology (Kelly, 1955; Landfeld & Leitner, 1980), we help children learn to bring into full awareness the dimensionalized personal attributes they use to think about themselves. We help them discover how they use these personal constructs to order and organize their behavioral world. We try to teach them how their own self-defined, personal attributes (such as dumb-smart, weak-strong, masculine-feminine, mean-nice, happy-sad, good-bad) are put into action by them in the same way they activate "inert" objects. We try to help them become aware that they use these attributes to compare, and to act in relationship to, significant other people in their own lives. All of these personal attributes originate within the children themselves; they cannot be put into children from outside. Thereby, we try to teach children to assume responsibility for their thinking selves and their own actions that flow from these personal constructions.

The initial personal construction exercise asks the children to think about one or two people they like most and one or two they like least (other than family), and then list what they like most or least about those people. We then have them think about one or two attributes they like most in themselves and one or two that they like least. We then provide an instrument through which the children are able to use these attributes to compare and rank themselves with these other nominated children. They then work out, with the teacher, a number of assignments using these personally salient attributes. Each child keeps a "self-book" or a "me-book" as a companion to the "think book," in which he or she records this critical personal attribute vocabulary and the various assignments tried out in using it. In these assignments the children attempt to modify their personal attributes or to develop substitutes for them in their everyday behavior both in and out of the classroom.

Flexibility of Thought

A child's personal construct repertoire is really only a part, although a significant part, of his or her overall personal worldview. Clinicians and special educators generally agree that children who are said to be psychologically, physiologically, or environmentally handicapped usually have relatively inflexible or rigid mental patterns of reality. Their range of tolerance for ambiguity or any contradictions to their own convictions about reality is very limited. Therefore, an important part of our thinking pattern instruction, designed to improve children's construction of reality, deals with the plasticity-rigidity of children's view of reality. In teaching or coaching children to mentally and physically manipulate and model reality as a whole, we employ a variety of phenomenologically familiar exercises and activities.

In all of the various tasks used in children's composite manipulation and modeling of reality, our purpose is to teach children increased mental flexibility and plasticity in projecting themselves into their personally known worlds. Examples of these holistic thinking exercises to increase plasticity in reality modeling include the classic use of a variety of black-and-white and colored inkblots into which children project their own constructions of the world. This not only allows children to see for themselves how much they project their "inner" thoughts and feelings into an "outer" world, but it provides an excellent medium for teaching children how they can perceive one thing and then shift their view and perceive something quite different. It gives them an opportunity to see how different people "see" different things. Another medium for this kind of teaching is the familiar figure-ground reversal so well known to students who take psychology courses. For example, one of the transparencies we flash on the classroom screen can be seen either as an ugly old hag or as a beautiful young girl. These reversal exercises are good because they give children direct experience in alternating realities where more than one perception is warranted and absolutely correct. Another exercise in the holistic reality construction category is the use of conflict between two or more children where each is confirmed, in the same situation, that he or she is the one who perceives and experiences the incident correctly. We have a variety of instrumentalities in which each child has an opportunity to state his or her own reality, is then exposed to the reality of the opponent, and finally has to reconcile, in his or her own mind, the differences between the two realities.

Preliminary Results

The population to which we are currently introducing the curriculum is a small cohort of severely emotionally disturbed, physically and sexually abused, White, "disadvantaged" adolescent and preadolescent children in a totally self-contained residential setting. At the end of the 1988-1989 school year, the following trends seemed to be emerging from our data:

(1) Children were consistently learning to generalize the coaching and teaching from the experimental classroom into their lives outside of classroom.

(2) The experimental program appeared to be helping to change children's measured self-concept and self-confidence.

(3) Previously rigidly structured thinking processes of children in the program were becoming more flexible in terms of their reality constructions, conceptions, and convictions, and more tolerant of the reality convictions of others.

Other potential trends that seemed to be emerging, on which we have collected test data to confirm or disconfirm, include the following: (a) The frequency of conflict between children within the group appeared to be decreasing; (b) the rate of learning in traditional subject-matter classes outside our experimental one seemed to be increasing; and (c) the level of general intellectual functioning seemed to be following other "thinking skills" curricula in improving over time.

Hope for the Future

Any of these changes, or any combination of them, is important to the present goals of education, lending credibility to this particular experimental program of instructional research. However, our goal for the long-run importance of this type of research is much more basic. We would like our efforts to encourage other educators to search for ways to bring about healing and wholeness in the troubled and troubling minds of our young. Even envisioning such educational possibilities could help foster unity where there is divisiveness and fragmentation in their relationship to their world. We would like education to respond to their unanswered cry for meaning in their lives, rather than simply providing them with a way to earn their daily bread. We feel that this is a rational goal for education.

References

Belenky, M., Clinchy, B., Goldberger, N., & Tarule, J. (1986). *Women's ways of knowing: The development of self, voice, and mind.* New York: Basic Books.

Bohm, D. (1984). *Wholeness and the implicate order.* London: Routledge & Kegan Paul.

Bohm, D. (1988). *Science, order, creativity.* New York: Bantam.

Boole, G. (1958). *An investigation of the laws of thought, on which are founded the mathematical theories of logic and probabilities.* New York: Dover.

de Bono, E. (1983). The direct teaching of thinking skills. *Phi Delta Kappan, 64*, 703-708.

Elvee, R. (Ed.). (1982). *Mind in nature: Nobel Conference XVIII.* New York: Harper & Row.

Feuerstein, R. (1979). *The dynamic assessment of retarded performers.* Glenview, IL: Scott Foresman.

Feuerstein, R. (1980). *Instrumental enrichment: An intervention program.* Glenview, IL: Scott Foresman.

Gribbin, P. (1987). *Particles and paradoxes.* New York: Cambridge University Press.

Heisenberg, W. (1958). *Physics and philosophy: The revolution in modern science.* New York: Harper.

Heisenberg, W. (1974). *Across the frontiers.* New York: Harper & Row.

Kelly, G. (1955). *The psychology of personal constructs* (2 vols.). New York: W. W. Norton.

Landfeld, A., & Leitner, L. (1980). *Personal construct psychology: Psychotherapy and personality.* New York: John Wiley.

Lipman, M. (1984). The cultivation of reasoning through philosophy. *Educational Leadership, 42*(1), 51-56.

Pagels, H. (1984). *The cosmic code: Quantum physics as the language of nature.* New York: Bantam New Age Books.

Piaget, J. (1950). *The psychology of intelligence.* New York: Basic Books.

Piaget, J. (1971). *The child's conception of time.* New York: Ballentine.

Piaget, J. (1975). *The origins of intelligence in children.* New York: International Universities Press.

Piaget, J. (1981). *The psychology of intelligence.* Totowa, NJ: Littlefield Adams.

Piaget, J. (1983). *The child's conception of the world.* Totowa, NJ: Rowman & Allanheld.

Piaget, J. (1986). *The construction of reality in the child.* New York: International Universities Press.

Schrodinger, E. (1958). *Mind and matter.* Cambridge: Cambridge University Press.

Stapp, H. (1971). S-matrix in interpretation of quantum theory. *Physical Review D, 3*, 1303.

Sternberg, R. (1984). How can we teach intelligence? *Educational Leadership, 42*(1), 38-48.

Vygotsky, L. (1978). *Mind in society.* Cambridge, MA: Harvard University Press.

Vygotsky, L. (1987). *Thought and language.* Cambridge: MIT Press.

Wheeler, J. (1982). Bohr, Einstein and the strange lesson of the quantum. In R. Elvee (Ed.), *Mind in nature: Nobel Conference XVIII.* New York: Harper & Row.

Wigner, E. (1967). *Symmetries and reflections: Scientific essays.* Bloomington: Indiana University Press.

Wolf, F. (1984). *Starwave: Mind, consciousness, and quantum physics.* New York: Macmillan.

9

Drug and Alcohol Use
Among Adolescents

Social Context and Competence

KEVIN ALLISON
PETER E. LEONE
ELLEN ROWSE SPERO

Problems associated with alcohol and other drug use by adolescents are pervasive in the United States. Parents, educators, community groups, and adolescents themselves have expressed concern about the numbers of youths using and abusing drugs and our seeming inability to stem the tide of relatively cheap and readily available substances.

In addition to problems associated with physical and psychological dependency and the risk of automobile fatality, the danger associated with drug sales currently places some adolescents at increased risk for violent death. The present drug crisis is also of particular concern for adolescents at higher risk for HIV infection due to unprotected sex or the use of unsterilized needles. This may be particularly important for adolescents in the Hispanic and Black communities, where incidence rates are disproportionately high (Selik, Castro, & Pappaioanou, 1988).

In a recent study, 92% of high school seniors reported some past experience with alcohol, 66% indicated alcohol use within the past

AUTHORS' NOTE: Special thanks to Ray Lorion for suggestions made on a preliminary draft of this chapter.

month, and 4.8% reported using alcohol daily (Johnston, O'Malley, & Bachman, 1988). Some 57% of senior high students surveyed in 1987 indicated illicit drug use at some point during their lives, with 36% of those subjects reporting illicit drug use other than marijuana (Johnston et al., 1988). The pervasive nature of adolescent experiences with drugs and alcohol requires that a distinction be made between the terms *use* and *abuse* regarding these substances. Within the context of a society where alcohol and cigarette use are socially sanctioned, the drug and alcohol use of adolescents may fall within a "normal," or culturally acceptable, range of involvement. Not all adolescents who use alcohol or other drugs experience problems or problem use, and use is not necessarily associated with problem or delinquent behavior. For our purposes, alcohol and/or drug *abuse* (or problem use) will be used to designate any pattern of drug use that results in dysfunction in any of an adolescent's major areas of functioning (e.g., social, academic, physical, emotional). In contrast, alcohol and/or drug *use* will refer to any pattern of involvement, regardless of consequence.

Discussion of substance abuse among adolescents typically raises issues related to etiology, prevention, and appropriate treatment. In recent years there has been interest in assessing the relationships among environmental demands, interpersonal resources, and drug use (Marlatt & Donovan, 1981; Wills & Shiffman, 1985). While biological factors certainly play a role in the physiological response to drugs and alcohol, biological reactivity alone does not explain the wide variability in the prevalence of drug use among adolescents.

In this chapter we focus on youths who are troubled or troubling by virtue of their alcohol and/or drug use. The discussion incorporates literature from four conceptually differentiated groups. These include studies of alcohol and drug *use* among (a) "normal" adolescents and among (b) adolescents with behavioral, social, emotional, or cognitive disabilities; and data concerning alcohol and drug *abuse* among (c) general samples of adolescents and within (d) samples of adolescents with behavioral, social, emotional, or cognitive disabilities (i.e., the "dually diagnosed").

As the title of the chapter indicates, the present discussion of drug and alcohol use during adolescence will be structured in relation to the concepts of *context* and *competence*. While much of the research concerning the etiology and maintenance of dysfunctional behaviors attributes variables of influence to "nature" (i.e., biogenic factors) or "nurture" (i.e., environmental factors), these distinctions tend to minimize the complexity of the relationships among sources of influence. In examining the contextual and competency aspects of adolescent drug use, complex relationships exist between individuals and the ecology in which they live. Within this framework, *context* is used to refer to a range of social environmental variables that include ethnic and cultural identity and peer and family factors associated with drug-taking behavior. In contrast, *competence* is used to indicate variables that would denote "traits" or "crystallized" abilities, that is, functional potential within environments. For the purposes of this chapter, we use children's categorization by social agents such as educators, psychiatrists, psychologists, and social workers to characterize low competence in learning, social, behavioral, and emotional arenas. Before examining these two broad concepts, we begin with a brief discussion of adolescent development and theories of drug use. In this first section we also discuss the contextual issues of ethnic, cultural, and gender differences, and peer and family factors related to drug-taking behavior.

The second part of this chapter examines youths' competence in relation to drug and alcohol use. We review studies that have investigated drug use in relation to adolescents' perceived social and emotional competence, school performance, juvenile delinquency, and coping behaviors. The chapter concludes with implications for treatment and research.

Developmental Issues

Adolescence has been described as a tumultuous time during which many important developmental issues are to be resolved. Adolescents are viewed as struggling to define their identities (Erikson, 1959; Koocher, 1974) and to attain autonomy and independence (Thornburg, 1982). Miller (1986) suggests that certain children may be at higher risk for substance abuse during adolescence due to a biological predisposition that might be latent during childhood (e.g., offspring of substance-abusing parents). Substance abuse and other dysfunctional behaviors are not viewed as part of a normal developmental process, but as maladaptive attempts to cope with the demands of independence. This conceptualization seems to reflect an apparent consensual shift in American values related to adolescent substance use since the 1970s. At that time, adolescent drug use was often viewed as a "normal" expression of youthful defiance.

The understanding of drug and alcohol use during adolescence has been enhanced by research addressing the developmental course of drug and alcohol use itself. Kandel (1984) has proposed a stage or "gateway drug" theory of use based on data including her cross-cultural investigation of substance use among adolescents in France and Israel. The study found sequential patterns of drug use; that is, alcohol and cigarette use tended to precede the use of marijuana, which, in turn, more often preceded other illicit drug use.

Theories of Adolescent Drug Involvement

While the literature as a whole does not present a consistent, clear picture of the problem of substance use and abuse among adolescents, it does begin to describe a complex, multidimensional problem. Jessor, Chase, and Donovan (1980) have suggested that adolescent drug involvement is not a solitary phenomenon, but fits within a pattern of greater behavioral disturbance. This complexity may be further augmented by the variety of adolescent drug-use patterns manifest in the form of different coexisting subcultures (Dembo, Blount, Schmeidler, & Burgos, 1986).

Recently, several researchers have applied different theories to the prediction of adolescent drug use. White, Johnson, and Horwitz (1986) evaluated the predictive value of *social control* (i.e., the bonds to social institutions such as family, school, and church that help provide behavior controls), *strain* (i.e., the stress resulting from the effects of life events), and *differential association* (i.e., differences in social environment that may determine behavior, such as hanging out with drug users) to predict adolescent drug use. Differential association was found to be most predictive of adolescent drug use. In a separate investigation, social learning and social control theories were found to be equally helpful in understanding adolescent drug use, but the researchers noted that additional factors, such as ethnicity and specific drug types, continued to have a significant impact on adolescent drug involvement independent of those theories (Winfree, Theis, & Griffiths, 1981).

Blum and Singer (1983) suggest that understanding the genesis of substance use involves examining six factors: (a) value development, (b) institutional provision and opportunity, (c) peer group, (d) family, (e) personality and self-image, and (f) biogenic. This conceptualization and the research comparing predictive models of adolescent drug involvement suggest that there is not a single pathway, but rather multiple, interactive influences that lead to alcohol and drug use (Kaplan, Martin, & Robbins, 1984).

Survey and other research data indicate that over time, the nature of drug and alcohol use among adolescents changes; new substances are introduced and become popular and consumption reflects not only availability, but also legal, geographic, political, and cultural forces (Johnston, O'Malley, & Bachman, 1986; Kozel & Adams, 1986; Penning & Barnes, 1982; Ryser, 1983). The acknowledgment of these factors requires research and treatment models that are inclusive of the temporal and contextual nature of these changes.

Who Is Not Counted

Despite a large body of literature regarding substance use and abuse during adolescence, data available on the extent and nature of the problem among certain groups of youth potentially underestimate prevalence. For example, Johnston et al.'s (1986, 1988) annual surveys of drug use among high school seniors and college students employ national samples of age-specific cohorts from senior high schools. However, the authors themselves estimate that approximately 15% of the age cohorts are lost due to the dropout rate, and that this is not an unimportant segment, since illicit drug use tends to be higher than average in this group. While the attrition rate due to dropouts may be 15%, it is unclear from Johnston et al. (1988) whether they also accounted for students who may have been overlooked due to psychiatric or medical hospitalization, incarceration, or placement in residential or day treatment settings, or those who had died before they had reached their senior year in high school. The selection bias in excluding these subpopulations may not obscure general trends among "mainstream" adolescents; however, when considering the issue of substance abuse, these omitted subgroups may contain the troubled youth most in need of assistance.

The Context

Understanding the context within which substance use occurs involves examining more than adolescent development and theories of substance use. Factors that have contextual significance such as the ethnic, cultural, and gender identities and the peer and family social ecologies in which adolescents live also must be considered.

Cultural and Ethnic Differences

While the literature is inconclusive and often contradictory, a variety of different patterns of drug and alcohol use have been suggested by researchers sampling adolescents within differing ethnic and cultural groups. Other than marijuana and alcohol, Black, Hispanic, and Native American youth have reported higher rates of drug use and show a different pattern of drug involvement than that found among their White peers (Brunswick, 1979; Galchus & Galchus, 1978; Kandel, 1978; Padilla, Padilla, Morales, Olmedo, & Ramirez, 1979). While other investigators have not found differences between Black and White adolescents with respect to alcohol and marijuana use (Dembo et al., 1986), some have reported that Black adolescents are more likely to be nondrinkers and are underrepresented among heavy drinkers compared with White (Zucker & Harford, 1983) or Hispanic teens (Welte & Barnes, 1987). High proportions of heavy drinkers have been reported among Native American adolescents, who also have higher rates of delinquency and suicide than their White peers (Welte & Barnes, 1987). Among Asian youth, whom researchers suggest may experience a genetic intolerance of ethanol, general rates of alcohol consumption are thought to be low (Miller, Goodwin, Jones, & Pardo, 1987).

Other investigators have examined drug and alcohol consumption across cultures. Marcos and Johnson (1988) found similar rates of lifetime alcohol and cigarette use among Greek and American adolescents. Kandel's (1984) cross-cultural study comparing the alcohol, cigarette, and illicit drug use of French and Israeli adolescents found higher rates of use, earlier use, and greater prevalence of use among French teens. Kandel suggests that these differences may be attributed to sociocultural variables affecting availability and social acceptance of substance use. In general, the literature reporting ethnic and cultural differences in adolescent drug use indicates that there is considerable variation in patterns of teen drug involvement.

Gender Differences

Most of the research on adolescent substance use and abuse has focused on males or has failed to examine gender differences. However, prevalence surveys indicate that drug use among girls may be comparable to that of boys (Beschner & Treasure, 1979). Although female adolescents may use drugs for many of the same reasons as males and follow a similar developmental pattern of drug involvement, female drug users face unique problems and risks because of their gender. The most striking difference is that female abusers are often victims of physical or sexual abuse (Spero, 1989). A second problem facing adolescent girls in relation to drug use is pregnancy. Yamaguchi and Kandel (1987) found that young women who had used or were currently using illicit drugs were twice as likely as nonusers to have premarital pregnancies.

Family Context

In reviewing the etiology of drug and alcohol use among the general adolescent population, several investigators have noted that adolescents from families where members use cigarettes, alcohol, or drugs are more likely to become involved in substance use than those adolescents who live in families where the members are nonusers (Brook, Lukoff, & Whiteman, 1977; O'Connell et al., 1981; Pressons et al., 1984). In addition, Dishion, Patterson, and Reid (1988) have identified poor parental monitoring and parental modeling of drug use as factors that increase the risk of early drug exploration. In homes where adolescents perceive close and loving family, the prevalence of alcohol, cigarette, and marijuana use was two times lower than in families that were not seen as close or loving (Reynolds & Rob, 1988). Children of clinically depressed parents have higher rates of major depression, substance abuse, psychiatric treatment, poor social functioning, and school problems than children of nondepressed parents (Weissman et al., 1987). Self-reported alcohol use is also higher among adolescents who report parental approval of drinking than among teens who do not report parental permission to drink (Wright, 1985).

Peer Context

Relative to the influence of parents, peers have been noted to have a greater impact on adolescent drug use in the general adolescent population (Jessor & Jessor, 1978; Kandel, 1973; Kandel & Adler, 1982; Needle et al., 1986; O'Connell et al., 1981). Dishion and his colleagues (1988) found early experimentation into drugs to be related to "deviant" peers; this, in turn, was apparently related to poor parental monitoring practices. Association with drug-using peers, including siblings, provides "easy access" to drugs and is linked to higher rates of drug involvement (Huba, Wingard, & Bentler, 1979; Needle et al., 1986).

Huang (1981) found that subjects identified as mildly mentally retarded perceived more peer-related motivation to drink, with more retarded than nonretarded participants responding that they drank "to be with the crowd" (22% versus 15%), "to avoid being laughed at" (14% versus 6%), or because "their friends drink" (31% versus 20%). Clements and Simpson (1978) presented findings from a survey of 47 adolescents from a state inpatient mental health center who were diagnosed as "behavior disordered" or "socially maladjusted." All subjects had a history of illicit drug use and indicated peer pressure as motivation for initial use. This correlate may be particularly important for "special populations" placed in separate treatment programs who become members of a concentrated "deviant" peer group or culture. Due to their separation from "normal" peer groups and probable experience with social rejection, these teens may have an exaggerated need to belong or to seek a group identity, and therefore might be more susceptible to peer influence.

In considering influences on adolescent drug use, the areas discussed above—contextual influence; ethnic, cultural, and gender differences; and the family and peer contexts—all appear to have their own significant impacts on adolescent drug use. A variety of other variables (e.g., geographic location and socioeconomic status) are known to be associated with substance use but are beyond the scope of this chapter.

Competence

Although examining the context within which adolescent drug use occurs is important in furthering our understanding of this phenomenon, it is insufficient to consider these variables in isolation. Adolescents vary in their perceived abilities on social-emotional, behavioral, and learning constructs, and these variations may have important implications for the examination of adolescent drug use and behavior.

Emotional and Behavioral Difficulties and Substance Use

A review of the literature on the drug use of adolescents experiencing emotional or behavioral disorders shows that the research focuses on several specific diagnostic groupings: attention deficit disorders with hyperactivity, depression and suicidality, and eating disorders.

Several investigations with adult psychiatric patients found that alcoholism was more frequent in patients who were identified as having childhood hyperactivity (HA) than in a psychiatric control group of patients who did not report childhood HA (De Olbidia & Parsons, 1984; Morrison, 1979; Tarter, McBride, Buonpane, & Schneider, 1977). As young adults, individuals who had been diagnosed as hyperactive during childhood had higher rates of substance abuse and court involvement over a five-year period compared with normal controls, although there were few significant differences between the groups during the year prior to evaluation (Hechtman, Weiss, & Perlman, 1984).

Gittleman, Mannuzza, Shenker, and Bonagura (1985) found higher rates of substance use among adolescents and young adults who had been hyperactive as children, but similarly found that conduct disturbance associated with hyperactivity predicted later increased substance use. Substance abuse disorders appeared to follow the onset of conduct disturbance in most cases (Gittleman et al., 1985). These findings, similar to the work of August, Stewart, and Holmes (1983), suggest that it is perhaps the combination of hyperactivity *and* other conduct disturbances that leads to higher probability of substance involvement.

A number of other investigators have found an association between depression and alcohol use (e.g., Lie, 1984; Reichler, Clement, & Dunner, 1983). Paton, Kessler, and Kandel (1977) surveyed 8,206 adolescents attending public high schools in New York State and found depressed mood to be positively associated with the use of illicit drugs, especially drugs other than marijuana, among White teens. Kashani, Keller, Solomon, Reid, and Mazzola (1985) investigated the relationship between adolescent depression and drug use, including alcohol, among new referrals to a psychiatric clinic at a midwestern youth drop-in center. These clients had not been prescribed psychotropic medications. The investigators found no differences between depressed and nondepressed adolescents with respect to alcohol abuse; however, there were more continuous alcoholics among the depressed group than among other subjects, and individuals with a history of amphetamine abuse tended to come from the depressed group.

Further support for a link between adolescent depression and adolescent substance abuse comes from assessment research indicating that a major affective disorder (such as major depression or bipolar illness) doubles the risk of later drug abuse or dependence among young adults

(Christie, Burke, Reiger, & Rae, 1988) and that preadolescent alcohol-ism is predictive of major affective disorders during adolescence (Famularo, Stone, & Popper, 1985). Deykin, Levy, and Wells (1987) suggest the possibility of self-medication among depressed college students, as both alcohol and drug abuse were associated with major depression and the onset of the depression reportedly preceded that of substance abuse.

In addition to adolescent depression, alcohol and drug abuse appear associated with adolescent suicide (Garfinkel, Froese, & Hood, 1982; Robbins & Alessi, 1985). Of a sample of 20 children and adolescents who committed suicide, 70% had histories of alcohol and drug abuse (Shafii, Carrigan, Whittinghill, & Derrick, 1985). In an investigation of suicidal thoughts among high school seniors and college students, those who saw themselves as having drug or alcohol problems were more likely to report histories of serious suicidal thought (Wright, 1985).

Eating disorders, which are more prevalent among adolescent fe-males than among males (Quay & Werry, 1979), also appear to be strongly associated with alcohol and drug use (Muuss, 1986; Winstead & Willard, 1983). In a study of 259 consecutive callers to the National Cocaine Hotline, 32% met DSM III criteria for anorexia, bulimia, or both (Jonas, Gold, Sweeney, & Pottash, 1987). One-third of bulimic patients studied by Mitchell, Hatsukami, Eckert, and Pyle (1985) indi-cated a history of problems with drugs and/or alcohol. There has been the suggestion of a biological link between eating disorders and drug abuse as higher rates of substance abuse depression have been found among first- and second-degree relatives of anorexic patients (Rivinus et al., 1984).

In sum, there is substantial research evidence to indicate that a wide range of behavioral and emotional disorders during adolescence are frequently associated with alcohol and drug use. The literature does not clearly demonstrate whether alcohol and drug abuse are the cause or the effect of other disturbances. Studies of the relationship between sub-stance use and attention deficit disorders are even less clear. Among adolescents who received psychotropic medication for treatment of an attention deficit disorder or hyperactivity as children, studies have found both higher ratings of alcohol use (Blouin, Bronstein, & Trites, 1978) and lower rates of alcohol and illicit drug use (Beck, Langford, MacKay, & Sum, 1975; Henker & Whalen, 1980) when compared with their peers. The inconsistency of the results from these three studies may be due to differing sampling and control group criteria and operational definitions used in the various studies. In addition, general investigations into adolescent substance use have not typically identified adolescents with undiagnosed or untreated attention deficit disorders who may use drugs as a means of "self-medication."

School Performance and Substance Use

Several studies have found high correlations among substance use, school failure, and low commitment to school. Other reports have identified school failure and low commitment to school as predictors of both delinquent behavior and substance use (Hawkins, Lishner, Jenson, & Catalano, 1987), although causality within these relationships remain unclear.

Jessor and Jessor (1978) conducted a three-year study of drug use among 483 students in the Rocky Mountain region. Their analyses revealed that nonusers were more likely to value academic achievement and to expect academic success, while drug users were more likely to show a lack of interest in school.

Smith and Fogg (1978) conducted a five-year study on the psychological predictors of marijuana use among 651 high school students in Boston. They found that nonusers were more likely to value study habits and to have higher grade point averages than users.

Kandel, Kessler, and Margolies (1978) examined the relationship of student drug use to parental use of drugs (including prescription), friends' use of drugs, and students' personal values and life-styles among 5,423 high school students in New York State. The study did not identify a clear relationship between drug use and school performance, number of classes cut, or absenteeism. However, Kandel et al. (1978) note that their sample did not survey students who dropped out or were absent at the time of the survey. Bias may exist in all three of these studies, given that all subjects were volunteers, predominantly White, and middle-class, and sample attrition occurred between testing points.

Studies by Anhalt and Klein (1976) and Friedman, Glickman, and Utada (1985) support the results of these longitudinal studies. Anhalt and Klein (1976) surveyed 3,807 eighth and ninth graders in five school districts in Nassau County, New York, and found that illegal drug use was highly correlated with low academic achievement, family conflict, and personal problems. In a similar study, Friedman et al. (1985) compared the school dropout rate among adolescent nonusers, occasional or casual drug users, and regular drug users in two Philadelphia high schools. The study also found that students who did not like school were more likely to be involved with drugs. In addition, 26% of the nonusers and 30% of the casual users dropped out, compared with 51% of the regular users. These findings suggest that estimates of adolescent drug use based on Johnston et al.'s (1986, 1988) surveys may be substantially deflated due to sampling bias. Friedman et al. (1985) also note that the temporal relationship between school problems and drug involvement remains unclear. Drug use and school dropout could in fact be "concomitant" effects of a "more basic state of dissatisfaction" (Friedman et al., 1985, p. 363). Overall, these studies support the conclusion that substance-using adolescents are less committed to education and at greater risk for leaving school before graduating.

Juvenile Delinquency and Substance Use

The link between substance abuse and juvenile delinquency has been well established in the research literature. Studies also suggest that delinquency precedes drug use (Dishion et al., 1988; Farrow & French, 1986; Kandel, Simcha-Fagen, & Davies, 1986). While some researchers have concluded that there is a causal relationship between delinquent behavior and adolescent drug use, others agree with Jessor et al. (1980) that drug use as well as delinquency may be related outcomes of some generalized factor.

Kandel et al. (1986) examined 15 risk factors for adolescent drug use and delinquent behavior to identify commonalities. Their findings suggest that etiological factors such as depression and lack of attachment to conventional roles and institutions are common to both drug use and delinquency. One of the more interesting findings from this study is that the same factors that predicted male delinquency also predicted female illicit drug use (Kandel et al., 1986). Similarly, Hawkins et al.'s (1987) review of the literature also suggests that a number of variables predict *both* drug abuse and juvenile delinquency. These factors include early antisocial behavior, familial dysfunction, school failure, delinquent peers, social alienation, community disorganization, high mobility, and personality variables.

Dishion and his colleagues (1988) conducted a longitudinal study of drug use by conduct-disordered youths. They found that early maladjustment, antisocial behavior, low self-esteem, depression, and coercive family interactions were all significant predictors of drug use.

These studies indicate that the relationship between drug use and delinquent behavior is complex and interactive. The data also suggest that drug use and delinquency may be different responses to similar problems, such as depression, family conflict, and lack of attachment to conventional roles.

Coping and Substance Use

Wills and Shiffman (1985) have proposed a conceptual framework that integrates substance use, stress, and coping skills. From their perspective, drug and alcohol use may be seen as a coping mechanism to reduce negative affect or to increase positive affect. Similarly, coping skills can be identified as behavioral or cognitive responses to environmental stressors or as responses to temptation to use drugs.

Pentz (1985) investigated drug use and social competence among a group of adolescents. In the first of two studies she examined the relationship between drug use and social competence over time among 254 sixth- through ninth-grade students. Her results indicated that a bidirectional relationship between competence and drug use exists and that prior drug use had the strongest influence on subsequent drug use. Further, higher levels of drug use at time 1 led to decreased self-efficacy, social skills, and higher levels of later drug use. Her data also suggest that, over time, drug use may increase rather than alleviate stress.

In a second study, Pentz (1985) examined the efficacy of social competence training with 1,193 sixth- through ninth-grade students. Results indicated that social competence training, in combination with individual behavior and grades, produced higher achievement and social competence and decreased drug use.

Allison (1989) surveyed 283 junior high and high school students about their life events, coping strategies, friends' and parents' drug use, and their own initial and current drug use. The results of stepwise multiple regressions on the frequency of cigarette, alcohol, marijuana, and PCP use revealed that different coping strategies were associated with different drugs. "Anesthetic" drugs (i.e., marijuana, PCP, alcohol) were associated with an "escape/self-destructive" coping factor, while an "aggressive" coping factor was associated with alcohol and cigarette use.

Studies that have examined drug and alcohol use in relation to coping behavior suggest that the etiology of adolescent drug use cannot be considered a unitary, isolated phenomenon (Blum & Singer, 1983; Kaplan et al., 1984; White et al. 1986). The ability of adolescents to employ specific coping strategies is embedded within both contextual and competence or interpersonal factors.

Conclusions

This chapter reviewed the current literature on substance use of adolescents in general and troubled and troubling adolescents in particular. Unfortunately, although a number of investigators have examined alcohol and drug use and abuse by adolescents, including samples of youth *with* and *without* behavioral, social, emotional, or cognitive disabilities, only circumscribed conclusions can be drawn about various groups. These limitations are due to the restrictive range of dysfunctional groups studied, the correlational nature of the majority of data, and the questionable comparability of assessment instruments, questions, and constructs. While there is no definitive indication that alcohol and drug use is higher among already troubled or troubling youth, the convergence of findings suggests a trend in this direction.

Implications for Research

Despite the shortcomings of the literature, evidence suggests that a complex matrix of interacting factors influence adolescent use of drugs and alcohol. Future studies might attempt to ascertain differences in both rates of substance use and abuse between samples of dysfunctional and nondysfunctional adolescents. Further, studies might help clarify the direction of the etiological relationship between substance and abuse and other troubling experiences during adolescence.

Although the majority of the research reviewed within this chapter is empirical or deterministic, integration of findings suggests certain limits to the knowledge that this methodological approach can generate. In response to the complications and complexity of studying real-world problems, some advocate tightening up the link between theoretical and empirical literatures and developing an "intellectual core" (Blalock, 1984, p. 159) in specific areas of the social sciences. However, the rich and complex web of factors associated with substance use that we have chosen to group together as either "context" or "competence" variables suggest that we can also further our understanding by using other research traditions and by devoting greater attention to contextual influences.

Too often, traditional research efforts ignore economic and sociopolitical factors that are likely to have a significant influence on the drug use of adolescents. As most of our theoretical models in the past considered singular variables, a new model of drug-use behavior would require further extension of present concepts. While Blum and Singer (1983) have produced an excellent point of departure for understanding the complex factors that affect adolescent drug use, their concepts must be stretched even further. To understand contextual issues related to adolescent drug use better, we must examine the historical, ethnic, and cultural (including value orientations), social network, economic, and sociopolitical variables that affect drug use. Those concerned with troubled and troubling youth need to understand meaning associated with drug use; that is, we need to understand not only how, when, and where drug use occurs, but also why drug use occurs in specific contexts. In addition to these broad contextual issues, drug use cannot be understood without discerning issues of competence, including biogenic "personality" or learned-response-style variables. The model of understanding must also acknowledge that factors within both categories (i.e., context and competence) are subject to temporal processes of maturation and development. Unfortunately, once a comprehensive model is developed that comfortably accounts for drug use at time 1 and location a, we cannot assume that it will account for drug use at time 2 and location b or that we will ultimately be able to control for all the variables that are relevant to drug-use phenomena. Despite the complex and seemingly overwhelming nature of adolescent drug use, practitioners do not have the luxury of waiting for better theoretical concepts to become available. Adolescents, their families, and society continue to suffer the costly emotional, social, and financial sequelae of teen substance abuse.

Implications for Treatment

The current state of knowledge suggests a number of implications for the prevention and treatment of substance abuse. It is apparent that adolescents experience different types of substance use and may become involved with drugs for varied reasons and by diverse means. Treatment models must, as suggested by Blum and Singer (1983), move beyond linear conceptualizations of etiology and treatment to appreciate and address the complex issues of individual competence and social context. To treat a child without providing alternative and culturally appropriate coping skills or to return the child to an ecology that will not support recovery is poor treatment and is ethically questionable. Prevention programming must begin to focus systematically on young children at risk for learning and behavior problems in efforts to delay early drug use, alter social ecologies that promote drug involvement, and provide alternative coping skills. These prevention programs must be specifically tailored to the contextual influences and cognitive and behavioral characteristics of troubled and troubling children. Human service workers, researchers, politicians, and parents must begin to share knowledge in order to address the interactive influences that increase the risk of adolescent drug use. Training for the parents, professional groups, and others who come in contact with substance-involved adolescents must provide a common language and promote collaboration in both research and practice.

There are myriad other issues relevant to substance use of troubled and troubling adolescents in applied settings (see Spero, Leone, Walter, & Wilson, 1989). For example: Should drug use at school be treated as a disciplinary or a treatment issue? Which is primary in treatment, substance abuse or troubling behavior? Are drug- and alcohol-dependent adolescents entitled to the protections of Section 504 of the Vocational Rehabilitation Act of 1973 or the Education for All Handicapped Children Act (P.L. 94-142)? There are, unfortunately, no simple answers to these questions.

To improve our ability to address the reality of adolescent alcohol and drug involvement, researchers and practitioners can collaboratively focus on well-defined communities and develop local knowledge useful in designing treatment and prevention programs. Traditional empirical investigations as well as naturalistic studies will be useful in developing an accurate and relevant understanding of adolescent drug use. While studies that develop local knowledge may not provide neat and broad-based cause-and-effect relationships, they may ultimately be more useful in addressing the complex problem of adolescent drug use.

References

Allison, K. (1989). *Substance use among adolescents in special education placements.* Unpublished doctoral dissertation, DePaul University, Chicago.

Anhalt, H. S., & Klein, M. (1976). Drug abuse in junior high school populations. *American Journal of Drug and Alcohol Abuse, 3*, 589-603.

August, G. J., Stewart, M. A., & Holmes, C. S. (1983). A four-year follow-up of hyperactive boys with and without conduct disorder. *British Journal of Psychiatry, 143*, 192-198.

Beck, L., Langford, W. S., MacKay, J., & Sum, G. (1975). Childhood chemotherapy and later drug abuse and growth curve: A follow-up study of 30 adolescents. *American Journal of Psychiatry, 132*(4), 436-438.

Beschner, G. M., & Treasure, K. G. (1979). Female adolescent drug use. In G. M. Beschner & A. S. Friedman (Eds.), *Youth drug abuse: Problems, issues, and treatment* (pp. 169-212). Lexington, MA: D. C. Heath.

Blalock, H. M., Jr. (1984). *Basic dilemmas in the social sciences.* Beverly Hills, CA: Sage.

Blouin, A. G., Bronstein, R. A., & Trites, R. L. (1978). Teenage alcohol use among hyperactive children: A five year follow-up study. *Journal of Pediatric Psychology, 3*(4), 188-194.

Blum, A., & Singer, M. (1983). Substance abuse and social deviance: A youth assessment framework. *Child and Youth Services, 6*, 7-21.

Brook, J. S., Lukoff, I. F., & Whiteman, M. (1977). Correlates of marijuana use as related to age, sex and ethnicity. *Yale Journal of Biology and Medicine, 50*, 383-390.

Brunswick, A. F. (1979). Black youths and drug use. In G. M. Beschner & A. S. Friedman (Eds.), *Youth drug abuse: Problems, issues, and treatment* (pp. 443-492). Lexington, MA: D. C. Heath.

Christie, K. A., Burke, J. D., Reiger, D. A., & Rae, D. S. (1988). Epidemiologic evidence for early onset of mental disorders and higher risk of drug abuse in young adults. *American Journal of Psychiatry, 145*, 971-975.

Clements, J. E., & Simpson, R. (1978). Environmental and behavioral aspects of glue sniffing in a population of emotionally disturbed adolescents. *International Journal of the Addictions, 13*, 129-134.

Dembo, R., Blount, W. R., Schmeidler, J., & Burgos, W. (1986). Perceived environmental drug use risk and the correlates of early drug use or nonuse among inner-city youths: The motivated actor. *International Journal of the Addictions, 21*, 977-1000.

De Olbidia, R., & Parsons, O. A. (1984). Relationship of neuropsychological performance to primary alcoholism and self-reported symptoms of childhood minimal brain dysfunction. *Journal of Studies on Alcohol, 45*, 386-392.

Deykin, E. Y., Levy, J. C., & Wells, V. (1987). Adolescent depression, alcohol and drug abuse. *American Journal of Public Health, 77*, 178-182.

Dishion, T. J., Patterson, G. R., & Reid, J. D. (1988). Parent and peer factors associated with sampling in early adolescence: Implications for treatment. In E. R. Rahdert & J. Grabowski (Eds.), *Adolescent drug abuse: Analysis of treatment research* (Research Monograph No. 77) (pp. 69-93). Rockville, MD: National Institute on Drug Abuse.

Erikson, E. H. (1959). Identity and the life cycle. *Psychological Issues, 1*(1).

Famularo, R., Stone, K., & Popper, C. (1985). Preadolescent alcohol abuse and dependence. *American Journal of Psychiatry, 142*, 1187-1189.

Farrow, J. A., & French, J. (1986). The drug abuse-delinquency connection revisited. *Adolescence, 84*, 951-960.

Friedman, A. S., Glickman, N., & Utada, A. (1985). Does drug and alcohol use lead to failure to graduate from high school? *Journal of Drug Education, 15*, 353-364.

Galchus, D. S., & Galchus, K. E. (1978). Drug use: Some comparisons of Black and White college students. *Drug Forum, 6*, 65-76.

Garfinkel, B. D., Froese, A., & Hood, J. (1982). Suicide attempts in children and adolescents. *American Journal of Psychiatry, 139*, 1257-1261.

Gittleman, R., Mannuzza, S., Shenker, R., & Bonagura, N. (1985). Hyperactive boys almost grown up. *Archives of General Psychiatry, 42*, 937-947.

Hawkins, J. D., Lishner, D. M., Jenson, J. M., & Catalano, R. F. (1987). What the evidence suggests about prevention and treatment programming. In B. S. Brown & A. R. Mills (Eds.), *Youth at risk for substance abuse* (DHHS Publication No. ADM 87-1537). Washington, DC: Government Printing Office.

Hechtman, L., Weiss, G., & Perlman, T. (1984). Hyperactives as young adults: Past and current substance abuse and antisocial behavior. *American Journal of Orthopsychiatry, 54*, 415-425.

Henker, B., & Whalen, C. K. (1980). The changing faces of hyperactivity, retrospect, and prospect. In B. Henker & C. K. Whalen, *Hyperactive children: The social ecology of identification and treatment.* New York: Academic Press.

Huang, A. M. (1981). The drinking behavior of the educable mentally retarded and nonretarded students. *Journal of Alcohol and Drug Education, 26*(3), 41-50.

Huba, G. J., Wingard, J. A., & Bentler, P. M. (1979). Beginning adolescent drug use and peer and adult interaction patterns. *Journal of Consulting and Clinical Psychology, 47*, 265-276.

Jessor, R., Chase, J. A., & Donovan, J. E. (1980). Psychosocial correlates of marijuana use and problem drinking in a national sample of adolescents. *American Journal of Public Health, 70*, 604-613.

Jessor, R., & Jessor, S. L. (1978). Theory testing in longitudinal research on marijuana use. In D. Kandel (Ed.), *Longitudinal research on drug use* (pp. 41-72). Washington, DC: Hemisphere.

Johnston, L. D., O'Malley, P. M., & Bachman, J. G. (1986). *Drug use among American high school students, college students, and other young adults: National trends through 1985.* Rockville, MD: National Institute on Drug Abuse.

Johnston, L. D., O'Malley, P. M., & Bachman, J. G. (1988). *Illicit drug use, smoking, and drinking by America's high school students, college students, and young adults, 1975-1987.* Rockville, MD: National Institute on Drug Abuse.

Jonas, J. M., Gold, M. S., Sweeney, D., & Pottash, A. L. (1987). Eating disorders and cocaine abuse: A survey of 259 cocaine abusers. *Journal of Clinical Psychiatry, 48*(2), 47-50.

Kandel, D. B. (1973). Adolescent marijuana use: Role of parents and peers. *Science, 181*, 1067-1070.

Kandel, D. B. (1978). Convergence in prospective longitudinal surveys of drug use in normal populations. In D. B. Kandel (Ed.), *Longitudinal research on drug use: Empirical findings and methodological issues.* Washington, DC: Hemisphere.

Kandel, D. B. (1984). Substance abuse by adolescents in Israel and France: A cross-cultural perspective. *Public Health, 99*(3), 277-283.

Kandel, D. B., & Adler, I. (1982). Socialization into marijuana use among French adolescents: A cross sectional comparison with the United States. *Journal of Health and Social Behavior, 23*, 295-309.

Kandel, D. B., Kessler, R. C., & Margolies, R. Z. (1978). Antecedents of adolescent initiation into stages of drug use: A developmental analysis. In D. Kandel (Ed.), *Longitudinal research on drug use* (pp. 73-100). Washington, DC: Hemisphere.

Kandel, D., Simcha-Fagen, O., & Davies, M. (1986). Risk factors for delinquency and illicit drug use from adolescence to young adulthood. *Journal of Drug Issues, 16,* 67-90.

Kaplan, H. B., Martin, S. S., & Robbins, C. (1984). Pathways to adolescent drug use: Self-derogation, peer influence, weakening of social controls, and early substance use. *Journal of Health and Social Behavior, 25,* 270-289.

Kashani, J. H., Keller, M. B., Solomon, N., Reid, J. C., & Mazzola, D. (1985). Double depression in adolescent substance users. *Journal of Affective Disorders, 8,* 153-157.

Koocher, G. P. (1974). Emerging self-hood and cognitive development. *Journal of Genetic Psychology, 125,* 79-88.

Kozel, N. J., & Adams, E. H. (1986). Epidemiology of drug abuse: An overview. *Science, 234,* 970-974.

Lie, G. Y. (1984). A longitudinal and multivariate study of adolescent alcohol involvement. *Dissertation Abstracts International, 46,* 264A.

Marcos, A. C., & Johnson, R. E. (1988). Cultural patterns and causal processes in adolescent drug use: The case of Greeks versus Americans. *International Journal of the Addictions, 23,* 545-572.

Marlatt, G. A., & Donovan, D. M. (1981). Alcoholism and drug dependence: Cognitive social learning factors in addictive behaviors. In W. E. Craighead, A. E. Kazdin, & M. J. Mahoney (Eds.), *Behavior modification: Principles, issues, and applications* (2nd ed., pp. 264-285). Boston: Houghton Mifflin.

Miller, D. (1986). Affective disorders and violence in adolescents. *Hospital and Community Psychiatry, 37,* 591-596.

Miller, N. S., Goodwin, D. W., Jones, F. C., & Pardo, M. P. (1987). Histamine receptor antagonism of intolerance to alcohol in the Oriental population. *Journal of Nervous and Mental Disorders, 175,* 661-667.

Mitchell, J. E., Hatsukami, D., Eckert, E. D., & Pyle, R. L. (1985). Characteristics of 257 patients with bulimia. *American Journal of Psychiatry, 142,* 482-485.

Morrison, J. R. (1979). Diagnosis of adult psychiatric patients with childhood hyperactivity. *American Journal of Psychiatry, 136,* 955-958.

Muuss, R. E. (1986). Adolescent eating disorder: Bulimia. *Adolescence, 21,* 257-267.

Needle, R., McCubbin, H., Wilson, M., Reineck, R., Lazar, A., & Mederer, H. (1986). Interpersonal influences in adolescent drug use: The role of older siblings, parents, and peers. *International Journal of the Addictions, 21,* 739-766.

O'Connell, D. L., Alexander, H. M., Dobson, A. J., Lloyd, D. M., Hardes, G. R., Springthorpe, H. S., & Leeder, S. R. (1981). Cigarette smoking and drug use in school children: 11 factors associated with smoking. *International Journal of Epidemiology, 17,* 749-791.

Padilla, E. R., Padilla, A. M., Morales, A., Olmedo, E., & Ramirez, R. (1979). Inhalant, marijuana and alcohol abuse among barrio children and adolescents. *International Journal of the Addictions, 14,* 945-964.

Paton, S., Kessler, R., & Kandel, D. (1977). Depressive mood and adolescent illicit drug use: A longitudinal analysis. *Journal of Genetic Psychology, 131,* 267-289.

Penning, M., & Barnes, G. E. (1982). Adolescent marijuana use: A review. *International Journal of the Addictions, 17,* 749-791.

Pressons, C. C., Chassin, L., Sherman, S. J., Olshavsky, R., Bensenberg, M., & Corty, E. (1984). Predictors of adolescents' intentions to smoke: Age, sex, race and regional differences. *International Journal of the Addictions, 19*, 503-519.

Pentz, M. A. (1985). Social competence and self-efficacy as determinants of substance use in adolescents. In S. Shiffman & T. A. Wills (Eds.), *Coping and substance use*, (pp. 117-142). New York: Academic Press.

Quay, H. C., & Werry, J. S. (1979). *Psychopathological disorders of childhood* (2nd ed.). New York: John Wiley.

Reichler, B. D., Clement, J. L., & Dunner, D. L. (1983). Chart review of alcohol problems in adolescent psychiatric patients in an emergency room. *Journal of Clinical Psychiatry, 44*, 338-339.

Reynolds, I., & Rob, M. I. (1988). The role of family difficulties in adolescent depression, drug-taking and other problem behaviors. *Medical Journal of Australia, 149*(5), 250-256.

Rivinus, T. M., Bierderman, J., Herzog, D. B., Kemper, K., Harper, G. P., Harmatz, J. S., & Houseworth, S. (1984). Anorexia nervosa and affective disorders: A controlled family history study. *American Journal of Psychiatry, 141*, 1414-1418.

Robbins, D. R., & Alessi, N. E. (1985). Depressive symptoms and suicidal behavior in adolescents. *American Journal of Psychiatry, 142*, 588-592.

Ryser, P. E. (1983). Students and drug abuse. *Journal of School Health, 53*, 435-436.

Selik, R. M., Castro, K. G., & Pappaioanou, M. (1988). Racial/ethnic differences in the risk of AIDS in the United States. *American Journal of Public Health, 78*, 1539-1545.

Shafii, M., Carrigan, S., Whittinghill, J. R., & Derrick, A. (1985). Psychological autopsy of completed suicide in children and adolescents. *American Journal of Psychiatry, 142*, 1061-1064.

Smith, G. M., & Fogg, C. P. (1978). Psychological predictors of early use, late use, and nonuse of marijuana among teenage students. In D. Kandel (Ed.), *Longitudinal research on drug use* (pp. 101-114). Washington, DC: Hemisphere.

Spero, E. R. (1989). *Special education and the female juvenile offender.* Unpublished seminar paper, University of Maryland, College Park, Department of Special Education.

Spero, E. R., Leone, P., Walter, M. B., & Wilson, E. (1989). Substance abuse, school policy, and special education. *Counterpoint, 9*(3), 18.

Tarter, R. E., McBride, H., Buonpane, N., & Schneider, D. U. (1977). Differentiation of alcoholics. *Archives of General Psychiatry, 34*, 761-768.

Thornburg, H. D. (1982). *Development in adolescence* (2nd ed.). Monterey, CA: Brooks/Cole.

Weissman, M. M., Gammon, G. D., John, K., Merikangas, K. R., et al. (1987). Children of depressed parents: Increased psychopathology and early onset of major depression. *Archives of General Psychiatry, 44*, 847-853.

Welte, J. W., & Barnes, G. M. (1987). Alcohol use among adolescent minority groups. *Journal of Studies on Alcohol, 48*, 329-336.

White, H. R., Johnson, V., & Horwitz, A. (1986). An application of three deviance theories to adolescent substance use. *International Journal of the Addictions, 21*, 347-366.

Wills, T. A., & Shiffman, S. (1985). Coping and substance use: A conceptual framework. In S. Shiffman & T. A. Wills (Eds.), *Coping and substance use* (pp. 3-24). New York: Academic Press.

Winfree, L. T., Theis, H. E., & Griffiths, C. T. (1981). Drug use in rural America: A cross-cultural examination of complementary social deviance theories. *Youth & Society, 12*, 465-489.

Winstead, D. K., & Willard, S. G. (1983). Bulimia: Diagnostic cues. *Southern Medical Journal, 76*, 313-315.

Wright, L. (1985). High school polydrug users and abusers. *Adolescence, 20*, 853-861.

Yamaguchi, K., & Kandel, D. (1987). Drug use and other determinants of premarital pregnancy and its outcome: A dynamic analysis of competing life events. *Journal of Marriage and the Family, 49*, 257-270.

Zucker, R. A., & Harford, T. C. (1983). National study of the demography of adolescent drinking practices in 1980. *Journal of Studies on Alcohol, 44*, 974-985.

10

Troubled Families
and Troubled Youth

The Development of Antisocial Behavior
and Depression in Children

JAMES SNYDER
DEBRA HUNTLEY

The goal of this chapter is to describe how families contribute to the development of problem behavior in children. Four central theses are made about the role of the family. First, the influence of the family on child development occurs in the context of social interaction. Parent-child interaction is the proximal process affecting development. Global (e.g., socioeconomic status), distal (e.g., parent and child dispositions), and contextual (e.g., marital adjustment, stress) variables impinging on and operating within the family are important, but they exert their influence via proximal interaction. Second, children play an active role in their own development. Their behavioral, biological, and emotional characteristics evoke specific responses from others. As a result of these characteristics, children select certain environments and are affected by and experience those environments in a varying manner. Third, the role of the family changes as development progresses. The manner in which the family fosters competence or maladjustment changes with the child's maturation and previous learning, and with the salient experiences and transitions descriptive of a particular developmental period. Fourth, the family is only one of several socialization agents.

The impact of the family on child developmental outcomes varies according to the amount and nature of the child's contact with other socialization agents, and to the interaction of socialization processes occurring in familial and extrafamilial settings.

The chapter is divided into four main parts. In the first part, a general conceptual model of the role of the family in child development is described in the context of a developmental, social systems frame of reference. In the next two parts, research concerning the role of the family in the development of two prevalent child problems, antisocial behavior and depression, is described and organized using this model. Finally, the implications of the model for preventive and remedial interventions are briefly reviewed.

A Conceptual Model of Socioemotional Development in Children: The Role of the Family

Family Interaction as the Proximal Mediator of Development

Research in developmental psychopathology has identified a wide range of variables that influence a child's adjustment. These include dispositional characteristics and developmental history of the parents, the marital relationship of the parents, family socioeconomic status, parental stress, and gender and dispositional characteristics of the child. Whereas these factors are often reliably related to child developmental outcomes, each by itself accounts for a small amount of variance in those outcomes. For example, many children from low socioeconomic backgrounds fare well, and only a subset of children who have difficult temperaments evidence significant behavioral and emotional problems. These factors are marker variables, each of which provides a potential bias toward particular child developmental outcomes; they do not necessarily result in such outcomes. This leads to two questions. Why is the risk expressed in some cases and not others? What is the mechanism that serves as the transducer by which these dispositional, contextual, and historical factors influence development?

From a social interactional perspective, parent-child interaction is one central vehicle by which the child is socialized. Socioemotional and cognitive development entails learning, much of which occurs in myriad social interchanges between parents and their children. Both parents and children contribute to the nature of these interchanges. The unit of

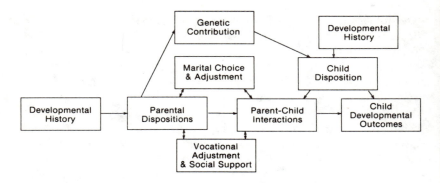

Figure 10.1. The Role of the Family in Child Development: A Conceptual Model

analysis is neither the child's nor the parents' behavior. Rather, it is the patterns of interaction that describe the systematic relationship between the behavior of one family member and the reaction of other members to that behavior. These patterns, or mutual behavior interdependencies, directly reflect the interpersonal teaching and social influence that are the core meaning of socialization. The influence of families on child development is not unidirectional and linear, but bidirectional and recursive.

Historical, contextual, and dispositional variables play out their child developmental influence in family interaction (Belsky, 1984). Parent-child interaction is the proximal transducer by which these distal variables affect child development. Distal variables have an impact on developmental outcomes to the degree that they affect interaction. It follows that a distal variable, such as parental stress, has a negative impact on child development only insofar as it disrupts family interaction. A model detailing the central transducer role of family interactional processes on child development is shown in Figure 10.1.

A Developmental Perspective on the Role of the Family

As children mature and learn, their behavior undergoes a progressive transformation and reorganization. The role of the family in child development is not static. Those quantitative and qualitative aspects of family interaction that foster competence or pathology depend on the developmental status of the child, which, in turn, is the product of prior maturation and learning. For example, in infancy the synchrony, contingency, and affective tone of parent-infant interaction influences the child's later attachment, social responsiveness, and emerging sense of self (Cairns, 1979; Watson, 1979). These developmental products, in turn, influence the manner in which parents try to foster the child's self-regulation and social and cognitive skills.

Child development also occurs in the context of parental development. The manner in which parents were socialized during their own development affects the availability to them of general instrumental and coping skills needed to engage successfully in work, marital, and social roles, and of specific skills needed to socialize their children effectively. Development of the parents continues concurrently with that of their children. Issues such as career orientation, marital adjustment, health, and economic stability influence how the parents view and interact with their children (e.g., Elder, Liker, & Cross, 1983; Forgatch, Patterson, & Skinner, in press). Child development unfolds in reference to a moving family context such that there is a dynamic interplay between the development of the child and that of the parents. The dynamic interplay between these developmental trajectories occurs in family interaction.

The Role of the Family
Relative to Other Socialization Agents

As a result of the child's increasing competence and independence, and of age-related cultural norms (e.g., going to school), the child comes into increasing contact with socialization agents outside of the family (e.g., peers and teachers). Extrafamilial agents play an important complementary role in socialization (see Hartup, 1983; also see Trickett & Zlotlow, Chapter 6, this volume; Dishion, Chapter 7, this volume).

The family influences the nature of children's interaction with these agents in two ways. First, early familial socialization provides children with "basic training" in socioemotional and cognitive skills that influence the nature of their transactions with peers and teachers (e.g., Putallaz, 1987; Sigel, 1982). Second, parents influence the nature of those transactions by choosing schools, selectively encouraging activities outside of the home, and monitoring the child's peer associates and school performance (e.g., Patterson, 1982). This monitoring function becomes increasingly important during late childhood and adolescence (Snyder, Dishion, & Patterson, 1986), and may serve a protective function in severely disadvantaged, high-risk environments (Wilson, 1980). The relationship between familial and extrafamilial socialization is reciprocal. Expansions in the child's repertoire, knowledge, experience, and opportunities resulting from extrafamilial socialization necessitate new adaptations in family interaction.

The Role of the Child in Family Interaction and Development

Children do not react passively to the family (or peer and school) environment. They contribute to that environment in evocative and active ways (Scarr & McCartney, 1983). The term *evocative contributions* refers to the notion that parents and other socialization agents differentially respond to children based on the observable physical (e.g., gender, attractiveness) and behavioral characteristics (e.g., temperament, aggression) of those children. *Active contributions* refers to children's selective attention and learning and differential responsiveness to environmental events. The characteristics of the child influence how a specific environment is experienced by the child in contrast to the type of environment to which the child is exposed. Children also make active contributions by selecting, to a degree, the environments to which they will be exposed. This selection is often based on the compatibility of the environment with their own characteristics.

The active contributions that children make to their own socialization are evident across development. For example, smiling, active babies receive more social stimulation than do sober, passive ones (Lytton, 1980). Difficult 2-year-old children are more negative and resistant to maternal attempts at control, and the mothers of such children more frequently use commands and physical control (Lee & Bates, 1985). As children mature and become more independent, they more actively select their own environments (e.g., peers, courses in school, athletic or other interests; Kandel, 1978). As a result, the parental role becomes more managerial and involves less direct instruction.

Summary

In the model just described, family interaction is a central arena in which dispositional, contextual, historical, and biological or maturational forces play out their role in child development. In the following sections, this conceptual model will be used to organize and interpret data relevant to two prevalent disorders in childhood and adolescence: antisocial behavior and depression. In each case, an effort will be made to describe the interface between the role of the family and that of other socialization agents in the development of these disorders.

The Role of the Family in the Development of Antisocial Behavior

Antisocial Behavior: Definition and Parameters

The term *antisocial behavior* refers to actions that have as their basic characteristic a violation of the rights of others and of societal norms. It includes behaviors such as noncompliance, physical and verbal aggression, destruction of property, stealing, lying, truancy, running away from home, and setting fires. The prevalence of antisocial behavior in the general population has been estimated to be 4-8%, and is observed more frequently in males than in females by a ratio of approximately 3 to 1 (Kazdin, 1985). It is the most frequent referral problem in outpatient child psychiatric settings, making up one-third to one-half of all referrals (Robins, 1981).

There is strong continuity in antisocial behavior across childhood and adolescence. Correlations between antisocial behavior measured at two time periods varies from .75 at 1-year intervals to .40 at 20-year intervals (Loeber, 1982). This continuity does not mean that antisocial behavior is isomorphic over development; the manner in which that behavior is expressed changes, but individuals tend to maintain their relative rank over time. Reliable predictors of antisocial behavior can be found as early as age 6, but they become more robust at age 10 (Loeber & Stouthamer-Loeber, 1987). This suggests that processes contributing to the development of antisocial behavior begin during early childhood and continue to operate through adolescence. Not all children evidencing high levels of antisocial behavior become antisocial adults. However, persistence of antisocial behavior into adulthood is more likely for individuals whose developmental history of antisocial behavior is characterized by one or more of the following: early onset, high rates, manifestation in several forms (e.g., hitting, lying, stealing), and performance in more than one setting (Loeber, 1982). As adults, those who were antisocial as children are also at greater risk for other types of psychiatric impairment, low educational attainment, poor vocational functioning, marital discord, and poor physical health (Kazdin, 1985).

A frequent concomitant to antisocial behavior is a failure to acquire adequate social, work, and academic skills. Antisocial children typically are rejected by peers, do poorly in school, evidence delays in behavioral and emotional self-regulation, and are rated as troublesome and lazy by teachers (Snyder & Patterson, 1987). Rejection and failure reduce opportunities for future involvement with normative socialization agents and activities. The behavioral excesses and deficits descriptive of antisocial behavior suggest a failure in socialization beginning early in the family environment and continuing in later family, peer, school, and community settings.

Family Interaction During Childhood and the Development of Antisocial Behavior

The family is the primary socialization agent during the first 3 to 5 years. One aspect of this early socialization critically related to the development of social and emotional competence is compliance training. At approximately age 2 to 3, when children show increased autonomy and mobility, parents begin making demands, imposing restrictions, and directing children's behavior. In doing so, the parents are communicating rules of conduct and social intercourse. The failure to achieve compliance is the first in a series of transitive steps leading to later, more serious manifestations of antisocial behavior (Patterson, 1982). Acquisition of compliance is prerequisite to the development of positive relationships with peers and family members, and to successful academic performance (Maccoby & Martin, 1983).

From a social interactional perspective, compliance training is accomplished during the frequent control episodes occurring in the daily interaction of young children and their parents. It is not a matter of a single act by the parent followed by a single act by the child. Compliance is shaped slowly over time. In any one control episode, the parent initially uses mild pressure to direct the child's behavior. If the child complies, the episode ends. If the child fails to comply, parents tend to escalate their pressure until compliance is achieved or the parent gives in. During these exchanges, reinforcement and punishment contingencies are in continuous operation. The effect of these contingencies is to produce slight but significant changes in the likelihood of compliance in future control episodes (Snyder & Patterson, 1986). The immediate goal is to gain compliance with minimal pressure, conflict, and negative emotionality (Maccoby & Martin, 1983).

Both parents and children contribute to compliance training. Let us first consider the parents' contribution. Research suggests that successful compliance training depends on three parental actions: (a) clear definition and careful tracking of desirable and undesirable child behavior; (b) communication of rules, expectations, and instructions in a direct, clear manner; and (c) consistent reinforcement of compliance and punishment of noncompliance (Forehand & Scarboro, 1975; Snyder, 1977). Most research on compliance training has used between-subject (family) cross-sectional designs. These designs utilize a one-time summary measure of family interaction and thus take a static "snapshot" of what is actually a dynamic process. However, a social interactional perspective maintains that compliance training is accomplished in a series of interactional trials over time. This dynamic learning process can be captured more aptly by observing families at intervals over an extended period of time, and then assessing the systematic relationships among the characteristics of family interaction at one time period with those observed at a later time period (i.e., a within-subjects approach). Rather than one "snapshot," this approach presents a "moving picture" of the social influence process as it unfolds in time.

The following discussion of research by Snyder and Patterson (1985) will clarify this notion. From a social interactional perspective, observation of compliance training within families over time should indicate that the probability of child compliance in a given control episode will be related to the clarity of the directive initiating the episode and to the type of consequences provided for compliance in previous episodes. To test this hypothesis, control episodes occurring during the interaction of five mother-child dyads were observed and coded for an hour each day for 8 days. After testing for homogeneity and stationarity, the data were collapsed over subjects and time. The probability of child compliance as a function of the type of maternal directive initiating an episode and the type of consequence she provided for the child's response to her previous command is shown in Table 10.1. The top half of Table 10.1 considers the case where the child complied in the previous episode, and the bottom half where the child did not comply in the previous episode. Presumably, fostering subsequent child compliance will necessitate different consequences for compliance and noncompliance. Regardless of compliance or noncompliance in the preceding episode, the

Table 10.1. The Probability of Compliance as a Function of Instructional Clarity and the Type of Consequence in the Previous Control Episode

Type of Consequence for Compliance in Previous Control Episode

Clarity of Instruction Initiating Current Episode	Positive Reinforcement	Ignore	Punish	
Command	78	65	10	67
Ambiguous command	62	41	00	50
Request	63	26	00	31
	69	53	06	60

Type of Consequence for Noncompliance in Previous Control Episode

Clarity of Instruction Initiating Current Episode	Punish	Ignore/Positive Reinforcement	
Command	75	48	59
Ambiguous command	49	43	45
Request	52	09	21
	62	39	51

SOURCE: Snyder and Patterson (1985). Based on 8 hours of observation in each of five families.

likelihood with which mothers obtained compliance increased with the clarity of their directives (command is associated with greater compliance than are ambiguous command and request). Mothers were also more likely to achieve child compliance when they had positively reinforced (rather than ignored or punished) child compliance in the previous episode (see top half of Table 10.1). Similarly, mothers were more likely to achieve compliance when they had punished (rather than ignored or reinforced) child noncompliance in the previous episode (see bottom half of Table 10.1).

A multivariate information analysis of these data indicates that the type of directive, the type of consequence, and their interaction are all significant predictors of child compliance, accounting for a total of 39-43% of the variance. Additional sequential analyses show that, within a given control episode, the likelihood of achieving compliance decreased after the child failed to comply with the initial maternal directive. The mean probability of noncompliance to initial directives was .33; to second directives after initial noncompliance, .46; and to third directives after the second noncompliance, .68. Obtaining compliance to initial directives with minimal pressure is critical.

Given that these parental skills promote child compliance, the next problem is to account for variation in the performance of those skills. Why are some parents clear and contingent whereas others scold and threaten but inconsistently follow through when teaching compliance? Two hypotheses seem reasonable. First, some parents may not have learned the requisite skills during their own development. Retrospective and prospective studies have found a significant covariation across generations in ineffective parenting (Caspi, Elder, & Bem, 1986; Patterson & Dishion, in press). Persons who evidenced conduct problems as children tend to be ill tempered and inconsistent in rearing their own children. Second, research indicates that skilled parenting may be disrupted by environmental stress, marital discord and divorce (Emery, 1982; Forgatch et al., in press), economic disruptions (Elder et al., 1983), and negative social contacts (Wahler, 1980). In fact, there is a powerful interaction between parental disposition and stress. Stress has the greatest negative impact on parenting for those parents who are marginally skilled in the first place (Patterson & Dishion, in press).

Children also contribute to compliance training. For example, children who are temperamentally difficult involve their parents in a higher frequency of control episodes and are less responsive to parental instructions and consequences (Lee & Bates, 1985), consequently evoking increased use of demands and physical means of control. Successful compliance training of difficult children may require that more attention be given to parental tracking, clarity, consistency, and contingency than is needed for temperamentally easy children.

The repeated measure, within-family method can be used to test the hypothesis that stress disrupts parenting behaviors requisite to successful compliance training. Using the same mother-child dyads as above, Snyder and Patterson (1985) calculated two indices of parenting relevant to compliance training for each day of observation: (a) maternal start-up (the conditional probability of a maternal directive given the child was not misbehaving—a measure of poor tracking), and (b) maternal noncontingency (the conditional probability of maternal reinforcement given child noncompliance and of maternal nonreinforcement given child compliance). The goal was to determine how much variance in these parenting behaviors can be accounted for by maternal stress. Maternal stress emanating from two sources was assessed on each observation day: (1) maternal self-reports of stress unrelated to the child, and (2) stress resulting from the child's misbehavior during the interaction (child start-up—the conditional probability of child's aversive behavior given mother's neutral or positive behavior). The temporal covariation of each parenting index with maternal self-reported stress and child start-up stress scores was assessed using a multilevel data array and disaggregated time-series analysis. This procedure controls for between-dyad differences and allows pooling of data across dyads.

Maternal self-reported stress was a reliable predictor of maternal start-up, accounting for 16% of the variance. Child start-up was not reliably associated with maternal start-up. Both maternal self-reported stress and child start-up were reliably associated with maternal noncontingency, uniquely accounting for 33% and 14% of the variance, respectively. On days of high maternal stress and frequent child misbehavior, the mothers less carefully tracked their children's behavior and less consistently encouraged compliance and discouraged noncompliance. This is consistent with the hypothesis that stress may disrupt the parenting skills requisite to teaching compliance to children, and that children contribute to compliance training.

The failure to achieve compliance has potent effects on subsequent development. Noncompliant children frequently use threats, whining, temper tantrums, and aggression as means of relating to family members. Parents often respond with increased irritability and with inconsistent and ineffective punitiveness. This results in a coercive interactional process to which both the parent and the child contribute (Patterson, 1976; Snyder, 1977). Over time, the child acquires a more coercive relational style, leading to parental rejection and reduced contact with the child. This reduction in positive, constructive parent-child interaction further interferes with the development of social and cognitive competence (Patterson, 1986; Patterson & Bank, in press).

Failure to teach adequate social and cognitive skills and continued reinforcement of coercive social behavior set the stage for problems outside of the home. The child's lack of skills and coercive repertoire generalize to interaction with peers and teachers. They are unable to discourage the child's antisocial behavior and to engage the child in constructive social interaction and learning. In a relatively short period of time, the child is rejected by peers (Dodge, 1983) and within a few years is identified as an academic failure (Patterson & Bank, in press). This rejection and failure set further limits on opportunities for positive socialization experiences. The range of peers and activities from which the child can select is reduced. The antisocial child associates with other antisocial peers who have compatible attitudes, behaviors, and interests (Snyder, 1988). Interaction with this peer group then reinforces and expands the antisocial repertoire of the child (Kandel, 1978).

Early development of antisocial behavior primarily occurs in family interaction. A number of converging factors interfere with family interactional processes requisite to the development of self-regulation and cognitive and social skills: difficult child temperament, unskilled/irritable parents, socioeconomic disadvantage, parental stress, and marital discord. Although not all antisocial children go on to become antisocial adolescents, the products of this early training (parental and peer rejection, school failure, association with antisocial peers) put children at risk for a continued drift into deviance.

Family Interaction and the Development of Antisocial Behavior During Adolescence

As children move into adolescence, they are increasingly independent and spend more time outside the home in the absence of adult supervision. They are establishing new roles and reconstructing their self-representation based on biological, social, and cognitive changes associated with maturation and culturally normative experiences. During this period, the parents' role becomes increasingly managerial and consultative. Adolescents become more active coparticipants with their parents in negotiating and selecting experiences inside and outside the home. Three aspects of family interaction are particularly germane to the continued development of socioemotional competence during adolescence: monitoring, discipline, and involvement.

Monitoring refers to parents' knowledge of their children's activities, peer associates, and whereabouts when outside the home. Effective monitoring entails the negotiation and communication of clear rules and expectations concerning curfews, drug use, school attendance and performance, persons with whom the child may associate, and places that are off limits to the child. Parents must track compliance with rules and engage in effective problem solving and discipline when the rules are violated (Snyder & Patterson, 1987).

In relation to antisocial behavior, monitoring has both preventive and corrective functions. Good monitoring limits contact with peers, activities, and locales that are the occasion for antisocial behavior, and ensures parents' attentiveness to indications of antisocial behavior (e.g., being high, truanting, ignoring curfews) requiring corrective action (Snyder et al., 1986). Poor parental monitoring and inconsistent discipline are associated with parent-, teacher-, peer-, and self-reported aggression, dishonesty, property damage, truanting, and official delinquency (Patterson, 1986; Patterson & Dishion, in press; Pulkkinen, 1983).

Monitoring and discipline are important in limiting adolescents' exposure to antisocial opportunities and learning experiences, and in promoting normative extrafamilial socialization opportunities. However, adolescents are becoming increasingly competent and individuated. Monitoring and discipline must be balanced with a reasonable assertion of independence and exercise of judgment by the adolescent, while simultaneously engendering respect and responsiveness to others' needs and viewpoints. Healthy individuation, self-competence, and good peer relations and school performance are also enhanced by good communication, continued mutual involvement of family members, and a willingness to negotiate, solve problems, and compromise (e.g., Grotevant & Cooper, 1985). Several longitudinal studies have demonstrated that parental coldness, passivity, and neglect and a lack of family cohesion and shared leisure time are associated with one-time and recidivist delinquency (McCord, 1979; Pulkkinen, 1983). Communication and problem solving in families with antisocial adolescents is characterized by a lack of intimacy and give and take, and by more blaming, anger, and defensiveness than in normal families (Alexander, 1973; West & Farrington, 1977).

In considering the role of the family in adolescent development, three developmental paths require explanation. First, we need to understand how children who are already oppositional continue on that path and become more involved in and committed to antisocial behavior. Second, we need to understand what factors operate to cause children who were antisocial during childhood to drop out of that process during adolescence. Third, we need to identify socialization processes that contribute to initiation into antisocial behavior during adolescence.

Children who are antisocial during childhood are at high risk for continuing along that developmental path (Wolfgang, Figlio, & Sellin, 1972). Parental dispositions and static contextual variables (e.g., poverty, low education) that disrupted early socialization practices and promoted the early development of antisocial behavior continue to operate. Parents with antisocial histories are less adept at monitoring and disciplining their children than parents lacking such histories (Wilson, 1980; Patterson & Dishion, in press). Parents who experience economic distress, who are poorly educated, who are raising their families in high-crime neighborhoods, and who lack supportive social networks are less likely to be involved constructively with their children and less likely to monitor and discipline their children adequately compared to their more advantaged counterparts (Forgatch et al., in press; Wilson, 1980). Continued disruption of competence-enhancing family interaction promotes the continuation and amplification of antisocial behavior during adolescence. Children who are already highly antisocial, associate with deviant peers, endorse deviant values, lack basic attention and work skills, and evidence poor academic performance present a much greater disciplinary and monitoring challenge. Further, because of the coercive manner in which these children relate to others, attempts at monitoring and discipline typically result in conflict (Alexander, 1973; McCord, 1979).

These continued disruptions in family interaction in combination with previous peer rejection and school failure exacerbate the deviant socialization process. Previous failure and rejection limit the child's learning opportunities and choice of peer associates. In the absence of corrective monitoring, discipline, and constructive involvement in the family setting, the antisocial child selects activities, experiences, and people consistent with his or her antisocial values, behavior, and interests. This reduces contact with normative, competence-enhancing learning experiences, and provides the child with "advanced training" in antisocial behavior (Patterson & Bank, in press; Snyder & Patterson, 1987).

The second developmental path entails the onset of antisocial behavior during adolescence. Relatively little research has focused selectively on this group of "late starters." It is reasonable to hypothesize that parents and adolescents jointly contribute to this process. Adolescent development entails a number of stressors, such as developing effective heterosocial relationships, moves from elementary to junior high and high schools, and pressure to formulate vocational and educational plans (Compas, in press). The stress associated with these developmental tasks may increase adolescents' irritability and opposition to parents, and their susceptibility to peer influence. This, in turn, challenges effective family functioning. Parents may fail to make timely shifts to more management-oriented and coparticipatory interactional strategies congruent with the increased competence and independence of their developing children. Changes in marital, social, vocational, and emotional functioning, or transient stressors that constitute the parents' own developmental context, may diminish the consistency and skill with which they monitor and discipline their children, and constructively engage them in problem solving and mutually satisfying activities. As a consequence, children who have not previously displayed serious antisocial behavior may drift toward peers and activities that appear cool, daring, or macho (Elder, Caspi, & Van Nguyen, 1984; Patterson & Bank, in press).

The third developmental path involves those individuals who are antisocial as children, but who later drop out of this process. Approximately one-half of antisocial children do *not* continue their antisocial behavior during adolescence (Patterson, 1982). Clinical and epidemiological research suggests that such shifts are most likely to occur at earlier ages, prior to repeated school failure, peer rejection, and commitment to deviant peers, activities, and values. Why does this shift occur? Parents who were relatively ineffective socialization agents for their young children may, because of either experience or a diminution in background stress and disadvantage, gain (or regain) the ability to track their children's behavior inside and outside the home, to use effective discipline strategies, and to engage their children constructively in problem solving, communication, and shared activities. Clinical interventions that teach these skills to parents produce significant and lasting reductions in child antisocial behavior (e.g., Patterson, Chamberlain, & Reid, 1982).

The relationship of improved family functioning (i.e., monitoring, discipline, and problem solving) to decreased adolescent antisocial behavior has not been clearly established. A necessary but not sufficient criterion to establish this relationship is to demonstrate temporal covariation between family functioning and antisocial behavior. Previous research has also not delineated the role of family contextual variables in the alteration of antisocial behavior. It is reasonable to suppose that parental stress disrupts family functioning, which, in turn, is associated with exacerbation of adolescent antisocial behavior. In order to identify family processes associated with change in antisocial behavior, we measured monitoring, discipline, parental stress, and antisocial child behavior in 10 foster families at 1-, 5-, 12-, 26-, 52-, and 76-week intervals after the placement of an adolescent with severe conduct disorders. Each of the constructs was assessed by multiple indicators using different methods or informants. This arrangement provides a

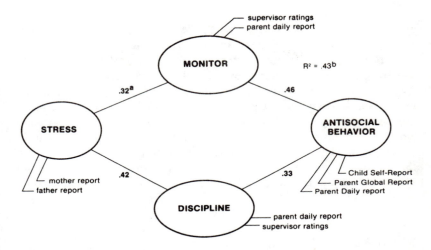

Figure 10.2. A Causal Model of the Impact of Parental Stress, Monitoring, and Discipline on Antisocial Behavior

a. Path coefficients are beta weights; all are significant at $p < .05$.
b. Amount of variance accounted for by the model.

sensitive test of the natural covariation of these variables while controlling for the effects of previous family history. The causal model shown in Figure 10.2 was tested using a multilevel data array and disaggregated time-series analysis.

Each of the path coefficients (standardized beta weights) shown in Figure 10.2 is significant. The model accounted for 43% of the variance in the adolescents' antisocial behavior. This suggests that parental stress was associated with disruptions in monitoring and discipline, and that these disruptions were in turn related to displays of increased child antisocial behavior. With a few exceptions, the foster parents consistently displayed high levels of discipline and monitoring, but there were large temporal variations in the adolescents' antisocial behavior. This suggests that in the case of well-established antisocial child behavior, the deleterious effects of relatively small disruptions in discipline and monitoring are amplified. After extended progression along the developmental path of antisocial behavior, remediation requires extremely consistent, high-level family functioning.

In summary, the family's contribution to the development of antisocial behavior during adolescence entails a set of issues and interactional processes somewhat different from those operating during childhood. Adolescents are more independent and exercise more control over the route of their development. They spend more time outside of the home and are strongly influenced by extrafamilial socialization agents. Family interaction becomes more managerial and coparticipatory. The failure of families to engage in effective monitoring, discipline, and problem solving may lead to a late initiation into antisocial behavior, and amplifies the deviance training process in those who started earlier in development. The successful acquisition and consistent performance of those skills may remedy earlier expressions of antisocial behavior, but are most likely to be successful if this remediation is initiated early in the developmental process.

The Role of the Family in
the Development of Child Depression

Although there has been controversy over the existence of childhood depression, most psychologists currently agree that a depressive disorder can occur in children. Recent research has shown that the full syndrome of depression can be reliably identified in children as young as 6 to 8 years (Puig-Antich, Blau, Marx, Greenhill, & Chambers, 1978; Zahn-Waxler et al., 1988). The term *childhood depression* does not refer to transitory moments of sadness or disappointment; rather, it is a condition characterized by long duration (longer than three months), severe impairment of the child's scholastic and social adjustment, and disturbances in vegetative functions, especially food intake and sleep (Cytryn & McKnew, 1972).

Many professionals identify child depression using adult diagnostic criteria, such as those in DSM III-R. However, the symptoms of depression in children can take a variety of forms, dependent on the child's developmental level (Deuber, 1982; Rie, 1966). Child, Murphy, and Rhyne (1980), for example, note that depression in infancy is evidenced by apathy, listlessness, lack of appropriate response to stimuli, weight loss, poor feeding, lack of crying, gross motor retardation, and an increased susceptibility to infection. In preschoolers, depression is most typically manifested by sad affect, withdrawal, irritability, difficulty with other children, sleep and appetite disturbances, lack of interest and enjoyment, and rocking and other repetitive activities. In the school-aged child, depression is indicated by monotone voice, slow movement, somatic complaints, temper tantrums, running away from home or school, tearfulness, spending an inordinate amount of time to complete assignments, avoidance of eye contact, difficulty in simple mental activities, avoidance of group activities, indifference to success, frequent crying, and excessive daydreaming. In late adolescents, depression is similar to adult depression. The classical or cardinal features of adult depression, hopelessness and despair, frequently can be observed, although these features are not yet present in early adolescent depression (Hudgens, 1974).

Whereas the symptoms of a depressive disorder may change as the child matures, research indicates that the depressive disorder itself may be very stable and enduring. Cytryn, McKnew, Zahn-Waxler, and Gershon (1986) report that 50-77% of the depressed children they studied were still depressed as young adults. Those who do not evidence continuity in depression often manifested other forms of psychopathology as adults. Signs of depression in childhood and adolescence are not merely benign, transitory phenomena, but tend to foreshadow important psychiatric maladjustment in adulthood (Fard, Hudgens, & Welner, 1978; Welner, Welner, & Fishman, 1979).

Epidemiological studies assessing the frequency of childhood depression in the general population are relatively rare, and the wide variance in reported prevalence is probably due to differences in diagnostic methodology. Kashani and Simonds (1979) reported that 2% of a sample of 103 children were depressed, while Rutter, Tizard, and Whitmore (1981) reported that .4% of 2,199 prepubertal children were depressed. The literature indicates that there is an increase in incidence of depression from prepubescence to adolescence (Rutter, 1986), although this has not been systematically researched from a longitudinal perspective. In the Isle of Wight general population study, 13% of 10- to 11-year-old children showed a depressed mood at interview (Rutter et al., 1981). When the same children were reassessed at ages 14 to 15, over 40% of the adolescents reported substantial feelings of misery and depression. Pearce (1978), in an investigation of 547 clinic children, found that 11% of prepubertal children showed depressive symptomatology, compared to 25% of postpubertal children. Rutter (1986) suggests that increased incidence of depression during adolescence may be due to hormonal changes accompanying puberty, increased stress, decreased family supports, or a developmental change in the ability to make depressive-type cognitive attributions (e.g., viewing failure as implying a stable and lasting limitation on performance).

To summarize, depression can occur at a very young age, perhaps as early as infancy. It is a clinically significant syndrome affecting children and adolescents, and can persist throughout childhood and into adulthood. This suggests that the development of depression starts early, often in the context of the family. Early treatment is important, as it may prevent future depressive episodes and accompanying developmental problems. Similarly, it is useful to examine family variables because family plays an important and influential role in child development, and because the family is a critical resource in the treatment of child depression.

The remainder of this section will look at recent research on the role of the family in child depression. Information is presented on the relationship between parental depression and child depression, examining behaviors that occur in depressed parents that may influence or lead to depression in the child. Then parental variables other than depression that may be related to the etiology of depression in the child will be discussed. This research focuses on child depression and attempts to identify familial factors.

Parental Depression

Several researchers have found that children of depressed mothers are more likely to be depressed themselves (Cytryn et al., 1986; Orvaschel, Walsh-Allis, & Ye, 1988). Three types of hypotheses could account for these findings: (a) Parental depression causes child depression, (b) child depression causes parental depression, and (c) child and parental depression occur in response to the same precursors or events. Most studies focus on the first of the three; however, it should be noted that having a depressed child may also be stressful and may evoke depression in the parent. Additionally, depressed people are likely to report increased stress and decreased social support. Stress and poor social support may occur in response to such events as divorce, marital dissatisfaction, or death of a family member, and may lead to depression in both parent and child. This section, however, will focus on the manner in which parental depression facilitates child depression.

To understand how parental depression influences child depression, studies will be presented on the way in which depression affects parenting skills. Unfortunately, most studies have examined only maternal depression. However, the incidence of depression is greater for females than for males, and mothers are still the primary caretakers for children.

Most studies did not control for paternal depression or involvement in parenting, both of which may have an important impact on the development of depression in offspring.

The social and emotional development of children is strongly influenced by parents' behavior and affect. Even very young children are sensitive to and affected by their parents' emotional state (Zahn-Waxler & Radke-Yarrow, 1982). Tronick, Ricks, and Cohn (1982) asked mothers to simulate depression while interacting with their infants. The infants were observed to use gaze aversion in response to the depressed mothers. This may have been an attempt by the infants to regulate their own responses or negative feelings through avoidance. Gaze aversion may lead to decreased opportunities to observe the mother and to reduced reciprocity and role-taking, which are important sources of learning. If maintained over a significant length of time, these reduced opportunities could cause deficits in socialization in addition to depressive behavior in children. Termine and Izard (1988) found that the more frequently infants looked at depressed mothers, the more sadness they experienced. Although it is unclear as to why the infants expressed sadness (e.g., whether it is limitation, empathy, or "depressive" behaviors used to regulate affect), it is noteworthy that depression in mothers directly affects infants' emotional expression. Finally, there is some developmental research that suggests that the fluctuation of mood in the parents leads to the inability of the child to regulate his or her own affect (Termine & Izard, 1988; Zahn-Waxler et al., 1988).

Depressed mothers are less effective in child rearing (Anthony & Ittleson, 1980; Cohler, Grunebaum, Weiss, Hartman, & Gallant, 1976; Hops et al., 1987), which, in turn, affects the social-emotional development of the child. Studies have found that depressed mothers are more withdrawn, have less interaction with their children, and demonstrate less affection (e.g., Weissman & Paykel, 1974). Depressed mothers also feel more resentment toward their children, are more critical of them, and, in general, emit more negative statements (Boswell & Murray, 1981; Hammen & Peters, 1978; Libet & Lewinsohn, 1973; Rubinstein & Timmins, 1981). Depressed mothers take longer to respond to their children, smile less, keep their heads down more, speak in monotonous tones, use less eye contact, and speak for shorter periods of time (Hammen et al., 1987; Libet & Lewinsohn, 1973; Rubinstein & Timmins, 1981). In terms of communication, depressed mothers less frequently use compromise and negotiation when resolving conflict with their children (Orvaschel et al., 1988). Instead, they rely on avoidance or hostility when disagreements occur with the child. They are more frequently off task, less able to stay focused on completion of a task, and emit fewer task-productive remarks, such as guidance, feedback, or praise (Hammen et al., 1987). In terms of expectations and discipline, depressed mothers have been shown to demand unquestioning obedience and to attempt rigid control over their children's behavior. Again, this may be related to the depressed mother's anxiety when faced with conflict.

Another factor related to child depression may be the level of family discord. Marriages in which one partner is depressed are typified by hostility and friction between the marriage partners and between the depressed parent and the children (Rubinstein & Timmins, 1981). Family conflict can directly influence depressive symptomatology in the child using Seligman's (1974) learned helplessness model, in which the child does not feel in control of a threatening situation. A family systems proponent may propose that the child engages in deviant behavior (e.g., depression) in an attempt to direct the focus of attention away from the family conflict and onto the child's symptomatology. Marital conflict can also indirectly influence child depression, as demonstrated in Figure 10.1; parental dispositions and marital adjustment can influence the parent-child interaction, which, in turn, can lead to child depression.

Finally, Anthony (1975) found that depressed parents have increased dependency needs, want to be taken care of (as opposed to meeting the needs of others), and make more demands of their children. He found that children of depressed parents often take the role of caretaker, and that this may lead to depression in the child.

In summary, research has demonstrated that parenting is influenced by parental depression. The mechanisms by which this may lead to child depression is not clear. However, some mechanisms that have been proposed or make conceptual sense from the developmental literature are as follows:

(1) A child may develop depressive symptomatology in order to focus the parents' attention away from a conflictual marital relationship, which the child perceives as very threatening. Subsequently, the parents must attend to the child's needs (Rubinstein & Timmins, 1981).

(2) The child's depression may result from identification with the parent. For example, the child may empathically respond to the parent's depression by becoming depressed in response to the parent's emotional state or in

response to environmental stimuli that normally elicit depression in the parent, such as a late night at the office.

(3) The child may be modeling or imitating the parent's depressive behavior. In this case, the child has learned how to handle moments of distress or conflict (when the child is most uncertain and most in need of a model) by looking to parental responses to stressful situations. These depressive child behaviors may then be reinforced by the parents. More specifically, a child's depressive behavior—such as helplessness, sadness, or self-disparagement—may result in parental attention and nurturance. This would be especially reinforcing if a depressed parent is usually withdrawn or inattentive.

(4) The low rate of positive reinforcement received by a child from a depressed parent may lead to depression in the child. Maternal depression can lead to reduction in the amount of positive reinforcement experienced by the child and to withdrawal from, less affection toward, and fewer positive reactions to the child, and less time spent in interaction with the child (Libet & Lewinsohn, 1973). For a young child, whose environment is dominated by parents, this can be even more overwhelming.

(5) Social isolation can occur in response to a parent's depression. The depressed parent may be less likely to take the child to activities or events after school, or to allow the child's friends to visit. Because younger children are dependent on their parents for socialization and involvement, socially isolated parents will have a child who is socially isolated. This isolation could further maintain child depression by not providing the child with other important role models who may handle stress in a nondepressive manner.

(6) Children may develop a depressive bias in terms of their cognitive attributions. Depressed parents tend to be more critical, rejecting, and hostile, and less reinforcing to the child. Consequently, the child may attribute negative outcomes or failure to him- or herself, and positive outcomes or success to external events (Abramson, Seligman, & Teasdale, 1978).

While this section has addressed the relationship between parental and child depression, it should be noted that parental depression can lead to other problematic child developmental outcomes. Zahn-Waxler et al. (1988) found that children with depressed parents have problems with relationship formation and social development, resulting in a lack of social skills and a sense of incompetence. Pound and Mills (1983) and Rickman, Stevenson, and Graham (1982) found that children whose parents are depressed demonstrate decreased cognitive performance compared to children whose parents are not depressed. One could hypothesize that poor cognitive performance leads to decreased self-esteem and a greater vulnerability to depression. Similarly, less involvement in social activities will lead to peer isolation, also contributing to the child's vulnerability to depression. To summarize, other developmental outcomes that may occur in response to parental depression, such as decreased cognitive performance or problems in developing relationships, will generalize outside of the home to the school and peers, affecting the child's relationship with others and influencing the child's view of self. This may lead to depressive behavior later in the child's development.

Other Parental Characteristics
Associated with Child Depression

Parental depression may facilitate child depression. However, there are parental characteristics other than depression that may lead to child and adolescent depression. These characteristics range from hostility and rejection to modeling ineffectual emotional regulation. The studies presented in this section identify depression in the child and contrast families of depressed children to families without a depressed child.

Several studies indicate that child and adolescent depression is likely to occur in unsupportive family environments. Although the mechanism by which an unsupportive family environment leads to child depression has not been delineated, unsupportive families may provide much less positive reinforcement, a factor associated with depression (e.g., Lewinsohn, 1974).

Lack of support, in general, has a direct relationship with depression (Huntley, 1988; Lin, Simeone, Ensel, & Kuo, 1979). Lack of support could occur through a specific event—such as moving to a new neighborhood, loss of contact with a family member, or changing schools—or through poor social skills, which may have the greatest impact on supportive relationships outside of the family, such as peers and school. Several studies have shown that a failure to develop good peer relations can lead to depression (Rutter, 1986; Lerner, Hertzog, Hooker, Hassibi, & Thomas, 1988). Rutter (1986) has proposed that failure to develop good peer relations eliminates a means of coping with stress and eliminates potential attachment figures, which can lead to a loss of self-esteem, to self-devaluation, and ultimately to depression in the child. Brugha et al. (1982) found that depressives spend less time in social interaction and have fewer friends.

In addition to an unsupportive family environment, depression is also more prevalent in families that are described as highly emotional, overreactive, critical, and rejecting (Cytryn & McKnew, 1980; Vaughan & Leff, 1976). Parents' deprecation and devaluation of the child could be internalized by the child, leading to low feelings of self-worth that predispose the child to depression. Similarly, the parent-child bond is important in the establishment of the child's sense of predictability and effectance. Children who do not develop this sense may experience what Seligman has identified as "learned helplessness." This, in turn, will facilitate depression.

Another precursor of depression is lack of autonomy. Wetzel and Redmond (1980) and Bemporad and Wilson (1978) found that depression was related to dependence in the individual and a failure to develop autonomy. Child depression is more frequent in overprotective and emotionally overinvolved families, and mothers of depressed children are less likely to grant autonomy (Asarnow, Ben-Meir, & Goldstein, 1987; Cytryn & McKnew, 1980; Garmezy, 1981). Taken together, these findings may suggest that child dependence fostered by overly protective families may increase vulnerability to depression. The mechanism by which dependence leads to depression has been demonstrated by the learned helplessness model (Seligman, 1974). Specifically, learned helplessness occurs when the child learns that he or she has no effect on the environment, and thus must rely on others perceived to be in control of that environment (e.g., parents). The relationship between dependency and depression has been observed in infants (Cicchetti & Schneider-Rosen, 1986).

Bandura (1977) and Garmezy (1981) have demonstrated that stringent or unattainable parental standards for a child's success may lead to depression in the child. Garmezy describes these mothers as being "neutral to successes but strongly negative to failure." These mothers also tend to use social comparison rather than individual norms for judging their children's achievements. Because of the parent's high standards, the child develops unrealistic goals for him- or herself. As a result, the child is more likely to administer low rates of self-reward and high rates of self-punishment, which may lead to depression. Along similar lines, Cole and Rehm (1986) found that parents of depressed children use less frequent reward and more frequent punishment than parents of nondepressed children. This failure to administer high rates of positive reinforcement while setting high standards is postulated to lead to depression in the child.

Cicchetti and Schneider-Rosen (1986) suggest that caregivers assume a large role in socializing affect. Masking and distortion of depression and sadness are typically learned during the second or third year. One hypothesis is that inhibition of an emotional response leads to the experience of that emotion as less intense. It may be that depressed children are not socialized to mask and distort, and thereby diminish the emotional experience of depressive affect. On the other hand, it has also been suggested that the child's inability to be aware of multiple emotions, even conflicting emotions, predisposes the child to depression (Cicchetti & Schneider-Rosen, 1986). More specifically, parents use of language referring to emotions (e.g., "I am sad when you get angry at me") facilitates the child's control over nonverbal emotional expressions (e.g., depression). Children, in assimilating their parents' emotional language and labeling affect, develop their own coping skills. Emotional language of a depressed parent may serve as a means of transmission of depression.

Theories relating poor parental skills and characteristics to child depression have been addressed. However, there is also a relationship between child depression and loss of a parent. It has been hypothesized by Brown and Harris (1978) that loss of a mother for a significant length of time in childhood, whether real or imaginary, leads to decreased self-esteem in the child, predisposing the child to depression. Loss may also lead to failure to mourn and inability to attach to a substitute, which have been hypothesized in the psychoanalytic literature as leading to depression.

This section has attempted to demonstrate some of the familial and extrafamilial factors that may predispose children and adolescents to depression. It has been demonstrated that the family context is critical to social and emotional development in children and adolescents, particularly in the instance of child depression. The family plays a role not only in the development of child depression, but also in the maintenance and alleviation of depressive symptomatology. The following section will discuss implications of prevention and intervention for child and adolescent disorders.

Implications

A conceptual model concerning the role of the family in the development of child psychopathology, with a special emphasis on antisocial behavior and depression, has been presented. Some aspects of this model have only tentative empirical support, but considerable progress has been made in delineating family processes associated with the development of socioemotional problems in children.

If we assume that this model is largely correct, there are several implications for social policy and efforts in prevention and clinical intervention. First, there are several sensitive periods in child development during which preventive and clinical interventions will have optimal effects. One period is around age 2 or 3, during which children are learning behavioral and emotional self-regulation. The successful attainment of self-regulation provides the base requisite to subsequent socialization tasks. A second period occurs during the first few years of school, during which the child is developing peer relationships, learning to work in an academic setting, and establishing a sense of self-competence. Unsuccessful negotiation of these tasks leads to peer rejection and school failure, both of which interfere with subsequent normative socialization opportunities and experiences. This exacerbates existing problems and complicates the development of effective remedial interventions. A third period occurs during the transition from grade school to middle or junior high school. During this time, the child becomes increasingly independent, is faced with increased stress and peer pressure, is undergoing rapid physical change, is establishing a more integrated self-identity, and is learning new roles. In the absence of adequate supervision, support, and guidance, the child is at risk for the development of socioemotional problems.

The second implication of the proposed model is that early intervention is the most effective. This is not simply a truism. It is based on evidence suggesting that existing problems, in the absence of corrective experiences, are exacerbated, amplified, and generalized to multiple environments. This progression is apparent in both "positive symptoms" (i.e., problematic behavior) and "negative symptoms" (i.e., skills deficits). Prevention and early intervention require the development of economical and reliable means to identify children who are at risk. Different tools, informants, and strategies will be needed to assess risk at different points in child development. It also requires the development and implementation of effective preventive interventions. Such interventions may focus on reducing the risk of child rearing by individuals (e.g., adolescents) who are physically, psychosocially, and economically unprepared for effective parenting. They may also focus on systematic education concerning child development and effective parenting as a part of high school curriculum or community education.

Third, the family is a central agent in the development of child psychopathology, and consequently should be a focal point of preventive and clinical interventions. This is particularly evident for preschool-age children, for whom the family is the primary socialization agent. We would also argue that family involvement is a critical ingredient in successful interventions for children during subsequent developmental periods as well. Even though the family is no longer the sole (or perhaps even primary) socialization agent, effective child-focused interventions in systems outside of the family require the active support, cooperation, and involvement of the family, particularly when addressing serious child problems. This is the result of the natural and socially prescribed role of the family as the pivotal agent in socializing the child and in managing the child's contacts with and commitments to other social systems. This does not preclude a role for school-, peer-, and community health-based interventions. However, the impact of interventions by these systems will be more powerful, generalizable, and lasting insofar as they engender the support and involvement of the child's family (e.g., Head Start; Scarr & Weinberg, 1986). If we are to develop effective multisystem (e.g., family and schools, family and peers) interventions successfully, research on the interactive effects of family and other systems on child development needs increased attention.

The fourth implication entails identifying targets of intervention by which social policy and programming can support the family system and foster optimal family functioning, and thereby promote the development of child competence. Referring back to the proposed model (see Figure 10.1), there appear to be two general family-oriented strategies. The first involves enhancing the general context in which the family system resides: vocational opportunities, economic assistance, adequate housing, and medical/nutritional assistance. These policies and programs are laudable, and arguably effective. However, enhancing the context in which the family resides does not ensure that parents are sufficiently skillful to promote optimal child development. Such enhancement enables but does not ensure good family functioning. These contextual supports must be complemented by experiences through which parents can acquire the specific skills needed to foster socio-emotional and cognitive competence of their children.

References

Abramson, L., Seligman, M., & Teasdale, J. (1978). Learned helplessness in humans: Critique and reformulation. *Journal of Abnormal Psychology, 87*, 49-74.

Alexander, J. F. (1973). Defensive and supportive communication in normal and deviant families. *Journal of Consulting and Clinical Psychology, 40*, 223-231.

Anthony, E. (1975). The influence of a manic-depressive environment on the developing child. In E. Anthony & T. Benedek (Eds.), *Depression and human existence*. Boston: Little, Brown.

Anthony, E., & Ittleson, B. (1980). *The effects of maternal depression on the infant*. Paper presented at the Third Annual Symposium on Infant Psychiatry, San Francisco.

Asarnow, J., Ben-Neil, S., & Goldstein, M. (1987). Family factors in childhood depressive and schizophrenia-spectrum disorders: A preliminary report. In K. Hahlweg & M. Goldstein (Eds.), *Understanding major mental disorder: The contribution of family interaction research*. New York: Family Process Press.

Bandura, A. (1977). *Social learning theory*. Englewood Cliffs, NJ: Prentice-Hall.

Belsky, J. (1984). The determinants of parenting: A process model. *Child Development, 55*, 83-96.

Bemporad, J., & Wilson, A. (1978). A developmental approach to depression in childhood and adolescence. *Journal of the American Academy of Psychoanalysis, 6*, 325-352.

Boswell, P., & Murray, E. (1981). Depression, schizophrenia, and social attraction. *Journal of Consulting and Clinical Psychology, 49*, 641-647.

Brown, G., & Harris, T. (1978). *Social origins of depression*. London: Tavistock.

Brugha, T., Conroy, R., Walsh, N., DeLaney, W., O'Hanlun, J., Donero, E., Hickey, N., & Bourke, G. (1982). Social networks, attachments and support in minor affective disorders: A replication. *British Journal of Psychiatry, 114*, 249-255.

Cairns, R. B. (1979). *Social development: The origins and plasticity of interchanges*. San Francisco: W. H. Freeman.

Caspi, A., Elder, G., & Bem, D. (1986). *Moving against the world: Life patterns of explosive children*. Unpublished manuscript.

Child, A., Murphy, C., & Rhyne, M. (1980, July/August). Depression in children: Reasons and risks. *Pediatric Nursing*, pp. 9-13.

Cicchetti, D., & Schneider-Rosen, K. (1986). An organizational approach to childhood depression. In M. Rutter, C. E. Izard, & P. B. Read (Eds.), *Depression in young people: Developmental and clinical perspectives*. New York: Guilford.

Cohler, B., Grunebaum, H., Weiss, J., Hartman, C., & Gallant, D. (1976). Child care attitudes and adaptation to the maternal role among mentally ill and well mothers. *American Journal of Orthopsychiatry, 46*, 123-133.

Cole, D., & Rehm, L. (1986). Family interaction patterns and childhood depression. *Journal of Abnormal Child Psychology, 14*, 297-314.

Compas, B. E. (in press). Stress and life events during childhood and adolescence. *Clinical Psychology Review*.

Cytryn, L., & McKnew, D. (1972). Proposed classification of childhood depression. *American Journal of Psychiatry, 129,* 149-155.

Cytryn, L., & McKnew, D. (1980). Affective disorders of childhood. In H. Kaplan, A. Friedman, & R. Sadock (Eds.), *Comprehensive textbook of psychiatry* (3rd ed.). Baltimore: Williams & Wilkins.

Cytryn, L., McKnew, D., Zahn-Waxler, C., & Gershon, E. (1986). Developmental issues in risk research: The offspring of affectively ill parents. In M. Rutter, C. E. Izard, & P. B. Read (Eds.), *Depression in young people: Developmental and clinical perspectives.* New York: Guilford.

Deuber, C. (1982, September). Depression in the school-aged child: Implications for primary care. *Nurse Practitioner,* pp. 26-30.

Dodge, K. A. (1983). Behavioral antecedents of peer social status. *Child Development, 54,* 1386-1399.

Elder, G., Caspi, A., & Van Nguyen, T. (1984). Resourceful and vulnerable children: Family influences in hard times. In R. Silbereisen & K. Eyferth (Eds.), *Development in context: Integrative perspective on youth development.* New York: Springer.

Elder, G. H., Liker, J. K., & Cross, C. E. (1983). Parent behavior in the Great Depression: Life course and intergenerational influences. In P. Baltes & O. Brim (Eds.), *Life span development and behavior* (Vol. 6, pp. 373-396). New York: Academic Press.

Emery, R. (1982). Interparental conflict and the children of discord and divorce. *Psychological Bulletin, 92,* 310-330.

Fard, K., Hudgens, R., & Welner, A. (1978). Undiagnosed psychiatric illness in adolescents: A prospective study and seven-year follow-up. *Archives of General Psychiatry, 35,* 279-282.

Forgatch, M. S., Patterson, G. R., & Skinner, M. L. (in press). A mediational model for the effect of divorce on antisocial behavior in boys. In E. M. Hetherington & J. D. Aresteh (Eds.), *Impact of divorce, single parenting, and step-parenting on children.*

Forehand, R., & Scarboro, M. E. (1975). An analysis of children's oppositional behavior. *Journal of Abnormal Child Psychology, 3,* 27-31.

Garmezy, N. (1981). The current status of research with children at risk for schizophrenia and other forms of psychopathology. In D. A. Regier & G. Allen (Eds.), *Risk factor research in the major mental disorders* (DHHS Publication No. ADM 81-1068). Washington, DC: Government Printing Office.

Grotevant, H. D., & Cooper, C. R. (1985). Patterns of interaction in family relationships and the development of identity formation in adolescence. *Child Development, 56,* 415-428.

Hammen, C., Gordon, D., Burge, D., Adrian, C., Jaenicke, C., & Hiroto, D. (1987). Communication patterns of mothers with affective disorders and their relationship to children's status and social functioning. In K. Hahlweg & M. Goldstein (Eds.), *Understanding major mental disorder: The contribution of family interaction research.* New York: Family Process Press.

Hammen, C., & Peters, S. (1978). Interpersonal consequences of depression: Responses to men and women enacting a depressed role. *Journal of Abnormal Psychology, 87,* 322-332.

Hartup, W. W. (1983). Peer relations. In E. M. Hetherington (Ed.), *Handbook of child psychology* (4th ed., Vol. 4, pp. 104-196). New York: John Wiley.

Hops, H., Biglan, A., Sherman, L., Arthur, J., Friedman, L., & Osteen, V. (1987). Home observations of family interactions of depressed women. *Journal of Consulting and Clinical Psychology, 55*, 341-346.

Hudgens, R. (1974). *Psychiatric disorders in adolescence.* Baltimore: Williams & Wilkins.

Huntley, D. (1988). *Depression and social support in adolescence.* Unpublished doctoral dissertation, University of Houston.

Kandel, D. B. (1978). Homophily, selection and socialization in adolescent friendships. *American Journal of Sociology, 84*, 427-436.

Kashani, J., & Simonds, J. (1979). The incidence of depression in children. *American Journal of Psychiatry, 136*, 1203-1205.

Kazdin, A. E. (1985). *Treatment of antisocial behavior in children and adolescents.* Homewood, IL: Dorsey.

Lee, C., & Bates, J. (1985). Mother-child interaction at age two years and perceived difficult temperament. *Child Development, 56*, 1314-1325.

Lerner, J., Hertzog, C., Hooker, K., Hassibi, M., & Thomas, A. (1988). A longitudinal study of negative emotional states and adjustment from early childhood through adolescence. *Child Development, 59*, 356-366.

Lewinsohn, P. (1974). A behavioral approach to depression. In R. M. Friedman & M. M. Katz (Eds.), *The psychology of depression: Contemporary theory and research.* New York: John Wiley.

Libet, J., & Lewinsohn, P. (1973). Concept of social skill with special reference to the behavior of depressed persons. *Journal of Consulting and Clinical Psychology, 40*, 304-312.

Lin, N., Simeone, R., Ensel, W., & Kuo, W. (1979). Social support, stressful life events, and illness: A model and an empirical test. *Journal of Health and Social Behavior, 20*, 108-119.

Loeber, R. (1982). The stability of antisocial and delinquent behavior: A review. *Child Development, 53*, 1431-1446.

Loeber, R., & Stouthamer-Loeber, M. (1987). Prediction. In H. C. Quay (Ed.), *Handbook of juvenile delinquency.* New York: John Wiley.

Lytton, H. (1980). *Parent-child interaction: The socialization process observed in twin and singleton families.* New York: Plenum.

Maccoby, E. E., & Martin, J. A. (1983). Socialization in the context of the family: Parent-child interaction. In E. M. Hetherington (Ed.), *Handbook of child psychology* (4th ed., Vol. 4, pp. 1-102). New York: John Wiley.

McCord, J. (1979). Some child rearing antecedents of criminal behavior in adult men. *Journal of Personality and Social Psychology, 19*, 1477-1486.

Orvaschel, H., Walsh-Allis, G., & Ye, W. (1988). Psychopathology in children of parents with recurrent depression. *Journal of Abnormal Child Psychology, 16*, 17-28.

Patterson, G. R. (1976). The aggressive child: Victim and architect of a coercive system. In L. A. Hamerlynck, L. C. Handy, & E. J. Mash (Eds.), *Behavior modification and families: Theory and research* (Vol. 1, pp. 267-316). New York: Brunner/Mazel.

Patterson, G. R. (1982). *Coercive family process.* Eugene, OR: Castilia.

Patterson, G. R. (1986). Performance models for antisocial boys. *American Psychologist, 41*, 432-444.

Patterson, G. R., & Bank. L. (in press). Some amplifying mechanisms for pathological processes in families. In M. Gunnar (Ed.), *Minnesota Symposium on Child Psychology.* Hillsdale, NJ: Lawrence Erlbaum.

Patterson, G. R., Chamberlain, P., & Reid, J. (1982). A comparative evaluation of parent training procedures. *Behavior Therapy, 13*, 638-650.

Patterson, G. R., & Dishion, T. J. (in press). Multilevel family process models: Traits, interaction and relationships. In R. A. Hinde & J. Stevenson-Hinde (Eds.), *Relations between relationships within families*. Oxford: Oxford University Press.

Pearce, J. (1978). The recognition of depressive disorder in children. *Journal of the Royal Society of Medicine, 71*, 494-500.

Pound, A., & Mills, M. (1983). *The impact of maternal depression on young children*. Paper presented at the Tavistock Centre Scientific Meeting.

Puig-Antich, J., Blau, S., Marx, N., Greenhill, L. L., & Chambers, W. (1978). Prepubertal major depressive disorder: A pilot study. *Journal of the American Academy of Child Psychiatry, 17*, 695-707.

Pulkkinen, L. (1983). Finland: The search for alternatives to aggression. In A. P. Goldstein & M. H. Segal (Eds.), *Aggression in global perspective* (pp. 104-144). New York: Pergamon.

Putallaz, M. (1987). Maternal behavior and children's sociometric status. *Child Development, 58*, 324-340.

Rickman, N., Stevenson, J., & Graham, P. (1982). *Preschool to school: A behavioral study*. London: Academic Press.

Rie, H. (1966). Depression in childhood. *Journal of the Academy of Child Psychiatry, 5*, 653-685.

Robins, L. N. (1981). Epidemiological approaches to natural history research: Antisocial disorders in children. *Journal of the American Academy of Child Psychiatry, 20*, 566-680.

Rubinstein, D., & Timmins, J. (1981). Depressive dyadic and triadic relationships. In G. Berenson & H. White (Eds.), *Annual review of family therapy* (Vol. 1). New York: Human Sciences Press.

Rutter, M. (1986). The developmental psychopathology of depression: Issues and perspectives. In M. Rutter, C. E. Izard, & P. B. Read (Eds.), *Depression in young people: Developmental and clinical perspectives*. New York: Guilford.

Rutter, M., Tizard, J., & Whitmore, K. (1981). *Education, health, and behavior*. Huntington, NY: Krieger.

Scarr, S., & McCartney, K. (1983). How people make their own environment: A theory of genotype-environment effects. *Child Development, 54*, 424-435.

Scarr, S., & Weinberg, R. A. (1986). The early childhood enterprise. *American Psychologist, 41*, 1140-1146.

Seligman, M. (1974). Depression and learned helplessness. In R. J. Friedman & M. M. Katz (Eds.), *The psychology of depression: Contemporary theory and research*. New York: Winston-Wilet.

Sigel, I. (1982). The relationship between parental distancing strategies and the child's cognitive behavior. In L. Laosa & I. Sigel (Eds.), *Families as learning environments for children* (pp. 83-102). New York: Plenum.

Snyder, J. J. (1977). A reinforcement analysis of interaction in problem and non-problem families. *Journal of Abnormal Psychology, 86*, 528-535.

Snyder, J. J. (1988). *Peer sociometric status: Social interactional antecedents and consequences*. Paper presented at the annual meeting of the Association for the Advancement of Behavior Therapy, New York.

Snyder, J. J., Dishion, T. J., & Patterson, G. R. (1986). Determinants and consequences of associating with deviant peers during preadolescence and adolescence. *Journal of Early Adolescence, 6*, 29-43.

Snyder, J. J., & Patterson, G. R. (1985). *Child compliance to parental commands: A social interaction analysis.* Unpublished manuscript, Wichita State University.

Snyder, J. J., & Patterson, G. R. (1986). The effects of consequences on patterns of social interaction: A quasi-experimental approach to reinforcement in the natural environment. *Child Development, 57*, 1257-1268.

Snyder, J. J., & Patterson, G. R. (1987). Family interaction and delinquent behavior. In H. C. Quay (Ed.), *Handbook of juvenile delinquency.* New York: John Wiley.

Termine, N., & Izard, C. (1988). Infants' responses to their mothers' expressions of joy and sadness. *Developmental Psychology, 24*, 223-229.

Tronick, E., Ricks, M., & Cohn, J. (1982). Maternal and infant affective exchange: Patterns of adaptation. In T. Field & A. Fogel (Eds.), *Emotion and early interaction.* Hillsdale, NJ: Lawrence Erlbaum.

Vaughn, C., & Leff, J. (1976). The influence of family and social factors on the course of psychiatric illness. *British Journal of Psychiatry, 129*, 125-137.

Wahler, R. G. (1980). The insular mother: Her problems in parent-child interaction. *Journal of Applied Behavior Analysis, 13*, 207-219.

Watson, R. S. (1979). Perception of contingency as a determinant of social responsiveness. In E. Thomas (Ed.), *Origins of infants' social responsiveness* (Vol. 1, pp. 33-64). New York: Halstead.

Weiner, A., Weiner, Z., & Fishman, R. (1979). Psychiatric adolescent inpatients: Eight- to ten-year follow-up. *Archives of General Psychiatry, 36*, 698-700.

Weissman, M., & Paykel, E. (1974). *The depressed woman: A study of social relationships.* Chicago: University of Chicago Press.

West, D. J., & Farrington, D. P. (1977). *The delinquent way of life.* London: Heinemann.

Wetzel, J., & Redmond, F. (1980). A person-environment study of depression. *Social Service Review, 54*, 363-375.

Wilson, H. (1980). Parental supervision: A neglected aspect of delinquency. *British Journal of Criminology, 20*, 203-235.

Wolfgang, M. R., Figlio, R. M., & Sellin, T. (1972). *Delinquency in a birth cohort.* Chicago: University of Chicago Press.

Zahn-Waxler, C., Mayfield, A., Radke-Yarrow, M., McKnew, D., Cytryn, L., & Davenport, U. (1988). A follow-up investigation of offspring of parents with bipolar disorder. *American Journal of Psychiatry, 145*(4), 506-509.

Zahn-Waxler, C., & Radke-Yarrow, M. (1982). The development of altruism: Alternative research strategies. In N. Eisenberg (Ed.), *Development of prosocial behavior.* New York: Academic Press.

PART III

Structural and Cultural Perspectives

11

Understanding African-American Teen Fathers

JOHN LEWIS McADOO

When many authors discuss fatherhood, they assume that a beginning father is in his 20s, has completed his education, is gainfully employed, and is married to the prospective mother of his child. However, when we discuss teen fatherhood, we usually associate it with problematic relationships that are out of cycle (Montemayer, 1986), at risk for lower educational and occupational attainment (Marsiglio, 1986), and in general represent a high level of stress (Elster & Hendricks, 1986).

The purpose of this chapter on unmarried and married African-American teenage fathers is to explore the literature from a modified social exchange theoretical perspective. Racial, educational, and economic barriers to these fathers' positive contribution to their families and communities will be explored, and some promising programs will be discussed that attempt to deal with negative economic, social, and psychological effects that may result from the fatherhood experience.

The assumption here is that the costs and rewards for becoming a father between the ages of 13 and 19 are similar for youths of all ethnic groups; however, for the African-American teenage father, the interactions among the values related to his African heritage, his castelike status (Ogbu, 1988), and the effects of long-term institutional racism may limit the range of choices and raise the social and economic costs.

Russell's (1980) review on the transition into parenting suggests that while studies on the process of becoming a first-time parent have noted substantially less crisis for African-American teens than for other groups, there is reason to believe that the severity of the crisis has been understated in the professional literature. She notes in her own and other studies that families with premarital conception, a state usually associated with high crisis scores, are less likely to return their questionnaires.

Research on African-American fatherhood has traditionally focused on the man's participation in the family, and the many roles associated with that participation. The following facts summarize the literature on the African-American father's role as a provider. Economically sufficient fathers provide for their families in much the same manner as fathers of other ethnic groups (Casenave, 1979; McAdoo, 1988; Price-Bonham & Skeen, 1979). African-American fathers perceive themselves as egalitarian in the family decision-making process (Dietrich, 1975; Hill, 1971; Lewis, 1975; Reuben, 1978; Staples, 1978; Tenhouten, 1970; Willie & Greenblatt, 1978). African-American fathers are more nurturing than restrictive in their interaction patterns with their children (McAdoo, 1988; Radin, 1972). However, very few studies have evaluated the effects of age differences at the time of assuming the father's role in the family.

Development theories lacking historical and cultural context are inadequate for understanding problems associated with becoming a father at an early age (Teti, Lamb, & Elster, 1987). Rather, I suggest that a choice and exchange model may provide us with a broader perspective in viewing the teen father in his many environmental perspectives. The review begins with a brief overview of the theory in terms of things that affect teen fathers: economic barriers, education, marital status, and paternal roles. After a discussion of these factors, a review is presented of some of the programs that have been initiated to prevent teen pregnancy and to provide educational and employment counseling for teenage fathers.

Background

Choice and exchange theory (Nye, 1979) provides us with a conceptual framework for understanding the context in which the African-American male chooses to become a biological father (Lamb & Elster, 1986) or a social father (Marsiglio, 1986, 1987). Further, this theory helps us to understand the consequences related to that choice within the urban experience. Choice and exchange theory leads us to believe that adolescents will choose to become fathers when other social rewards (i.e., jobs, higher education) are perceived as unavailable to them. Further, they will choose to become fathers or to participate in activities related to fathering when the rewards appear to be greater than the costs.

The theory assumes that, other rewards being equal, adolescent males are more likely to have intimate relationships with, marry, or form other relationships with equals rather than with those above or below them. Equity is seen as the sum of abilities, performances, characteristics, and statuses that determines one's desirability in the social marketplace (Nye, 1979).

For African-American adolescent fathers, there are societal-structural barriers that limit accessibility to the reward structure within the society. Employment and educational barriers may force them to choose financial and other rewards through crime, dropping out of school, and/or becoming involved in a peer culture that sees making babies as their major rewarding activity.

Economic Barriers

Sociological, psychological, and educational researchers pay very little attention to the historic impact of economic barriers in the African-American community. There seems to be little concern for evaluation in which one really controls for socioeconomic level. Many African-Americans are considered in the lower socioeconomic bracket along with many Whites or other ethnic groups. However, belonging to the same socioeconomic group in which African-Americans make 57% of the salary earned by White Americans in that group logically does not make African-Americans and Whites similar. One cannot say the groups are similar when a "glass ceiling" is placed on occupational attainment (Gibbs, 1988).

I have noted in earlier work that fathers who are economically sufficient in their role as provider are more nurturing in their interaction patterns (McAdoo, 1988). The problem for many African-American fathers is that there appears to be a glass ceiling on their earnings and their ability to move into higher levels of employment. A review of Bureau of Labor Statistics data for the years 1954-1984 found that unemployment rates for African-Americans aged 16 and over were twice the national average during that period (Wilson, 1987).

Joe (1987) has noted that we should use both the unemployment data and labor force participation data to measure the economic status of African-American men more accurately. His analysis of the 1985 census data reveals that 43% of all working-age Black men may be without jobs: 11% are unemployed, 19% are out of the labor force, 2% are in correctional institutions, and 11% are unaccounted for. He notes that for every man who is counted as unemployed, another two are out of the labor force.

Another key to economic status may be family income. Swinton (1988) notes that African-American families tend to be worse off than White families regardless of socioeconomic status. He found, for example, that the lowest fifth of African-American families averaged only 45% the income of the lowest fifth of White families. The second-lowest fifth of African-American families averaged 53% of the income of their White counterparts.

In sum, the African-American male suffers from an unemployment rate that has continued to be twice that of White males since 1954. For almost 35 years, his labor participation rate has fallen, while the labor participation rate of White males has remained the same. For those who are employed over the same period, working-class Black fathers' family income has remained at about half that of working-class White fathers. We can surmise that many teen fathers may have come from families characterized by chronic unemployment, underemployment, and lower wage scales.

Wilson's (1987) analysis of national labor force participation for African-American males ages 16 and 17 notes that their participation has dropped from 46% in 1960 to 27% in 1984. The rates for those ages 18 to 19 dropped from 71% to 47% during the same period. White teens' participation has remained rather stable, with slight increases in employment participation during the same periods. The rates for White teenage males in 1984 were 47% for 16-17-year-olds and 71% for 18-19-year-olds. Gibbs (1988) reports that the unemployment rate among African-American youth in 1987 was 34%, and in large metropolitan areas their unemployment rate has ranged between 40% and 50% during the past decade.

Similarly, Edelman (1985) reviewed national unemployment rates for 1982 and found that the rates were high for African-Americans who completed high school and those who dropped out. For those who completed high school, 58% were unemployed, 30% were not in the labor force, and only 29% had jobs. Of the Whites who graduated from high school, 67% were working. Of the African-American school drop-outs, 51% were in the labor force; only 15% of these were employed, and 71% were unemployed. The corresponding employment rate for Whites who had dropped out was 43%.

Sullivan has noted that massive structural and economic deterioration of the inner cities has resulted in fewer employment opportunities for ethnic minority males and is creating enormous problems (cited in Poinsett, 1988). The movement of many small businesses to the suburbs has decreased employment opportunities and left adults and adolescent teens to compete for low-paying jobs. Most of the new jobs are to be found in the suburbs, where African-American males are less likely to be hired, partly because they usually do not have the resources to get to the jobs—public transportation, if available at all, may not meet their needs. Wilson has reported that employers who are likely to hire inner-city residents rank African-American males at the bottom of the potential employment pool because they are perceived as threatening and dangerous, and therefore employers prefer not to take chances with them (cited in Poinsett, 1988).

We can see that when youths are blocked from gainful employment by a combination of personal, racial, and structural factors, they cannot develop the necessary work attitudes, habits, and skills that are appropriate and necessary in a competitive, highly technical society (Gibbs, 1988). Lack of available employment may be a major cause of African-American fathers' not seeking further educational training or a way to provide necessary financial support to their families or children. The glass ceiling and walls around available jobs may lead these males to become discouraged and to drop out of the job-seekers' market completely (Auletta, 1982; Gibbs, 1988). Blocked from gainful employment by racial barriers, these youths may turn to the illegal alternative economy of the urban community—that is, bartering in drugs, stolen goods, gambling, and prostitution (Clark, 1965; Gibbs, 1988; Glassgow, 1981).

Educational Barriers

A second structural barrier to satisfactory parenting relationships for young African-American fathers is education. The African-American community feels that education is the key to upward mobility. It has generally allowed the schools to miseducate children because of (a) the lack of needed political skills to force accountability on the educational system and (b) the lack of economic resources to provide the kinds of supports generally found in middle-income White communities. As a result, African-American adolescent males leave school with a less than adequate education, and many are poorly equipped to take advantage of a limited job market. Too often, Black males are blamed for the schools' failure, and unless they receive special help to develop occupational skills, many will never be totally economically self-sufficient.

Reed (1988) points to education as the key that unlocks the door to social, economic, and political mobility. He sees education as prerequisite to adolescent African-American males' self-fulfillment, employability, and participation in a rapidly growing information- and technology-based society. However, as Glassgow (1981) notes, the educational institution presents a fundamental paradox for African-American males. Education is held up as the ideal by the broader society and by the African-American community as the vehicle for upward mobility or movement into the mainstream. Yet these same adolescents' encounters with it result in destroyed aspirations and failure.

The American Council on Education (1988) has reported that the high school completion rate for 18- to 24-year-old African-American males has increased from 62% to 76%. Between 1970 and 1975, the percentages of Black high school graduates 24 years old or younger increased from 39% to 48%. However, between 1975 and 1985, the report continues, while the college participation rates for Whites rose to 55%, the rates for Blacks declined to 44%. The summary to this report indicates that both public schools and institutions of higher education tend to have lower expectations of African-American males and to react to them in a disproportionately punitive way, with frequent suspensions and expulsions. The report also provides support for the findings presented by other African-American researchers, who found that Black males were generally given lower grades and received less academic support than Black females and White students (Gary, 1981; Glassgow, 1981; Ogbu, 1988; Patton, 1981).

More often than not, the American Council on Education report continues, African-American males who experience learning problems in school are diagnosed as learning disabled, mentally retarded, or emotionally disturbed. Many of these males are placed out of the mainstream early in their educational careers, with little likelihood of return. This process increases the likelihood of their dropping out of school and being ill prepared for higher education.

Reed's (1988) analysis of U.S. Census Bureau data on education reaches the same conclusions as the Council on Education report and finds African-American males to be at risk for school failure. While graduation rates have improved, school completion rates for these males are lower than for other groups and their SAT scores are lower. African-American males are far more likely than Whites to be placed in general education and vocational high school curricular tracts than in academic tracts. Reed found them to be suspended more often and for longer periods than other ethnic groups. Those who do go to college tend to enroll in two-year colleges where the dropout rates are high and transfers to four-year colleges are low.

In a longitudinal study on high school completion of 12,686 adolescent African-American, Hispanic, and White teen fathers and nonfathers, Marsiglio (1986) found almost equally high graduation rates between African-American teen fathers (68%) and nonfathers (76%). While he was unable to present data on the married father who lives with the child, we may assume that these fathers are more likely to drop out and, when possible, pursue a G.E.D. The report was also not able to shed any light on the quality of the teen father-mother relationship or the quality of the teen parent-child relationship.

The educational environment for the African-American male does not differentiate by fertility status. As Gibbs (1988) observes, inner-city students are confronted with insurmountable barriers to learning and achievement in the schools, such as poorly trained teachers, low teacher expectations, ineffective administrators, and chronic violence. Many inner-city schools do not have the technical and other resources that are found in suburban schools and are not able to communicate effectively with parents or others in the community.

In summary, economic and educational factors present formidable barriers to the African-American male. The empirical literature that is available on the employment and education of African-American teen fathers provides us with very little information about how their needs in those areas differ from those of African-American teens who do not father children; both appear to be equally endangered (Gibbs, 1988). Teen fathers graduate high school at about the same rate, experience the same inferior education, and experience the same high unemployment and underemployment rates as their nonfather peers.

Marital Status

A few researchers have examined the marital status of African-American adolescents. Furstenberg (1981), in a longitudinal study of 350 African-American teen mothers, found in almost all instances that the father of the child remained active in providing emotional support and some financial support. Of those fathers, 64% married the teen mother by the time of the first follow-up, five years later. The adolescent fathers in this study tended to marry their children's mothers when they were financially able to provide for the children. Westney, Cole, and Munford (1986) note that 86% of the teen fathers in their study reported they planned to work to provide partial support for their children.

One longitudinal study of adolescent males found that those who choose to marry as adolescents had significantly more educational, financial, and occupational negative consequences compared with their peers who married as adults (Teti et al., 1987). The subjects were not able to recover these losses even after periods of 30 to 40 years. Both the African-American and White married teens in this study and others tended to have more marital disruptions and divorces than their peers (Burchinal, 1965; DeLissovoy, 1973).

The findings of these studies and others are consistent with choice and exchange theory (Nye, 1979), which suggests that the greater the economic resources, the more likely adolescent fathers of all ethnic backgrounds are to provide economic and emotional support for their children (McAdoo, 1988; Casenave, 1979). Bowman and Sanders (1988) and others suggest that rapid postindustrial displacement of unskilled jobs, with gender-specific academic problems in the public schools, places African-American fathers at alarming risk for chronic joblessness, provider role failure, familial estrangement, and high levels of personal distress (Farley & Allen, 1986; Wilson, 1987).

Parental Roles

Research has been unable to determine the degree to which age is related to the assumption of a paternal role in the family. Some authors claim that American fathers generally do not help around the house and others claim that fathers' participation in house and child care is increasing because of dual employment (Barnett & Baruch, 1988; Hoffman, 1983; Pleck, 1983).

African-American teen fathers provide some financial support for their offspring (Furstenberg, 1976; Lorenzi, Klearman, & Vogel, 1977). Lorenzi et al. found that 64% of unmarried teen fathers were supporting their children's mothers. The couples appeared to have reached an understanding about such support, because 81% of the mothers who expected some support received it.

There is little known about the relationship between the adolescent father and the mother of his child. As noted in one study (Westney et al., 1986), most of the studies conducted thus far have employed small nonprobability samples and their generalizability is limited. Hendricks and Montgomery (1983) report that most of the fathers in their study seemed to be unready for but accepting of fatherhood. The relationships between many of the teen couples seemed to be stable and close regardless of their marital status or living arrangements (Furstenberg, 1976; Westney et al., 1986). The adolescent males in one study reported that their relationships with the mothers of their children were ones of love (Hendricks & Montgomery, 1983).

In one study, a large number of the teen expectant fathers expressed an interest in continuing their relationships after their babies were born on the same emotional and social level as before the pregnancy (Westney et al., 1986). As noted earlier, the adolescent male is likely to provide close emotional support for the mother of his child even if he has no plans to marry (Furstenberg, 1976). Popular literature leads us to believe that teens are not responsible in the nurturing of their pregnant partners or their young. However, some scientific studies have cast some doubt on this view. Some adolescent fathers have been found to be equally as proficient as older fathers in caring for their partners and children, regardless of marital status.

Furstenberg (1976) has noted that emotional support given to his pregnant partner by the teen father is peculiarly important during adolescence in light of the high degree of social prejudice and interpersonal tension characterizing adolescent pregnancy and parenthood. For example, when tensions between the adolescent mother and her parents are high as a result of the changed relationship, the adolescent father sometimes can provide needed emotional support to reduce the tensions.

Even after their children's birth, many teen fathers are reportedly involved with the children's mothers on a regular basis. Almost half (46%) of the mothers in one study had either married the father after the birth of the child or were seeing him on a regular basis 26 months after the birth (Lorenzi et al., 1977). In his five-year Baltimore study, Furstenberg (1976) found that 20% of the fathers were married to the mothers of their infants, 20% visited the mothers and children on a regular basis, and another 20% visited occasionally. The study noted that two-thirds of the teen fathers reported spending time every day playing with their children.

One of the many myths concerning teen father-child interactions suggests that the interaction patterns may be immature because of the presumed immaturity or self-centeredness of the father. Lamb and Elster (1986) found no differences in patterns of father-child interactions as a result of age. Their study notes that mothers of all ages interact more with their infants than do fathers. Several studies have provided support for the notion that fathers are less likely than mothers to participate in infant care (Park & O'Leary, 1976; Park & Sawin, 1980) and child care (Kotelchuck, 1976).

Park, Power, and Fisher (1980), in reviewing the literature on adolescent parental involvement, note that the involvement in routine caretaking, emotional investment in the infant, and the stimulation level of paternal play are positively related to the male infant's attachment to his father. The quality and quantity of adolescent father-child interactions have also been found to be positively related to the child's cognitive development, lower level of behavioral problems, higher efficacy, trust, and self-esteem, but not delayed gratification (Furstenberg, 1976; Park et al., 1980).

Park and his colleagues also suggest that teen father-infant interactions occur more frequently through the structural characteristics of play, and this fosters the child's cognitive and social development. Unmarried fathers who visit their children regularly are probably more involved in play activities than in caregiving. While little empirical evidence exists in this area, it seems likely that adolescent males may be more ready to engage in and enjoy play. This play activity may have some effect on the child's development and on the development of the teen father.

Belsky, Gilstrap, and Rovine (1984), who studied the correlation of parent-infant and parent-parent interactions, suggest that the quality of father-infant interaction is significantly correlated with the quality of father-mother interaction patterns. It is suggested that teen fathers who nurture teen mothers and receive nurturing in turn are able to provide positive support for their infants' and young children's development. In earlier work, I have noted that positive ethnic identity and positive self-esteem in African-American preschool children may be the result of continuing nurturance of the mother by the father (McAdoo, 1988).

In summary, some evidence has been presented that many African-American teen fathers marry the mothers of their children. Some are able to provide nurturance to their children's mothers and their infants, and some are able to provide child care and other supports in the same manner as older fathers, and their children develop just as well. It should be recognized that some young men may do a good job in making the transition to parenting in spite of the social and economic costs of early fatherhood.

At the same time, it must be noted that other teen fathers have trouble in making that transition to parenthood. They may be, like some of their older counterparts, emotionally immature, affected by their economic circumstances, and vulnerable to peer pressure, and may have low self-esteem. They may lack the necessary parenting skills and the skills needed to seek and hold jobs, and they may experience academic difficulty. Parenting for these individuals may create more stress and strain and could lead to spouse or child abuse if they and their families do not receive some programmatic help. The final section of this chapter will discuss some of the programs that seek to help teen fathers. However, before turning to programs, I would like to make an observation.

We are led to believe that many African-American males, along with males of other racial and ethnic groups, do not face the same kind of negative educational, social, economic, and occupational consequences for parenting a child as do African-American teenage mothers. We are also led to believe that they do not experience the same psychological risks as the mothers of their children. There seems to be some question as to the proportion of teenage pregnancy that can be attributed to teen males. For the few teen fathers who choose to marry the mothers of their children, there are some indications of both personal and familial distress that may be related to educational and occupational disadvantages. A major weakness of the studies involving these teens is that researchers consistently view them as a monolithic group.

Programs

A few programs have been developed to address the needs of African-American teen males. However, many of the programs related to adolescent pregnancy are based on antiquated social casework models that seemed to punish rather than provide some real help to the adolescents involved, both males and females. The African-American male is an endangered species (Gibbs, 1988) because of his educational and economic circumstances. Becoming a father at an early age without occupational skills or educational background compounds the problem for many African-American adolescents. Programs are needed for these individuals that will tie educational and occupational training to real jobs with decent wages.

Mitch Snyder, a leading advocate for the homeless, has often remarked on television that many people living in shelters for the homeless are working every day, making $4.00 an hour. The reality for some adolescents and adults is that they cannot find affordable housing when they are making $4.00 an hour. If teen fatherhood programs are unable to shift from the antimale welfare bias and find their clients jobs that enable them to provide shelter and support for their families, they will continue to have high school dropout rates and low success rates. Some of these fathers as a result may fall victim to the urban drug culture, where they can earn significantly large amounts of money in a short period of time. Unfortunately, the life expectancy of those who fall prey may not be more than five years.

Dryfoos (1988) has reviewed several programs that attempt to promote sexual responsibility among younger males. Most of the programs attempt to promote prevention through the use of teen theater, sex education, condom distribution, male outreach, and family planning clinics. Most of the programs reviewed by Dryfoos did not provide us ethnic breakdowns concerning the provision of services. She notes that the National Urban League has become heavily involved in pregnancy prevention efforts through its 113 affiliate members. The impact of those programs has been difficult to evaluate.

In a telephone conversation with Mr. Furgeson of the Alexandria, Virginia, Urban League office in March 1989, I learned that his office has a contract with the local Boys' Club to educate African-American males about sexuality and to help change their attitudes regarding females. In addition, they help teens by providing them with in-house referrals for education, job training, and employment in the community. In the first year of the program, 60 boys received peer and group counseling.

The teen fatherhood project (Klinman, Sander, Rosen, & Longo, 1986) has evaluated seven demonstration projects across the country. The Family Service Agency of San Francisco has a project called the Teenage Pregnancy and Parenting Project. It is a school-based program, and African-Americans are 41% of the caseload. The project provides peer counseling, a caseworker, an employment counselor, public health nurses, and an outreach worker. Teen father counseling is offered once a month, and weekly peer discussion groups, couples counseling, a

well-baby program, vocational guidance, and some job placement services are also offered. The San Francisco project is the largest in the
network, serving 120 teen fathers a year. The fathers' outreach component of the YMCA of Dutchess County in Poughkeepsie, New York, is
the smallest in the collaboration, serving 15 teen fathers a year. Almost
half (46%) of the fathers in the program are African-Americans. The
services these young men receive are similar to those in other projects.

The teen fathers program at the medical college of Pennsylvania
Hospital has over 60% African-American males in its programs. The
fathers are recruited to take part in this program when they accompany
their female partners to clinic appointments. A counselor offers them a
range of services related to individual counseling as well as prenatal
counseling and classes.

Klinman et al. (1986) have noted several barriers to service delivery
encountered by all of the service providers in the collaboration project:

(1) lack of agencywide support of teen fathers as clients in their own right
(2) inadequate funding, which results in assigning low priority to male
    clients in the competition for scarce resources (money, space, equipment,
    staff time), and failure to sustain funding for innovative programs over
    time
(3) insufficient numbers of trained male service workers and a less than
    optimal match between the skills and attitudes of staff people and the
    particular characteristics of the male clients they serve
(4) failure to attract an adequate number of young fathers to the program
    through the use of the right combination of aggressive, streetwise out-
    reach strategies and individualized follow-up
(5) inability to retain reasonable numbers in the programs by failing to
    develop comprehensive programs related to these fathers' real-life needs

In regard to the last item in this list, Klinman et al. point out that young
fathers will not enter programs unless they provide job-related skills
and training. In addition, they will not stay in programs over time if
they are not helped with their personal, relationship-oriented problems.

The Klinman et al. report was an interim one and presented descriptive data on only 245 of the fathers from the different projects. No data
are given on the dropout rate or the rate at which clients are successfully
placed in gainful employment. Many of the descriptive data note that,
regardless of marital status, 89% of the teen fathers reported they
considered themselves and the mothers of their children to be intact

couples. Only 13% of the teens were married, and 82% of the men had known their partners for two or more years. Approximately 78% of the fathers saw their children every day and, similarly, most of the fathers-to-be (83%) said they planned to see their children on a regular basis. Just over half (55%) of the teen fathers and 40% of the expectant fathers said they were able to contribute financially to their children on a daily basis.

In summary, the few national and local programs that are able to reach African-American teen fathers and fathers of other ethnic groups are yet to be evaluated. It is reasonable to suspect that the results will be somewhat mixed. Those programs that are able to provide job training and support during the first few years on the job will be seen as successful. Those able to offer help in developing house, child, and spousal care skills may be also seen as successful in reducing stress and enhancing stable family relationships. Those programs that are unable to provide help in those two areas are more likely to be plagued with high dropout rates.

Programs that focus exclusively on prevention or contraception devices may need to reevaluate and expand their mission. Most teen fathers are aware of contraception devices thanks to television and movies that focus on plots related to that issue. What teen fathers seem to need most is some help in understanding and coping with relationship issues that come about as a result of their premature transition to parenthood. Many of the troubled teens' problems can be resolved through help in these areas and in finding gainful employment. If, in addition, the jobs provide economic sufficiency and longevity, many of the problems that trouble these youths would disappear.

Choice and exchange theory suggests that when African-American teen fathers are not able to overcome educational and economic barriers they are less likely to provide resources to the mothers of their children. The limited literature that is available indicates that when African-American teen fathers are able to overcome economic and educational barriers, they are, like other fathers, able to provide the social, emotional, and material support for the mothers of their children. Social programs need to help remove economic and educational barriers to traditional economic rewards so that African-American teen fathers can more fully participate in providing material and emotional support to their families.

References

American Council on Education, Commission on Minority Participation in Education and American Life. (1988). *One-third of a nation.* Washington, DC: Author.

Auletta, K. (1982). *The underclass.* New York: Random House.

Barnett, R. C., & Baruch, G. K. (1988). Correlates of fathers' participation in family work. In P. Bronstein & C. P. Cowan (Eds.), *Fatherhood today: Men's changing role in the family* (pp. 66-79). New York: John Wiley.

Belsky, J., Gilstrap, B., & Rovine, M. (1984). The Pennsylvania Infant and Family Development Project, I: Stability and change in mother-infant and father-infant in a family setting at one, three and nine months. *Child Development, 55,* 692-705.

Bowman, P. J., & Sanders, R. (1988). *Black fathers across the life cycle: Provider role strain and psychological well-being.* Paper presented at the 12th Empirical Conference on Black Psychology, Ann Arbor, MI.

Burchinal, L. G. (1965). Trends and prospects for young marriages in the United States. *Journal of Marriage and the Family, 27,* 243-254.

Casenave, N. (1979). Middle income Black fathers: An analysis of the provider role. *Family Coordinator, 28,* 583-593.

Clark, K. B. (1965). *Dark ghetto: Dilemmas of social power.* New York: Harper & Row.

DeLissovoy, V. (1973). High-school marriages: A longitudinal study. *Journal of Marriage and the Family, 35,* 245-255.

Dietrich, K. T. (1975). A reexamination of the Black matriarchy. *Journal of Marriage and the Family, 37,* 367-374.

Dryfoos, J. G. (1988). *Putting the boys in the picture: A review of programs to promote sexual responsibility among young males.* Santa Cruz, CA: Network Publications, ETR Associates.

Edelman, M. W. (1985). The sea is so wide and my boat is so small: Problems facing Black children today. In H. P. McAdoo & J. L. McAdoo (Eds.), *Black children: Social, educational and parenting environments* (pp. 72-85). Beverly Hills, CA: Sage.

Elster, A. B., & Hendricks, L. E. (1986). Stresses and coping strategies of adolescent fathers. In A. B. Elster & M. E. Lamb (Eds.), *Adolescent fatherhood* (pp. 55-67). Hillsdale, NJ: Lawrence Erlbaum.

Farley, R., & Allen, W. R. (1986). *The color line and the quality of American life.* New York: Russell Sage Foundation.

Furstenberg, F. F., Jr. (1976). *Unplanned parenthood.* New York: Free Press.

Furstenberg, F. F., Jr. (1980). Burdens and benefits of early childbearing on the family. *Journal of Social Issues, 36*(1), 64-87.

Furstenberg, F. F., Jr. (1981). The social consequences of teen parenthood. In F. F. Furstenberg, Jr., R. Lincoln, & J. Menken (Eds.), *Teen sexuality, pregnancy and childbearing* (pp. 184-210). Philadelphia: University of Pennsylvania Press.

Gary, L. E. (1981). A social profile. In L. E. Gary (Ed.), *Black men* (pp. 21-43). Beverly Hills, CA: Sage.

Gibbs, J. T. (1988). Young Black males in America: Endangered, embittered, and embattled. In J. T. Gibbs (Ed.), *Young, black, and male in America: An endangered species* (pp. 1-36). Dover, MA: Auburn House.

Glassgow, D. (1981). *The Black underclass.* New York: Vintage.

Hendricks, L. E. (1980). Unwed adolescent fathers: Problems they face and their source of social support. *Adolescence, 15,* 861-869.

Hendricks, L. E., & Montgomery, T. (1983). A limited population of unmarried adolescent fathers: A preliminary report of their views on fatherhood and the relationship with the mothers of their children. *Adolescence, 18*, 201-210.

Hill, R. (1971). *The strengths of Black families.* New York: Emerson-Hall.

Hoffman, L. W. (1983). Increased fathering: Effects on the mother. In M. E. Lamb & A. Sagi (Eds.), *Fatherhood and social policy.* Hillsdale, NJ: Lawrence Erlbaum.

Joe, T. (1987). The other side of female-headed families: The status of adult Black men. *Family Planning Perspectives, 19*, 74-76.

Klinman, D. G., Sander, J. L., Rosen, J. L., & Longo, K. R. (1986). The teen father collaboration: A demonstration and research model. In A. B. Elster & M. E. Lamb (Eds.), *Adolescent fatherhood* (pp. 155-170). Hillsdale, NJ: Lawrence Erlbaum.

Kotelchuck, M. (1976). The infant's relationship to the father: Experimental evidence. In M. E. Lamb (Ed.), *The role of the father in child development.* New York: John Wiley.

Lamb, M. E., & Elster, A. B. (1986). Parental behaviors of adolescent mothers and fathers. In A. B. Elster & M. E. Lamb (Eds.), *Adolescent fatherhood* (pp. 89-106). Hillsdale, NJ: Lawrence Erlbaum.

Lewis, D. K. (1975). The Black family: Socialization and sex role. *Phylon, 36*, 221-327.

Lorenzi, M. E., Klearman, L. V., & Vogel, J. F. (1977). School age parents: How permanent a relationship? *Adolescence, 12*, 13-22.

Marsiglio, W. (1986). Teenage fatherhood: High school completion and educational attainment. In A. B. Elster & M. E. Lamb (Eds.), *Adolescent fatherhood* (pp. 67-88). Hillsdale, NJ: Lawrence Erlbaum.

Marsiglio, W. (1987). Adolescent fathers in the United States: Their initial living arrangements, marital experiences and educational outcomes. *Family Planning Perspectives, 19*, 240-251.

McAdoo, J. L. (1988). Changing perspectives on the role of the Black father. In P. Bronstein & C. P. Cowan (Eds.), *Fatherhood today: Men's changing role in the family* (pp. 79-93). New York: John Wiley.

Montemayor, M. (1986). Boys as fathers: Coping with the dilemmas of adolescence. In A. B. Elster & M. E. Lamb (Eds.), *Adolescent fatherhood* (pp. 1-18). Hillsdale, NJ: Lawrence Erlbaum.

Nye, F. I. (1979). Choice and exchange theory. In W. R. Burr, R. Hill, F. I. Nye, & I. L. Reiss (Eds.), *Contemporary theories about the family* (pp. 1-42). New York: Free Press.

Ogbu, J. U. (1988). Black education: A cultural-ecological perspective. In H. P. McAdoo (Ed.), *Black families* (2nd ed., pp. 169-184). Newbury Park, CA: Sage.

Park, R. D., & O'Leary, S. E. (1976). Father-mother-infant interaction in the newborn period: Some findings, some observations and some unresolved issues. In K. Reigel & J. Meacham (Eds.), *The developing individual in a changing world: Vol. 2. Social environmental issues.* The Hague: Mouton.

Park, R. D., Power, T. G., & Fisher, T. (1980). The adolescent father's impact on the mother and child. *Journal of Social Issues, 36*(5), 88-106.

Park, R. D., & Sawin, D. B. (1980). The family in early infancy: Social interactional and attitudinal analysis. In F. A. Pederson (Ed.), *The father-infant relationship: Observational studies in the family setting.* New York: Praeger.

Patton, J. M. (1981). The Black male's struggle for an education. In L. E. Gary (Ed.), *Black men* (pp. 199-213). Beverly Hills, CA: Sage.

Pleck, J. H. (1983). Husband's paid work and family roles: Current research issues. In I. Lopata & J. H. Pleck (Eds.), *Research in the interweave of social roles: Vol. 3. Families and jobs*. Greenwich, CT: JAI.

Poinsett, A. (1988). *Young Black males in jeopardy: Risk factors and intervention strategies* (Conference Report). New York: Carnegie Corporation.

Price-Bonham, S., & Skeen, P. (1979). A comparison of Black and White fathers with implications for parents' education. *Family Coordinator, 28*(1), 53-59.

Radin, N. (1972). Father-child interaction and intellectual functioning of four year old boys. *Developmental Psychology, 6*, 353-361.

Reed, R. J. (1988). Education and achievement of young Black males. In J. T. Gibbs (Ed.), *Young, Black, and male in America: An endangered species* (pp. 37-93). Dover, MA: Auburn House.

Reuben, R. H. (1978). Matriarchal themes in Black literature: Implications for family life education. *Family Coordinator, 27*, 33-41.

Russell, C. S. (1980). Unscheduled parenthood: Transition to parent for the teenager. *Journal of Social Issues, 36*(1), 45-64.

Staples, R. (1978). The myth of the Black matriarchy. In D. Wilkerson & R. Taylor (Eds.), *The Black male in America*. Chicago: Nelson-Hall.

Sullivan, M. L. (1985). *Teen fathers in the inner city: An exploratory study*. Washington, DC: U.S. Department of Labor.

Sullivan, M. L. (1989). Absent fathers in the inner city. *Annals of the American Academy of Political and Social Science, 501*, 48-58.

Swinton, D. H. (1988). Economic status of Black Americans 1987. In J. Dewart (Ed.), *The state of Black America 1988* (pp. 129-153). New York: National Urban League.

Tenhouten, W. (1970). The Black family: Myth or reality. *Psychiatry, 2*, 145-173.

Teti, D. M., Lamb, M. E., & Elster, A. B. (1987). Long-range socioeconomic and marital consequences of adolescence marriage in three cohorts of adult males. *Journal of Marriage and the Family, 49*, 499-506.

Westney, I. E., Cole, O. J., & Munford, T. L. (1986). Adolescent unwed prospective fathers: Readiness for fatherhood and behavior toward the mother and the expected infant. *Adolescence, 21*, 901-911.

Willie, C. V., & Greenblatt, S. (1978). Four classic studies of power relationships in Black families: A review and look to the future. *Journal of Marriage and the Family, 40*(4), 691-696.

Wilson, W. J. (1987). *The truly disadvantaged: The inner-city the underclass, and public policy*. Chicago: University of Chicago Press.

12

Changing School Structures to Benefit High-Risk Youths

DENISE C. GOTTFREDSON

A variety of adolescent problem behaviors—drug and alcohol use, delinquent behavior, teenage pregnancy, dropout, and poor school performance—are related (Bachman, Green, & Wirtanen, 1971; Elliott & Voss, 1974; Jessor & Jessor, 1977; Thornberry, Moore, & Christenson, 1985), and they have common antecedents in early educational difficulties, including grade retention, poor school attendance and performance, and negative attitudes about school (Bachman, O'Malley, & Johnston, 1978; G. D. Gottfredson, 1981; Hirschi, 1969). These school-related correlates of adolescent problems converge with our theories about the sources of adolescent problem behavior to suggest the school as a potentially powerful place to intervene to reduce the risk of these problems (G. D. Gottfredson, 1981; Hawkins & Lishner, 1987).

In this chapter, I focus on the task of educating troubled or troubling youths who are at high risk for adolescent problem behaviors, including drug use, delinquency, and dropout. I present a model of the sources of these adolescent problem behaviors, draw implications from the model about the changes in schooling with potential for ameliorating adoles-

AUTHOR'S NOTE: This chapter is based on a paper presented at the National Center on Effective Secondary Schools Symposium on Structural Change in Secondary Education, Madison, Wisconsin, May 12, 1987. The research reported here was supported by a grant from the Office of Juvenile Justice and Delinquency Prevention to the Center for Social Organization of Schools at the Johns Hopkins University. I appreciate the editorial assistance of Gary D. Gottfredson, Lois Hybl, and Peter Leone.

cent problem behaviors, and assess the effectiveness of three school-based approaches to behavior change for high-risk youths.

A Model of Adolescent Problem Behavior

The Learning Process[1]

We learn by observing and imitating models, particularly models whom we perceive to be like ourselves. Once learned, behaviors are maintained when they are rewarded and extinguished when they are punished or when they fail to earn desired rewards. We often learn vicariously by observing the consequences of others' actions. Many behaviors are shaped through interaction with groups that provide models for behavior and that control the sources of reinforcement and punishment. The most important of these groups for adolescents are the peer group and the family, although teachers, school staff, and others may also be important.

Learning new behaviors depends not only on the kinds of behaviors modeled and reinforced in the present, but also on prior influences on the individual's pool of modelers and the attraction of the individual toward the model. The effectiveness of environmental consequences also depends on the individual's standards for self-reinforcement. Self-reinforcement occurs much more frequently than external rewards and is therefore a more powerful determinant of behavior. If an individual rewards him- or herself for deviant behaviors, the effectiveness of external rewards for conforming behaviors will be reduced.

This model of deviant behavior implies that restructuring the environment to control the available models and consequences for behaviors holds promise for modifying the behavior of high-risk youths, but that we must also take into consideration prior influences and developed personal characteristics that determine standards for self-reinforcement, the pool of potential models, and the likelihood that the individual will attend to the models.

Early schooling and family experiences influence later learning by shaping standards for self-evaluation and constraining values, interests, and associations. Parents and other adults reward children for meeting or exceeding their own standards for the children's behavior, and they punish children for falling short of those standards. Children exposed to low or conflicting standards for behavior are more inclined to reward themselves for lower levels of performance than are children exposed to models who consistently adhere to high standards of behavior (Bandura, Grusec, & Menlove, 1967).

Early family and school experiences that bond individuals to the social order are also essential to the development of prosocial behavior patterns. Social bonds hold deviant behavior in check by providing "stakes in conformity." Bonding gives an individual something to lose by indulging in impulses to engage in proscribed behaviors. One relevant element of the social bond is attachment to others. When we love or esteem another, we restrain impulses that would result in our losing the love or esteem of that person. A second element of the social bond is commitment. When we invest time and energy in the pursuit of a goal, we restrain our behavior for fear of losing our investment. Commitments to school, work, and family provide stakes in conformity.

Social bonding, then, restrains deviant behavior by increasing the cost of the deviant act. Bonding also reduces the likelihood of engaging in delinquent activities by constraining choice of associates. Individuals who are committed to conventional goals and attached to prosocial others choose not to associate with deviant individuals, reducing exposure to individuals who model deviant behaviors and techniques and who reward deviant behaviors.

Implications for Restructuring Schools

The model has implications for how schools should be structured. It implies that reward structures that provide clear expectations for behavior, apply frequent and consistent rewards for desired behaviors, and avoid rewards for undesirable behavior will reduce undesired behaviors. It also implies that providing prosocial models and grouping individuals to reduce the likelihood of association with deviant individuals will also reduce undesired behaviors.

But the model also suggests that manipulating the external reward structures and altering the pool of potential models is probably insufficient to alter established patterns of deviant behavior. Structures that promote bonding, commitment to education or work and attachments to others, and internalization of conventional standards for self-evaluation will be most effective for reducing deviant behavior in the long run.

It is more difficult to alter deviant behavior once patterns of association with delinquent peers have developed. Fortunately, schools can influence friendship choices by altering the pool of potential friends through deliberate groups in classes and extracurricular activities. Heterogeneous grouping in schools increases the probability of high-risk students choosing positive peers.[2] Classroom structures also affect friendship choices. The reward structure, level of participation in classroom activities, and cooperative nature of tasks all have been shown to influence friendship choices (Epstein, 1983; Hallinan & Tuma, 1978).

In addition to grouping and altering classroom activities to increase positive peer associations, efforts aimed at developing social bonds and decreasing social rejection are likely to increase positive peer associations during adolescence. Adolescents select friends on the basis of similarities in attitudes toward schoolwork, attitudes toward authority, involvement in conventional activities such as clubs and sports, and educational and occupational aspirations (Hallinan & Tuma, 1978). Early antisocial behavior, poor school performance, and poor socialization to prosocial norms increase the likelihood of rejection by prosocial peers, hence pushing the child into association with delinquent peers early in the schooling process (Patterson & Dishion, 1985).

Early interventions to increase social bonding might focus on increasing academic skills (especially for those children who have little support for academics at home), increasing rewarding experiences in school, strengthening attachments to teachers and other school staff, increasing opportunities for youths to become invested in conventional activities, and increasing social skills (especially among students who show early signs of inappropriate behavior).

These early measures to induce social bonding and provide the natural insulation of bonding have a higher potential payoff than do treatment strategies for youths already engaged in patterns of delinquent behavior. Elsewhere, my colleagues and I have documented the efficacy of delinquency prevention strategies that increase social bonding through structural change targeting the entire school population (D. C. Gottfredson, 1986c, 1987; D. C. Gottfredson & M. Cook, 1986b).

In the next section I examine alternative approaches schools can use to improve the behavior of youths who are already at high risk for engaging in problem behaviors. This examination is guided by the model described earlier, and it is intended to demonstrate that (a) restructuring the school and classroom environment is more likely to change the student experiences, behaviors, and attitudes necessary for reducing delinquent behavior than is providing more services to individuals; and (b) not all changes to the school or classroom structure are equal. Those targeted most directly at the experiences, attitudes, and behaviors most likely to reduce delinquent behavior will be most successful.

Three Attempts to Reduce Delinquency
Through Alternative Educational Experiences

This section summarizes the results of three school-based attempts to reduce delinquent behavior among high-risk youths. These examples are selected from 17 different programs that were part of the Delinquency Prevention Through Alternative Education Initiative funded by the Office of Juvenile Justice and Delinquency Prevention between 1980 and 1983 (see Office of Juvenile Justice and Delinquency Prevention, 1980).

A Pull-Out Program

Project PATHE (Positive Action Through Holistic Education; D. C. Gottfredson, 1983, 1986b, 1986c) was implemented in seven secondary schools in Charleston, South Carolina, between 1980 and 1983. It was a comprehensive school improvement program that simultaneously altered the organization and management structures in the seven schools and provided treatment for high-risk youths. The broad-based structural changes (changes in the discipline and management of the school, the testing practices, and the amount and kinds of activities available to staff and students) targeted the entire school population and were effective for increasing social bonding to the school and reducing disorder (D. C. Gottfredson, 1986c). Here I focus on the program component designed to reduce delinquency and increase learning for high-risk students.

The program for high-risk students called for diagnosis of student needs, prescription of services to meet those needs, and frequent monitoring of student progress. School system specialists carried out these activities with approximately 10% of the student population. The specialists were usually experienced teachers, but sometimes were assistant principals or guidance counselors.

The specialists were provided with historical information about each target student's school experiences. This information included standardized achievement test scores in detailed skill areas, school grades, and attendance and disciplinary records. Specialists met with each student, and sometimes with the student's parents and other teachers, before establishing behavioral objectives. Academic objectives, conduct objectives, or both were defined for each target student, and the specialists prescribed an individualized treatment program directed at those objectives. The programs most often called for regular counseling or tutoring sessions with the specialists during the school day, but they also involved target students in other school activities that were established as part of the larger prevention component. These other activities included peer counseling and "rap" sessions during which students were expected to discuss topics of concern in a constructive, prosocial environment, involvement in a student leadership team that involved students directly in planning for and implementing school change, field trips, and other extracurricular activities and clubs. In addition, specialists worked with the regular teachers of the target students to recommend teaching strategies that might help the students, and they referred students and their families to other community services when necessary.

The target students were closely monitored. Specialists recorded their attendance daily, and were immediately informed of any disciplinary incident involving a target student. The specialist called a target student's parents after three absences and met with the student and the student's parents following disciplinary incidents. Specialists also received each target student's grades and test scores throughout the project. Target students had an average of about two contacts per month with the specialists or some project activity. This average masks high involvement by some and low involvement by others.

The services provided were more intensive, systematic, and enduring than the services that typical schools are usually able to provide. The services were intended to increase attachments to the school specialists and commitment to school in the long run by increasing success experiences in school. But these services were provided as "add-on" services for students whose day-to-day existence in the school was unrewarding. The targeted students had a history of school failure, and had already developed patterns of association with other high-risk students and conceptions of themselves as not fitting into the required mold. The model described earlier would anticipate difficulty in altering the behavior of these high-risk youths with an intervention that did little to alter their day-to-day experiences in school.

The Alternative Class

Project STATUS (Student Training Through Urban Strategies) operated in one junior and one senior high school in Pasadena, California. The STATUS intervention for high-risk youths was an English and social studies class with a coordinated law-related education curriculum. The law-related curriculum and innovative teaching methods were expected to prepare delinquency-prone youths to become responsible, productive citizens. The philosophy behind law-related education is that the status of youth in our society isolates youths from meaningful and productive experiences with major social institutions. Isolating youths in a relatively sterile, book-learning environment cultivates low commitment to the educational process, alienation, low levels of belief in the validity of social rules and laws, and low self-esteem.

The alternative class was a year-long experience, involving five units. Each unit introduced youths to a different institution in American society. The first seventh-grade unit explored the school as an institution, and focused on the functions of school rules, decision-making processes in the school, rule enforcement, and students rights and responsibilities as school citizens. The second unit explored human nature and interpersonal relations. It focused on informal codes of conduct and how those codes are translated into more formal rules for behavior. The third unit examined the role of the family from personal, sociological, and legal perspectives. The fourth unit explored social contracts and their basis in the need for order in society, and the fifth unit covered the criminal justice system, including issues such as justice, fairness, and equity—it built on prior units to show how informal contracts and the need for order are expressed as laws in our society. The high school curriculum substituted units on the job market and life planning for the human nature and family units. The curriculum was intended to promote student understanding of society and its system of laws by showing students how they could function effectively within the law, clarifying students' attitudes, values, and perceptions regarding law and our legal system, and developing critical thinking abilities and problem-solving skills in students. This high-relevance curriculum was expected to increase the chance of academic success for the participants.

The methods used in the classes encouraged active participation. Field experiences included visits to a variety of organizations and agencies in the community, and guest speakers were frequently asked to speak to students on topics related to the curriculum. Structured role plays and simulations were common. Students were also expected to carry out research, both independently and in small groups, and to report the results of their work to the class. Teachers were trained to use heterogeneous student teams for tutoring and support, rewards for both individual and group progress, and individualized learning plans. The higher level of active participation of students in class activities was expected to increase the students' social competencies and communication and organizational skills. Through increased involvement in the school and community, youths were expected to see the school as an institution of legitimate authority and to believe that the institution's rules were fair.

The English and social studies classes were scheduled in a two-hour block to increase flexibility and coordination. The curriculum for the classes called for frequently combining the two classes to allow for activities (such as field trips and working with community volunteers) that required more than one hour. The English and social studies teachers worked as a team and used curriculum materials that coordinated activities for the two classes. When a particular theme was covered in social studies, the same theme was explored in the literature used in the English class.

The alternative class intervention is plausibly linked to delinquent behavior according to the model described earlier. It attempted to increase direct positive reinforcement for prosocial behavior and academic achievement, but it also attempted to increase social bonding and to alter peer influence. Helping students understand and accept law should have resulted in increased self-monitoring and accordance with the newly accepted higher standards for behavior. Students were also expected to gain a deeper appreciation for the function of school in our society and were expected to become more involved in school as a result of accepting their roles as school citizens. They also were expected to become more committed to school as their own success experiences increased and as they began to see themselves as successful, productive individuals.

The class also altered the pattern of associations. Youths were placed in classes with other delinquency-prone youths. This aspect of the class had the potential to increase delinquency by increasing negative associations. However, as we will see, the high degree of structure and the emphasis on prosocial behavior and attitudes resulted in altering the nature of the peer associations.

The Alternative School

The Academy for Community Education (ACE) was a small alternative school providing services to youths at high risk for delinquent behavior drawn from the Miami public schools. The program combined intensive basic skills training with community-based apprenticeship opportunities and a token economy system to provide incentives for appropriate behavior and academic achievement. The program was planned to increase students' commitment to education, academic achievement, persistence in school, and (eventually) their involvement in postsecondary training, education, and employment.

The academic component differed for students judged academically sufficient and those judged academically deficient. The Dade County Public School curriculum was used, but the approximately 50% of the students judged academically deficient received double the amount of basic skills instruction and were tutored individually at least one hour per week. Team teaching was used to facilitate homogeneous grouping for English instruction, and a standardized tutoring program was used for reading. Instruction was individualized. Teachers prepared lessons to cover the same content at different skill levels, and they prepared individual lesson plans for each student or small groups of students at each level.

The professional/vocational (PV) component was intended to expose students to various occupations so that they would become aware of the kinds of skills and training required, the work settings, employment opportunities, and financial benefits of different careers. The first few weeks of the course were spent in orientation, written and group self-awareness exercises, individual and group leadership development and employability skill exercises, and vocational assessment activities. The last activities were used to help students identify their potential vocational strengths and interests to help them choose a mini-apprenticeship.

Students in the PV component spent three periods a day, four days a week, in their field placement. They received three elective credits per semester for successful participation in PV in lieu of the usual elective credits they might take in ninth and tenth grades.

The PV placement worked as follows: Once a site in the student's area of interest agreed to provide a mini-apprenticeship, the student was taken to the site by an Academy staff person. A contract spelling out the commitments of both the student and the supervising employee was read, completed, and signed by four parties—the student, the PV coordinator, the supervising employee, and a parent. The supervising employee promised to familiarize the student with the job's responsibilities and the training and preparation needed to perform the job and to provide hands-on experience. The student agreed to be on time and to complete all assignments to the best of his or her ability. The student maintained a journal that included information about what he or she did, what skills he or she learned, and reflections on the experience.

Placements generally lasted at least six weeks, but they could extend to an entire year. At the end of a placement, both the student and the supervising employee completed evaluation forms. Periodic site visits were also made by ACE staff to each place, and a report was completed by the visitor.

ACE employed a token economy. Students earned points for appropriate dress and grooming, punctuality, helpfulness and cooperation during homeroom and lunch, homework completion, on-task behavior (spending time and effort working directly on academic assignments), and academic progress. The system also provided for point reductions for infractions and bonus points for extra effort. Classroom and homeroom teachers recorded points for each student each day in each period and totaled them weekly. Each Friday, students could exchange their points for material goods or accumulate points for a subsequent Friday. The menu of tangible items for which students could exchange their points was developed and modified through student suggestions.

The ACE intervention was partially consistent with the model of delinquent behavior described earlier. The token economy was based on the social learning principles of external reinforcement, particularly in its emphasis on clarity and consistency of rewards and punishments so that the student is better able to organize the environmental contingencies cognitively to enhance his or her ability to manipulate the environment to gain desired rewards. The ACE intervention was also clearly aimed at increasing commitment to education and work. Academic material was individualized and clearly tied to the world of work. Students who were not yet eligible for the prestigious PV component understood that they had to master basic skills to earn an apprenticeship. And students in the PV component were expected to learn those skills that were essential to obtain a job and perform well in it.

Methods

Evaluation Designs

A true experiment was used to evaluate the Charleston direct service pull-out components, and nonequivalent control group designs were used to evaluate the Pasadena alternative class and Miami alternative school programs.

For the Charleston experiment, a pool of high-risk students developed through teacher referrals and examination of academic and behavior records was randomly assigned to treatment and control conditions by researchers. Postrandomization checks indicated that the randomization resulted in equivalent treatment and control groups (see D. C. Gottfredson, 1986b, for details of the experimental design).

Random assignment was also attempted in each of the two Pasadena schools. Pools of students eligible for the options class were developed through school staff and self-nominations. Researchers randomly assigned students to the experimental conditions, but scheduling difficulties prevented randomization from being fully implemented. Nonequivalent treatment and control groups resulted: Postrandomization checks showed that the resulting treatment and control groups were slightly nonequivalent. D. C. Gottfredson and Cook (1986a) describe the experimental design in more detail and show results of postrandomization checks.

The Miami evaluation involved a nonequivalent control group design. ACE staff attempted to construct an equivalent control group by following a recruitment and screening procedure for selecting control group members similar to that used for treatment students. This process resulted in nonequivalent groups. Although the treatment and control groups were equivalent on age, gender, percentage Black, grade, socioeconomic status, and prior measures of suspensions, tardiness, absenteeism, and contact with the court, they differed significantly on Percentage White and Hispanic (D. C. Gottfredson, 1986a). Known nonequivalencies between the treatment and control groups were statistically controlled in outcome analyses for the Miami and Pasadena evaluations.

Treatment and control students in the true programs were assessed each spring with a standard survey to measure delinquent behavior and several relevant risk factors. Most measures are discussed in G. D. Gottfredson (1985). The program evaluations report the effects of each program on the entire range of outcomes. Only measures of the constructs included in the model of deviant behavior outlined earlier are discussed here. Measures from school and justice system records augment the self-reports. These are not parallel across projects.

The Appendix to this chapter describes each of the measures used, gives sample items, and reports the alpha reliability coefficients for each scale in a norming sample used to construct the scales (G. D. Gottfredson, 1985). Briefly, deviant behavior is measured by student self-reports of serious delinquent behavior and drug involvement and by counts of court contacts and school suspensions. The causes of delinquent behavior implied by the model described earlier are measured by student self-reports of negative peer influence and their reports of the rewards and punishments they experience in school. Also included as measures of success experiences in school are grades, promotion, and graduation. Standards for self-evaluation are measured by student self-reports of their belief in laws and their perceptions of themselves as law-abiding citizens. Attachment is measured by student self-reports of liking for teachers and others in the school and caring about the opinions of others in the school. Commitment to school is measured by school attendance and expectations to continue schooling.

Results

The comparisons of outcome measures for treatment and control groups in the three projects are shown in Tables 12.1 through 12.4. The tables show means and standard deviations for the two groups as well as effect sizes for the comparisons between treatment and control groups. Effect sizes are calculated by dividing the difference between the means for the two groups by the standard deviation for the control group. Analysis of variance was used for Charleston treatment and control group comparisons, and analysis of covariance was used for treatment and control group comparisons for the other two projects. Analyses of covariance controlled for each pretreatment measure for which significant treatment and control group differences were found. The specific covariates used in each analysis are noted in the tables.

Charleston: A Pull-Out Program

Table 12.1 shows the means and standard deviations for the Charleston treatment and control groups. Asterisks indicate that a significant treatment-control difference was found when the data for all schools were pooled. Treatment × school interactions are noted with superscripted as on the table. (Individual school results can be found in D. C. Gottfredson, 1986b.)

The table shows that the treatment had little measurable effect on delinquent behavior. The significant difference favoring the control group on drug involvement is entirely attributable to one high school in which the program was not well implemented and in which the treatment had a general negative effect.

The treatment did not alter negative peer influence, but treatment students experienced slightly more academic success than did the control students. Treatment students were promoted to the next grade at a higher rate at the end of the 1981-1982 school year. Treatment students also received significantly higher grades during the 1981-1982 school year (D. C. Gottfredson, 1986b). In the high school that implemented the program in the strongest form, treatment group seniors graduated at a higher rate than did control group members. These treatment student advantages in traditional school rewards were not accompanied by increases in reports of school as a rewarding place.

The effect of the program on the measures of social bonding differed by school. In general, the program did not increase attachment to school or belief in rules, and it did not alter the treatment students' self-concepts. In some schools the treatment appears to have increased time spent in school and in one school it reduced it.

In summary, the Charleston treatment had a small but generally positive effect on academic outcomes. Attachment to school, belief in rules, and self-concept were not affected by the program. The program did not reduce delinquent behavior, at least not in the short run.

Pasadena: The Alternative Class

Table 12.2 shows the treatment and control group comparisons for the alternative classes in the junior high school, and Table 12.3 shows the results for the senior high school. The tests of significance are from analyses of covariance using as covariates age for the junior high and race and gender for the senior high samples. The effect sizes were computed using unadjusted means. Effect sizes were also computed on

Table 12.1. Means and Standard Deviations for Treatment and Control Students on PATHE Program Outcomes (Pull-Out Program)

Outcome Measure	Treatment			Control			Effect Size
	M	SD	N	M	SD	N	
Delinquent Behavior							
Self-Reported Serious Delinquency	.07	.14	296	.07	.15	249	.00
Self-Reported Drug Involvement	.25*[a]	.30	301	.19	.26	253	.23
Number of Court Contacts	.02	.14	468	.02	.17	401	.00
Number of Suspensions	.18	.44	464	.17	.49	393	.02
Number of Expulsions	.01	.14	464	.03	.26	393	−.08
Number of Disciplinary Infractions	.28[a]	.53	464	.39	.80	393	−.14
Delinquent Associates							
Negative Peer Influence	.21	.20	329	.20	.19	291	.05
School Success/Failure Experiences							
Percent Seniors Graduated	.76**[a]	.43	41	.42	.50	31	.68
Self-Reported Grades	2.36[a]	.64	358	2.30	.67	306	.09
Average Grade, spring 1983	69.50	6.90	382	69.30	7.06	340	.03
Percent Promoted to Next Grade 1981-82	.77*	.42	410	.70	.46	352	.15
Percent Promoted to Next Grade 1982-83	.63	.48	309	.61	.49	273	.04
School Rewards	.28	.31	315	.27	.28	275	.04
School Punishments	.27	.27	314	.26	.27	275	.04
Stakes in Conformity							
Belief in Rules	.67	.23	278	.67	.24	240	.00
Positive Self-Concept	.77	.17	275	.76	.17	224	.06
Attachment to School	.70	.24	314	.72	.22	267	−.09
Percent Withdrew from School	.16[a]	.37	463	.13	.34	394	.09
Nonattendance	.34[a]	.39	351	.36	.41	303	−.05
Percent Days Absent (unexcused)	.05	.05	396	.05	.05	335	.00
Educational Expectations	2.38	1.64	346	2.41	1.63	303	−.02
Percent Outcomes Favoring Treatment Students	.45						

NOTE: Effect sizes indicate the ratio of the difference between the treatment and control means to the standard deviation for the control group.
a. Statistically significant school-by-treatment interaction was observed for the outcome
*F-statistic from analysis of covariance is significant at the $p < .05$ level.
**F-statistic from analysis of covariance is significant at the $p < .01$ level.

the means adjusted for differences on the covariates, but the adjustment made no substantive difference in the interpretation of the table. They are not reported here.

Table 12.2. Means and Standard Deviations for Treatment and Control Students on Options Program Outcomes—Junior High School (alternative class program)

Outcome Measure	Treatment			Control			Effect Size
	M	SD	N	M	SD	N	
Delinquent Behavior							
Self-Reported Serious Delinquency	.07	.10	42	.13	.18	48	−.33
Self-Reported Drug Involvement	.11*	.20	43	.21	.24	50	−.42
Number of Court Contacts	.02	.13	56	.04	.27	67	−.07
Percent Suspended	.02	.13	56	.00	.00	67	—
Percent Expelled	.00	.00	56	.03	.17	67	−.18
Delinquent Associates							
Negative Peer Influence	.16**	.16	47	.26	.19	56	.53
School Success/Failure Experiences							
Self-Reported Grades	2.62*	.68	47	2.33	.69	57	.42
Grade Point Average	2.32**	.77	52	2.00	.71	61	.45
School Rewards	.25	.28	46	.23	.24	54	.08
School Punishments	.19**	.26	46	.42	.28	54	−.82
Stakes in Conformity							
Belief in Rules	.65	.22	45	.66	.25	45	−.04
Positive Self-Concept	.76	.17	41	.74	.21	40	.10
Attachment to School	.70*	.22	45	.61	.19	53	.47
Months on Roll	9.04	2.56	56	9.54	1.56	67	−.32
Percent Withdrew from School	.16	.37	56	.10	.31	67	.19
Nonattendance	.21	.34	47	.26	.35	57	−.14
Educational Expectations	3.66	1.48	47	4.02	1.33	56	−.27
Percent Outcomes Favoring Treatment Students	.70						

NOTE: Effect sizes indicate the ratio of the difference between the treatment and control means to the standard deviation for the control group. Analyses of covariance control on age
*F-statistic from analysis of covariance is significant at the $p < .05$ level.
**F-statistic from analysis of covariance is significant at the $p < .01$ level.

The treatment students scored lower on the measures of delinquency than did the control students, and this was true for students in both schools. The self-reports are significantly lower for treatment students, and the court contact measures show lower rates of contact with the court, although the difference is not statistically significant.

The program reduced negative peer influence for both schools and resulted in greater academic success among treatment students. In both

Table 12.3. Means and Standard Deviations for Treatment and Control Students on Options Program Outcomes—Senior High School (alternative class program)

Outcome Measure	Treatment			Control			Effect Size
	M	SD	N	M	SD	N	
Delinquent Behavior							
Self-Reported Serious Delinquency	.02*	.05	44	.07	.12	32	−.42
Self-Reported Drug Involvement	.12*	.19	45	.21	.26	34	−.35
Number of Court Contacts	.05	.28	64	.14	.49	55	−.18
Percent Suspended	.03	.18	64	.02	.13	60	.08
Percent Expelled	.06	.24	64	.08	.28	60	−.07
Delinquent Associates							
Negative Peer Influence	.08*	.09	49	.15	.15	34	.47
School Success/Failure Experiences							
Self-Reported Grades	2.88**	.69	50	2.36	.72	36	.72
Grade Point Average	2.65**	.70	56	2.04	.66	44	.92
School Rewards	.25**	.29	45	.10	.14	34	1.07
School Punishments	.08*	.18	46	.20	.25	34	−.48
Stakes in Conformity							
Belief in Rules	.73	.19	33	.78	.20	37	−.25
Positive Self-Concept	.84**	.14	42	.72	.16	31	.75
Attachment to School	.84**	.16	42	.71	.23	33	.56
Months on Roll	9.42*	1.48	64	8.05	3.45	60	.40
Percent Withdrew from School	.16	.37	64	.27	.44	60	−.25
Nonattendance	.15	.31	49	.29	.37	36	−.38
Classes Missed	41.12	38.91	56	58.54	45.82	44	−.38
Educational Expectations	4.32	1.35	50	3.78	1.48	36	.36
Percent Outcomes Favoring							
Treatment Students	.89						

NOTE: Effect sizes indicate the ratio of the difference between the treatment and control means to the standard deviation for the control group. Analyses of covariance control on race and gender.
*F-statistic from analysis of variance is significant at the $p < .05$ level.
**F-statistic from analysis of variance is significant at the $p < .01$ level.

schools, alternative class students reported receiving higher grades, and the school records supported their reports. The treatment students also perceived school to be less punishing and more rewarding than did the control students.

The measures of social bonding show that the alternative class was effective at increasing social bonding. The effect was larger in the high school. Every measure of social bonding except belief favored the treatment students. When statistical controls were applied, the high school treatment students remained significantly more attached to school and had more positive self-concepts. They also persisted in school longer. The junior high school treatment students also were significantly more attached to school. No other bonding measures suggested an advantage for treatment students.

In summary, the alternative class program was a successful treatment for reducing delinquent behavior. The positive effect appears to have resulted from an increase in attachment to school, a change in the balance of peer influence, and an increase in success experiences at school.

Miami: The Alternative School

Table 12.4 shows the comparisons of treatment and control students from the Miami project. As for the Pasadena analysis, known non-equivalencies were controlled using analysis of covariance. Race is used as a covariate for all analyses. For measures taken from school and court records, the same measure covering the year prior to treatment (1980-1981) was usually used as an additional covariate. When such a measure was unavailable, another measure from the pretreatment year that was correlated with the outcome was used instead.

The ACE treatment appears to have *increased* delinquent behavior. Treatment students scored higher than controls on self-reported as well as official measures of delinquent behavior, and the difference on self-reports reached conventional statistical significance levels when controls were applied. No significant differences were observed among the measures of the learning variables, but ACE students received slightly more credits for their time spent in school, and they reported school to be somewhat more rewarding than did the control students.

The social bonding measures suggest that ACE decreased social bonding. The treatment group attended school more often (nonsignificant), but the control group scored higher on all other measures of bonding. The ACE treatment students reported significantly lower attachment to school than did members of the comparison group.

Conclusions and Implications

The Charleston pull-out counseling and tutoring program for high-risk youths, which was designed to increase high-risk youths' social

Table 12.4. Means and Standard Deviations for Treatment and Control Students on ACE Program Outcomes (alternative school program)

Outcome Measure	Treatment			Control			Effect Size
	M	SD	N	M	SD	N	
Delinquent Behavior							
Self-Reported Serious Delinquency	.15*	.21	79	.09	.15	17	.40
Self-Reported Drug Involvement	.48	.37	81	.40	.37	18	.22
Number of Court Contacts	.16[a]	.60	109	.12	.32	26	.12
Number of Suspensions	.44[ac]	.93	85	.10	.44	21	.77
Delinquent Associates							
Negative Peer Influence	.28	.19	86	.32	.24	29	−.17
School Success/Failure Experiences							
Credits Earned, 1982-83	9.67[bc]	3.66	86	8.81	3.50	21	.24
School Rewards	.37	.32	87	.15	.18	22	1.22
School Punishments	.32	.27	87	.33	.26	22	.04
Stakes in Conformity							
Belief in Rules	.65	.24	82	.74	.18	20	−.50
Positive Self-Concept	.70	.18	80	.76	.18	19	−.33
Attachment to School	.61*	.26	86	.72	.25	21	−.44
Days Enrolled in School, 1982-83	256.68[b]	73.10	109	262.62	62.56	26	−.09
Nonattendance	.45	.43	85	.61	.41	22	−.39
Number of Days Absent, 1982-83	19.21[ac]	18.01	86	25.62	24.62	21	−.26
Educational Expectations	3.17	1.82	88	3.41	1.82	22	−.13
Percent Outcomes Favoring							
Treatment Students	.40						

NOTE: Effect sizes indicate the ratio of the difference between the treatment and control means to the standard deviation for the control group. Covariates used in analyses of covariance are different for different comparisons. Race is always controlled. Notes a and b indicate which additional covariates were used.
a. Pretreatment measure of outcome for 1980-1981 school year is statistically controlled.
b. Absences during 1980-1981 school year are statistically controlled.
c. Only students enrolled in school at the end of the 1982-1983 school year are included in this analysis.
*F-statistic from analysis of covariance is significant at the $p < .05$ level.

bonding and success experiences in school, was ineffective for reducing delinquency. The program did not succeed at increasing social bonding, and the slight improvement on measures of school success was not sufficient to decrease delinquent behavior.

The model presented earlier helps to explain why. The kinds of behaviors modeled and the reinforcements experienced—most of which are self-imposed—affect behavior most directly. The pull-out intervention did not succeed at altering the self-concepts of the youths or their evaluation of the validity of rules and laws, either of which would indicate a change in the nature of the self-monitoring function. The program also failed to alter the level of negative peer influence. Although the program may have provided a positive adult model via the PATHE specialist, the most critical source of influence—peers—was not altered. The evaluation provides no evidence that the youths grew more attached to anyone in the school. In short, although the students who participated in the program were rewarded for academic accomplishments, these rewards were infrequent (promotion occurs only once a year, and report card grades only once per quarter) and are probably impotent compared to the rewards available through delinquent peer associations. At best, the increased achievement may have served to increase commitment to school somewhat.

The impression one gets from the Charleston direct service program is one of providing too little too late for the high-risk youths it served. Could a program resembling PATHE but strengthened considerably to provide for more tutoring and counseling contacts with the adult specialists be expected to alter the behavior of high-risk youths? This is an empirical question, but the level of resources required to upgrade the intensity of the services is likely to render the design infeasible.

A program model that integrates the extra support services to high-risks youths into the existing school structure would be more feasible. Rather than assigning a caseload of high-risk youths to special support staff, teachers could provide these services to youths identified as at high risk for social and academic failure. Each teacher might be designated as an adviser for a small group of high-risk youths. Such a structure would be expected to promote attachment to the adviser and perhaps to other students in the group.

The tutoring function of the PATHE specialist might also be integrated into the regular school structure. Rather than pulling students out of their regular classes for tutoring, an instructional system that diagnoses students' areas of weakness as part of the routine classroom operation and restructures the school day (at least for the targeted youths) to provide time for additional assistance in the relevant areas could have a higher probability of increasing success in the regular classroom. Such restructuring, although difficult to bring about, is probably necessary to bond disattached youths to the school and provide them with rewarding experiences. The PATHE experience suggests that tinkering with extra counseling and tutoring services without more basic changes to the schooling experience will usually fail.

The Miami project represents the other extreme of structural change. This project worked outside of the existing school structure and made drastic changes to the curriculum, school management and organization, governance, and instructional methods used. It also dramatically altered the student composition of the school by selecting only high-risk students. The Academy experience was intended to alter the balance of negative and positive experience in school, to change the students' self-concepts from academic losers to winners, to provide positive role models and frequent rewards and punishments for positive and negative behavior, and to increase commitment to school and careers. The Academy experience appeared intense compared to the traditional school experience.

Despite moderate success in school, the ACE students failed to develop attachments to prosocial others, commitment to schooling, belief in the validity of rules, and more positive self-concepts. Instead, the evidence implies that ACE students became less attached to school. The influence of the ACE students' peers did not change as a result of the program, and the ACE participants reported that they had committed significantly more rather than fewer crimes than the comparison students.

Like the Charleston project, the Miami project failed to alter the intervening attitudes and behaviors that the model implies must change in order to reduce delinquency. Although ACE increased the level of positive reinforcement for schoolwork and related conventional activities, the rewards were not sufficient to overcome the presumably more powerful rewards available from delinquent peers for engaging in delinquent behavior. Also, the Academy may have increased delinquency by removing adult sources of attachment. The formal, almost rigid, atmosphere of the Academy and the "shape up or ship out" attitude probably contrasted sharply with the attitudes of adults in the public schools. In the short run the program reduced attachment to school—an important source of social control—and failed to alter the peer reward structure or the belief structure that governs the self-monitoring function.

The design for this schooling alternative nevertheless appears promising. It could in principle be strengthened to take more explicit account of the importance of peer influence and attachments to adults. The climate of the school could be modified to be less rigid and formal and more supportive, giving students the opportunity to become attached to their teachers and to care about their opinions. Providing opportunities for informal student-teacher interactions, increasing student participation in clubs and activities that enhance their sense of belonging in the school, and engaging students in highly visible activities aimed at enhancing school pride are among the activities that have successfully increased school attachment for general school populations (D. C. Gottfredson, 1986c; D. C. Gottfredson & Cook, 1986a). Programs that improve the affective climate of the school while maintaining clear expectations for behavior and use a curriculum that increases the probability of success for these high-risk youths have promise for altering attitudes and behaviors.

The Pasadena alternative class restructured the school to accommodate to the needs of high-risk youths. The program involved changes to the school schedule, curriculum, teaching methods, and grouping of students for instruction. The changes were confined to the two classes of targeted youths, a strategy that may have been necessary in gaining support for the program and in maintaining a high quality of implementation.

The Pasadena program was successful. Students experienced considerably more success and less punishment in school, they liked school and the people in the school more and hence had more to lose by misbehaving, and negative peer pressure declined. Although we do not know precisely *how* the program altered negative peer influence, we expect that the high level of active participation in the class promoted positive peer influence. Students studied together and tutored each other, worked together on class projects, and frequently participated in *structured* role plays and other *structured* activities providing much more opportunity for interaction and potential for developing friendships than is found in traditional classes. Presumably, these structured peer contacts, centered on prosocial activities, were instrumental in the restraint of delinquent behavior for these students.

The critical difference between the successful alternative class program and the others was that the alternative class program succeeded in altering attitudes and behaviors tied directly to delinquency. Only for the alternative class students was peer influence altered. And, whereas, all three programs were at least partially successful at increasing academic achievement, only the alternative class treatment succeeded at increasing the attachment of students to prosocial others in the school. These students liked their teachers, counselors, and schools. This attachment presumably restrained them from involvement in delinquent activities by limiting their friendships to more prosocial peers and by increasing the effectiveness of rewards and sanctions applied by prosocial others.

Altering school structure has the potential for ameliorating the risk of academic and social failure for high-risk youths, but we are only beginning to understand the complexity of the task. The model of deviant behavior described in this chapter implies that as youths become more bonded to the school, are exposed to more positive models, and earn meaningful rewards for appropriate behavior, their behavior will change. It is unlikely that interventions that focus on changing the individual without changing the environment will be successful at bringing about these changes in attitudes and beliefs. It is more likely that intervention at both the individual and the organizational level will be required.

Some structural changes are effective; others are harmful. If we are to restructure our schools to change student behavior, we must have a clear idea about the sources of the behaviors we are trying to change, and we must carefully plan changes aimed at the sources of the problem behaviors. We must also study the effects of those changes to learn whether or not they are the ones that were anticipated. And we must refine our designs, implement them, and reevaluate. Structural changes, like any innovation, are most likely to succeed when they are guided by a clear theory of action and when they are undertaken in an experimenting spirit.

Appendix: Measures

Delinquent Behavior

- *Self-Reported Serious Delinquency:* A scale composed of items asking the student to report if he or she engaged in seven specific criminal activities in the last year. Examples of items are "Stolen or tried to steal something worth more than $50" and "Carried a hidden weapon." The alpha reliability of this scale is .83.
- *Self-Reported Drug Involvement:* A five-item scale composed of items asking the respondent to report whether he or she used certain drugs in the last year. Its alpha reliability is .75.
- *Number of Court Contacts:* The number of contacts each individual had with the court between September 1, 1982, and June 1, 1983. This measure is taken from court records.

- *Number of Suspensions:* The number of times the student was suspended during the 1982-1983 school year. Data taken from school records. For Pasadena, percentage of students in the treatment control groups suspended during the year is reported.

Delinquent Associates

- *Negative Peer Influence:* A nine-item scale asking students to describe the characteristics of their friends. Items include "Most of my friends think getting good grades is important" and "How many of your friends have been picked up by the police?" Its alpha reliability is .65.

School Rewards and Punishments

Most of these measures are indicators of academic success in a traditional sense. Students are rewarded for effort, diligence, and appropriate behavior with high grades, being promoted to the next grade, and graduating. The following scales are measures of these traditional rewards:

- *Percent Students Graduated:* Percentage of seniors graduated at the end of the 1982-1983 school year.
- *Self-Reported Grades:* This is a single-item measure asking students to report their grades at the end of the last school term. Responses ranged from "high (mostly As)" to "low (mostly Ds or Fs)."
- *Average Grade:* The average of the students' grades for the spring 1983 semester. Data taken from school records.
- *Percent Promoted to the Next Grade, Spring 1981 and Spring 1982:* This measure is taken from school records.

Students were also asked to report their perceptions of the extent to which they were rewarded and punished in school.

- *School Rewards:* A four-item scale that is an index of the positive sanctions an individual student experiences. It includes reports of incidents in which the teacher complimented the student's work or the student won an award or prize. The alpha reliability of this scale is .56.
- *School Punishments:* A four-item scale containing items asking students to report how many times in the last month they were punished (sent out of class, detained after school, given an extra assignment, or had their grade lowered). Its alpha reliability is .54.

Social Bonding

These measures are designed to tap the extent to which the individual is bonded to the social order. Hirschi's notion of belief in rules and the consequences of belief for the self-monitoring function are measured by the next two scales:

- *Belief in Rules:* A six-item scale including items such as "It is all right to get around the law if you can" and "Taking things from stores doesn't hurt anyone." Its alpha reliability is .53.

- *Positive Self-Concept:* A person who sees him- or herself as a law-abiding citizen is more likely to self-reward for appropriate behavior and self-punish for inappropriate behavior than one who sees him- or herself as a delinquent. This twelve-item scale contains general self-esteem items such as "I like myself" as well as items specific to the delinquent self-concept, such as "I am not the kind of person you would expect to get in trouble with the law." The alpha reliability coefficient is .61.

- *Attachment to School:* A ten-item scale including items such as "How important is what the teachers think about you?" and "I have lots of respect for my teachers." It is intended to measure the restraining influence of emotional attachments to others in the school. Its alpha reliability is .76.

The last set of measures is intended to measure the level of commitment to school. Individuals who attend school regularly and aspire to higher levels of educational attainment are expected to be more committed to school.

- *Self-Reported Nonattendance:* A two-item scale asking students to report how often they cut school in the last four weeks and how often they cut class. Its alpha reliability is .60.

- *Percent Days Absent (unexcused):* The percentage of days on the school roll that the student attended school. Data taken from school records.

- *Educational Expectations:* This single item asks students to report how far they think they will get in school. Responses range from "Less than high school graduation" to "Finish a four- or five-year college degree or more."

Notes

1. This section is based on social learning theory (SLT) as elaborated by Bandura (1971, 1977), on the concatenation of SLT with differential association theory (Akers, Krohn, Lanza-Kaduce, & Radosevich, 1979; Burgess & Akers, 1966), and on social

control theory (G. D. Gottfredson, 1982; Hindelang, 1973; Hirschi, 1969; Jensen, 1972; Linden & Hackler, 1973; Wiatrowski, Griswold, & Roberts, 1981).

2. The effect of grouping is complicated, however, by differences in the structure and the services provided in the different groups. Although placement in a non-college-bound track may increase the probability of association with delinquent peers, it also may increase the appropriateness of the educational experience and success experiences in school, hence increasing social bonding. Despite popular assertions that tracking produces delinquency, the empirical evidence shows that tracking is unrelated to delinquency (see, e.g., Wiatrowski, Hansell, Massey, & Wilson, 1982).

References

Akers, R. L., Krohn, M. D., Lanza-Kaduce, L., & Radosevich, M. (1979). Social learning and deviant behavior: A specific test of a general theory. *American Sociological Review, 44*, 636-655.

Bachman, J. G., Green, S., & Wirtanen, I. D. (1971). *Youth in transition: Vol. 3. Dropping out—problem or symptom?* Ann Arbor: University of Michigan, Institute for Social Research.

Bachman, J. G., O'Malley, P. M., & Johnston, J. (1978). *Adolescence to adulthood: Change and stability in the lives of young men.* Ann Arbor: University of Michigan, Institute for Social Research.

Bandura, A. (1971). *Social learning theory.* Morristown, NJ: General Learning Press.

Bandura, A. (1977). *Social learning theory.* Englewood Cliffs, NJ: Prentice-Hall.

Bandura, A., Grusec, J. E., & Menlove, F. L. (1967). Some social determinants of self-monitoring reinforcement systems. *Journal of Personality and Social Psychology, 5*, 449-455.

Burgess, R. L., & Akers, R. L. (1966). A differential association-reinforcement theory of criminal behavior. *Social Problems, 14*, 128-147.

Elliott, D. H., & Voss, H. L. (1974). *Delinquency and dropout.* Lexington, MA: Lexington.

Epstein, J. L. (1983). Selection of friends in differently organized schools and classrooms. In J. L. Epstein & N. Karweit (Eds.), *Friends in school: Patterns of selection and influence in secondary schools.* New York: Academic Press.

Gottfredson, D. C. (1983). Project PATHE: Second interim report. In G. D. Gottfredson, D. C. Gottfredson, & M. S. Cook (Eds.), *The School Action Effectiveness Study: Second interim report* (Report No. 342). Baltimore: Johns Hopkins University, Center for Social Organization of Schools.

Gottfredson, D. C. (1986a). *Academy for community education.* Unpublished manuscript, Johns Hopkins University, Center for Social Organization of Schools.

Gottfredson, D. C. (1986b). *An assessment of a delinquency prevention demonstration with both individual and environmental interventions* (Report No. 361). Baltimore: Johns Hopkins University, Center for Social Organization of Schools.

Gottfredson, D. C. (1986c). An empirical test of school-based environmental and individual interventions to reduce the risk of delinquent behavior. *Criminology, 24*, 705-731.

Gottfredson, D. C. (1987). An evaluation of an organization development approach to reducing school disorder. *Evaluation Review, 11*, 739-763.

Gottfredson, D. C., & Cook, M. S. (1986a, October). *Increasing school relevance and student decisionmaking: Effective strategies for reducing delinquency?* Paper presented at the annual meeting of the American Society of Criminology, Atlanta.

Gottfredson, D. C., & Cook, M. S. (1986b). *A test of a school-based program to reduce delinquency by increasing social integration: The Milwood Alternative Education Project.* Baltimore: Johns Hopkins University, Center for Social Organization of Schools.

Gottfredson, G. D. (1981). Schooling and delinquency. In S. E. Martin, L. B. Sechrest, & R. Redner (Eds.), *New directions in the rehabilitation of criminal offenders.* Washington, DC: National Academy Press.

Gottfredson, G. D. (1982). *Role models, bonding, and delinquency: An examination of competing perspectives* (Report No. 331). Baltimore: Johns Hopkins University, Center for Social Organization of Schools.

Gottfredson, G. D. (1985). *Effective school battery: User's manual.* Odessa, FL: Psychological Assessment Resources.

Hallinan, M. T., & Tuma, N. B. (1978). Classroom effects on changes in children's friendships. *Sociology of Education, 51*, 270-282.

Hawkins, J. D., & Lishner, D. M. (1987). Schooling and delinquency. In E. H. Johnson (Ed.), *Handbook on crime and delinquency prevention.* New York: Greenwood.

Hindelang, M. J. (1973). Causes of delinquency: A partial replication and extension. *Social Problems, 20*, 471-487.

Hirschi, T. (1969). *Causes of delinquency.* Berkeley: University of California Press.

Jensen, G. F. (1972). Parents, peers and delinquent actions: A test of the differential hypothesis. *American Journal of Sociology, 78*, 562-575.

Jessor, R., & Jessor, S. L. (1977). *Problem behavior and psychosocial development: A longitudinal study of youth.* Boulder: University of Colorado, Institute of Behavior Science.

Linden, E., & Hackler, J. C. (1973). Affective ties and delinquency. *Pacific Sociological Review, 16*, 27-46.

Office of Juvenile Justice and Delinquency Prevention. (1980). *Program announcement: Delinquency Prevention Through Alternative Education.* Washington, DC: Author.

Patterson, G. R., & Dishion, T. J. (1985). Contributions of families and peers to delinquency. *Criminology, 23*, 63-80.

Thornberry, T. P., Moore, M., & Christenson, R. L. (1985). The effect of dropping out of high school on subsequent criminal behavior. *Criminology, 23*, 3-18.

Wiatrowski, M. D., Griswold, D., & Roberts, M. K. (1981). Social control theory and delinquency. *American Sociological Review, 46*, 525-541.

Wiatrowski, M. D., Hansell, S., Massey, C. R., & Wilson, D. J. (1982). Curriculum tracking and delinquency. *American Sociological Review, 47*, 151-160.

13

Disruptive Behavior in Organizational Context

ROBERT B. EVERHART

This chapter concerns one of the paramount social issues facing our existence as a society, an issue that also happens to be an educational issue—it concerns the dynamics of being educationally "at risk." The educationally at risk form a group that sets off a societal chain reaction that challenges our immediate as well as our long-term prospects as a nation. I use the word *challenge* because, historically, our democracy has sponsored, advocated, and projected the ideology (and, at times, the reality) of upward social and economic mobility. There has been, then, a combination of myth and reality related to mechanisms that have permitted the poor, the disadvantaged, and traditionally oppressed racial and ethnic minorities to move ahead. I realize in saying this that many individuals who began life in poverty have stayed poor, and that racial lines have been caste lines in many situations (Wilson, 1987). Yet the dream of mobility, of improvement, of betterment has been a continual theme in our society. That vision of betterment is now fading among the less privileged, so much so that it is in danger of no longer being a realistic vision.

Education, of course, has always been perceived as a vehicle for personal and social betterment. For decades our classrooms and cloakrooms have been filled with children whose parents were less well educated than their progeny, but who wanted more for their own children. Today increasing numbers of these same children bring with them to school a complex and deep range of personal and social conditions that lead to the hindrance of their education. These difficulties overshadow, indeed can often suffocate, the learning that is designed to take place within the classroom. Teachers teach less and "manage" behaviors more; schools must increasingly cope with the problems that cannot be managed at the classroom level; society itself inherits the result of unsuccessful schooling. Of special note is the fact that there is increasing evidence that schools themselves exacerbate the very disadvantages that many students bring with them to school (Wehlage & Rutter, 1987). So, while it is true that many students are at risk, so too are schools.

I do not wish at this point to belabor the matter of "at riskness." I realize full well that the literature is brimming with arguments about dropout statistics, being at risk of "what," and whether the term *at risk* applies most appropriately to students, teachers, or schools (Hammack, 1987). My fundamental point focuses less on the strict definitions of *at risk* and more on the educational correlates of the general phenomenon. While the fact that the Chicago public school system, for example, classifies those students not in school into 19 different categories, only 1 of which is called "dropout," is not an unimportant finding, I do not want to dwell on it. The critical issue is that, according to a 1985 General Accounting Office report, 13% of young people ages 16-24 nationwide had dropped out of school and failed to finish (Hahn, 1987). When we understand who these students are likely to be, we better understand the impact of this problem.

Those students who do not benefit from a schooling that is challenging and productive are most likely to reject the educational agenda and to engage in disruptive behavior both in and out of school. Likewise, those schools that cannot offer an appropriate educational program for their students are likely to become disruptive schools. It is appropriate then to understand the characteristics of students who drop out of school, and this will be the first topic of investigation in this chapter. Next, I will examine one fundamental reason many students are educationally at risk, focusing on the match between schooling and cultural characteristics of student populations. The major focus of my analysis, however, is on the manner in which we as educators deal with disruptive students and school failure. Typically, we create "programs" to remedy the minimal congruence between schooling and student characteristics. These programs, however, usually lead to unimpressive results because we superimpose them on an organizational structure that is ill equipped to produce the desired results. Unless we seriously take into consideration the organizational context of schooling and how it affects the education of at-risk students, it is not just schools and students that are at risk; we as a society are clearly at risk as well.

Demographics and the United States

I noted above that the strategies we use to approach the at-risk agenda are crucial to our future as a democracy. I even went so far as to label educational failure as the paramount social issue that we face. This is true in part because the sector of the population growing most rapidly is the sector that, because it is societally at risk, tends also to be educationally at risk.

We know that the ethnic minority population of this country is growing at a faster rate than the Caucasian population. This fact is very clear when we realize that, in the United States, a fertility rate of 2.1 children per childbearing female is considered to be the "replacement rate," or that rate at which births and deaths are in equilibrium (Hodgkinson, 1986). For White women, the fertility rate currently stands at 1.7, which signifies a declining population for Caucasians. For Black women, the fertility rate is 2.4, and for Hispanics it is 2.9. Clearly, then, there are racial differences reflected in the differential population growth as well as in the overall population growth of the nation. Simple arithmetic tells us minorities will account for all of the population growth in the near future and, because the Caucasian population is decreasing in absolute terms, minorities will therefore become a larger proportion of the total population.

Yet if we disaggregate some of these data within racial cohorts, we arrive at an even more revealing set of conclusions. First, regardless of race or ethnic characteristics, women who have not completed high school have an average fertility rate of 2.5. At the other end of the continuum, again regardless of race or ethnicity, women who are college graduates have a fertility rate of 1.4, well below the replacement level.

Second, all families, regardless of race, with family income below $10,000 annually have a fertility rate significantly above the 2.1 replacement level. Conversely, family income of $35,000 or above is correlated with a fertility rate of 1.3, which, by the way, matches that of the nation with the lowest fertility rate in the world, West Germany.

It is clear then that while race and population growth are connected, this relationship is a spurious one in that social class accounts for most of the differential population increases. In recognizing this fact, it is clear that the most rapidly growing part of our population is that proportion that has the least access to the means and the results of economic production (Martin, 1988). Consider the following:

- The poorest 40% of all U.S. families in 1984 accounted for slightly less than 16% of the national income, while the wealthiest 40% accounted for 67% of the national income.
- From 1978 to 1984, the percentage of people living below the poverty line rose from 10% to 14%.
- In the first half of the 1980s, the poorest 40% of the population experienced a real annual income *drop* of an average $500, while the wealthiest 40% experienced a real income increase of an average of $1,800.
- Just 1% of the American population owns 36% of the nation's wealth. With such a concentration of wealth in the hands of so few, the decisions made by a relatively small number of people can affect a wide range of the economy.

These statistics relate to children in an even more dramatic fashion. Children (by definition, those under 18 years old) have for 15 years been the single poorest segment of our society. In that period of time, their economic condition has worsened. For example, in 1985, one of four children lived in poverty. Here race did make a difference, as 50% of Black children and 40% of Hispanic children lived in poverty. Of course, the poverty of children is also related to family situation, as single-parent, female-headed households account for much of the family poverty situation. One-third of all such families live in poverty, although for Blacks and Hispanics that figure is two-thirds.

The conclusions here are clear. In a nation that prides itself on democratic principles, in a system of supposed maximum access of the disenfranchised to the benefits of the society, in a system that supposedly is constituted by a vibrant and dominant middle class, many of these beliefs are in danger of becoming myths, if they are not already myths. The reality, then, is that the composition of our society is dramatically changing, that race and class are playing increasingly influential roles in the lives of our children. As a result, race and social class are playing increasingly dominant roles in the *education* of our children.

It is these children who constitute the bulk of the dropout statistics about which we hear so much. On the one hand, some of these figures are overstated to the degree that the dropout rate (that proportion between ages 16 and 24 who had not finished school) is actually less than it was 25 years ago (nationally, 20% in 1963 versus 14% in 1985). And even the current dropout figure is somewhat encouraging in that it is still somewhat less than the much-touted high school nongraduation rate of 30% (Hahn, 1987). Still, the dropout phenomenon tends to be characterized by some clear trends:

- While the dropout rates have declined in general, the rates by race are still significantly different. In 1984, more than 75% of 18-19-year-old Whites were high school graduates, while only 60% of Blacks and 50% of Hispanics could claim the same attainment.
- Dropping out is clearly related to social class. This should not be a surprise, considering the discussion above. Generally speaking, a student from a disadvantaged background is three times as likely to drop out as one not from such a background.
- Perhaps worst of all, these dropouts are least prepared for the complex labor market in the United States. Most of the jobs that have been created over the past decade have been relatively low-paying jobs in service and information sectors of the society. The reality is that the nation is rapidly heading for a bipolar labor force, with relatively few people holding higher-paying jobs and the vast majority of new jobholders occupying lower-paying jobs. As expected, these latter jobs are likely to be held by the poor and minorities.

One issue is eminently clear: A host of economic and social factors contribute to the disaffection that many of these young people experience in school. To the degree that they are in fact disaffected, they will participate on a decreasing basis in the educational experience of schooling. Furthermore, it does little good to search for individual causes of disaffection when such large numbers of students sharing characteristics are imprinted by this process. Rather, we must ask how our schools adapt to the special educational issues that race and class present. And by *adapt,* I mean more than adaptation as represented by the mere presence of Title I, bilingual education, or vocational education programs. I refer specifically to the manner in which the school *organizes its educational experiences to adapt to the special nature of a growing clientele that is poor and culturally different.*

Culture and Learning: The Black Experience

In the past, our schools have for the most part failed to adapt to many of the major accommodations that client differences require. A reading of history leads to a somewhat sorry review of the education of Blacks, Native Americans, and Hispanics, and demonstrates the manner in which minority cultures have been subverted by the educational process (Fuchs & Havinghurst, 1973; San Miguel, 1986; Weinberg, 1977). We tend to think of these days as past, as part of another era, but sadly they are not. Cultural diversity in this nation continues to be a matter to which our educational system has yet to adapt successfully. This factor is reflected nowhere more clearly than in the education of Black males, and I want to focus on Black males because they illustrate well the scope of the manner in which the structure of schooling influences student adaptation to schooling and learning.

For some time now, scholars have proposed that there are aspects of Black culture that affect the schooling of Black children. Wade Boykin (1986), for example, posits a number of interrelated dimensions of Afro-American culture that persist even though that culture over the centuries has existed in juxtaposition to the Afro-American ethos. Some of these dimensions of Black culture that are unique are noted below:

- *spirituality,* or an approach to life that is essentially vitalistic rather than mechanistic, with the conviction that nonmaterial forces influence people's daily lives
- *movement*, or an emphasis on rhythm, percussiveness, and dance as central to psychological health
- *oral tradition*, a preference for oral/aural modes of communication, where both speaking and listening are treated as performances and where oral virtuosity is emphasized and cultivated
- *expressive individualism*, or the cultivation of distinctive personality and proclivity for spontaneous personal expression

Given these and other attributes, one can imagine the conflicts that can arise for Black children in classrooms where order, passivity, and routine are the norms. One can imagine the difficulty that many Black children may have in a world where linear thought patterns prevail via the printed word and where "silence is golden." It brings meaning to

W.E.B. Du Bois's statement, made in 1903, that "one even feels his two-ness—an American, a Negro; two souls, two thoughts, two unreconciled strivings; two warring in one dark body, whose dogged strength alone keeps it from being torn asunder."

As humans often do when faced with what appears to be an irreconcilable social context, Black males who do not drop out develop coping mechanisms. While educators often treat them as students who cannot or will not learn, many of these students adopt either passive or active coping strategies. *Passive coping* consists of resignation to or acceptance of being on the outside, of being marginal. *Active coping* can range from insulation from the community to defying anything to do with "Whiteness," an attitude toward school adopted by many Black males (Fordham, 1988).

At the same time, teachers often believe that Black students who are failing are doing so because they have the wrong or bad attitudes, and therefore embark on an attempt to change these attitudes. These efforts take the form of attempting to modify students' penchant for communicating via talking rather than writing (e.g., emphasis on an oral tradition) and keeping students within the bounds of behavioral norms (seated, quiet, and so on) (McLeod, 1987; Williams, 1983). The students, of course, resist to various degrees being programmed into a learning style that is antithetical to their culture. This resistance in turn necessitates greater control on the part of the school. Teachers thus may have to spend more time managing the learning environment of Black males and, as a direct consequence, Black males may receive less direct instructional time. Since we know that "time on task" is a correlate of achievement, the achievement of Black males may be subsequently reduced.

How do we combat a situation such as this? Typically, well-intentioned educators propose a variety of remedies to assist teachers to work more effectively with "Blackness" and thereby reduce disruptive behavior. These may include (a) requirements for multicultural education at the preservice level, (b) in-service exposure to "at-risk" issues, and (c) the employment of Black aides who are "more sensitive" to the needs of Black children.

The above are all necessary steps that need to be taken, but it is clear that they are not sufficient (Grant, 1989). A more incisive, more radical strategy must also take place, one that enhances the education of Black children (especially males) within the context of Black culture. Such an education would mean a form of schooling very different from what is currently legitimated and supported by the dominant society. It would involve an education that does not condemn nonlinear thinking, personalized learning, an oral tradition, and active learning environments.

The real issue is whether our current organization of schooling can accomplish those ends. It seems not, and what may be required, especially in the early years and most particularly for many Black males from poor backgrounds, are special schools taught by Black males, not unlike day schools that have been designed for members of other races and cultures. This approach has been advocated by a number of Black educators, among them Spencer Holland (1987) (Washington, D.C., public schools), Janice Hale (professor, Cleveland State University), and Dr. Nathan Harr (Black studies, San Francisco State). These scholars have argued that, especially for Black males, the absence of an effective role model of the same gender and race is a primary contributor to the early negative experiences that subsequently feed the cycle of failure. If such schools were to exist, the emphasis would be on literacy within the context of the Black culture, with a primary emphasis on self-concept enhancement and motivational development. Only as such characteristics are developed would the student be able to make the transition into the skill-based "regular" curriculum.

I am raising the prospect of clear-cut departures from the current education of at-risk minority youth. By proposing the existence of separate schools, or at least schools within schools, I am advocating that, for lower-class Blacks, the standard primary curriculum be suspended for the first three years and be replaced by education centering on an oral tradition, expressivism, and the like. This approach is controversial and clearly has a "separate but equal" side to it that, in the end, could be dysfunctional for Blacks (Ogbu, 1978). Yet there are some parallels here to the "accelerated schools" advocated by Henry Levin (1986) and his colleagues at Stanford. Both models propose separate but temporary organizational units that focus on the creation of "total institutions." These total institutions emphasize focused activities that reinforce a given organizational culture. Such an approach rejects the standard approach to the at-risk agenda that results in the grafting of a compensatory or remedial program onto a conventional elementary school.

Such a drastic configuration is important because the education of low-income Black students suggests, quite fundamentally, that cultural differences among schools and their clients demand an organizational arrangement that explicitly reinforces important aspects of client cultures. Other, equally fundamental, issues suggest the critical nature of organizational arrangement in the education of at-risk youth; I turn now to further development of that topic.

Being At Risk and School Organization

In order to understand better how school organization is such an important influence on schooling and the behavior of at-risk students, let us leave the field of education for a moment and place ourselves in the role of another—that of a farmer. After years of attempting to make a living by raising corn, all the while fighting the weather, increased labor costs, and the high cost of mechanization, our farmer friend has finally found the potential for eternal profitability—a hybrid corn seed that is so effective it will yield double what his present seed yields. The farmer is ecstatic about this prospect and orders a year's supply of seed, all the while projecting future profits and calculating an early retirement. A year after planting the seed, our farmer meets an old friend, who asks for a progress report. The friend is amazed when informed that the plan did not work out so well after all. In fact, it was a money-losing proposition. The farmer mentions that he did not realize he would have to provide twice the nutrients and twice the water for the crop, which also meant that the demands on his farm equipment were far beyond their capacity, all of which resulted in the need to rent extra equipment. What is more, since now the farmer harvested two crops a year when previously he had harvested only one, he was short of qualified labor and had to pay a premium for the workers he did hire. Even more frustrating was the fact that the usual markets were not ready to absorb the surplus corn at the time it was produced, thus leading to difficulty with distribution. In short, what appeared to be a common-sensical remedy to the profitability of this farm was not realized because the basic organizational structures of the farming enterprise had not been recalibrated to account for the new patterns (Spicer, 1967).

We encounter similar problems constantly in social life. What was once an acceptable way of processing human routines becomes outmoded and no longer effective. The social units that recognize this precept and adapt to it are generally those that succeed and remain healthy. One of the recurring themes identified in *In Search of Excellence* is that successful companies have "simultaneous loose-tight properties." That is to say, they have adaptive organizational arrangements so as to account for variability in the environment. As Peters and Waterman (1982) note, "American companies [and, I might add, schools] are being stymied not only by their staffs but also by their structures and systems, both of which inhibit action."

It is clear that schooling for at-risk students is itself at risk for many of the same reasons that the farmer's hybrid corn experiment failed. In most schools where there are large numbers of low-achieving students or where the dropout rates are high, the organization of instruction is little different from that in any other school. While new programs are added with flair and ceremony, they fail to deliver, much as the hybrid corn failed to deliver. A basic problem is that the organizational structure and processes within the school have not been rearranged to account for the different rules and roles that the new program may need (Charters & Pellegrin, 1973).

It is virtually axiomatic that a failure to experiment with different organizational arrangements of schooling for at-risk youth only exacerbates the clear relationship noted earlier between economic disadvantage and poor schooling. In order to explore this thesis further, I want to examine an illustrative case that concerns a program in New York City, the Dropout Prevention Initiative (or DPI). I report on it because it illustrates the often futile attempts of "programmatic intervention" without commensurate organizational restructuring. Much of this discussion is based on the work of Gerics and Westheimer (1988), who have done extensive evaluation of the DPI.

The DPI reflects New York City's largest educational problem—a dropout rate of 42-50%, depending on the calculations used. Although students from all social classes drop out, the rate is highest, as one might imagine, for low-income students. In response to this problem, the Board of Education has developed a program that targets a range of services to students who evidence high absenteeism or low grades, or who repeatedly "cut" classes. These services, which have been applied to students in middle and high schools, are said to be "comprehensive" and involve a "wide range of community agencies" in a selected number of schools. These services include, but are not limited to, the following:

- a teacher at each school site whose responsibility it is to identify the targeted students and to coordinate services
- appropriate guidance and counseling services made available to each student in order to address problems that contribute to poor attendance

- a school linkage program designed to assist students in making the transition from middle to high school
- an alternative education program that incorporates basic skills instruction with individualized programs in order to encourage improved attendance and achievement

In examining how these and other dimensions in fact operate, it is clear that with the DPI, programs meant to accomplish these objectives were superimposed on an organizational structure ill suited to facilitate the attainment of the objectives. Let us examine, for example, the matter of attendance monitoring. The evaluation of the New York project evidenced a wide range of incentives used in order to keep students in school. Ways of motivating students included T-shirts with school slogans emblazoned on them, calculators, book bags, and pens for students—all of which served as rewards for students who had perfect attendance for a defined period of time. Program coordinators who were interviewed believed that rewards pertinent to "things that kids understand" were necessary to encourage students to stay in school.

Another facet of the DPI was a strong career education component, carried out through the extant guidance and counseling services. The career education function relied heavily on (a) teaching students how to search for jobs, stressing interviewing skills, job application strategies, and job search skills; and (b) placement procedures—that is, placing students in "appropriate" positions while they were school or once they finished school. An integral part of the placement process was a series of diagnostic procedures used to assess the types of jobs into which students could best be placed.

The evaluation of the DPI revealed, however, that the diagnosis of student skills became a driving force in determining the types of jobs students would attain. Since most students with problematical attendance patterns in the past had, by high school, experienced little school success and usually were many grade levels behind in achievement, they then were considered by counselors to lack the necessary skills needed for the majority of the jobs that could contribute to some upward mobility. Consequently, for many students who were at risk, the career education component served only to channel them into traditional jobs such as clerks, stock persons, and fast-food restaurant workers—all menial jobs that the students could have filled even without staying in school. Yet the message of the career education program was clear—students are fortunate to find any job, menial or not.

There were other, equally problematic, limitations to the DPI, but at this point it is sufficient to note that the program deficiencies relate to the fact that the DPI was predicated (at least in terms of practice) on *at-risk students adjusting to the school rather than the school significantly changing its way of educating to account for the characteristics of at-risk students.* In the DPI initiatives, a "deficiency model" was followed—at-risk students do not have the capability to make it in the "normal" schooling atmosphere and thus must, for example, be provided "incentives" to participate in schooling or be moved into an "alternative setting" that does little more than keep student-generated state revenue within the district coffers. Yet even when students did participate in the various alternative programs, they did not really "make it" (in conventional terms), so the school turned to serving these disadvantaged students by placing them in "appropriate" jobs, usually service sector jobs at the minimum wage.

There are a number of possible interpretations of this rather depressing but all too common scenario. One is that teachers seem not to have the dedication to get down to the serious business of educating at-risk students. After all, here in New York City is a comprehensive program that evidences the resolve of the Board of Education to deal with the fact that 40-50% of New York City students do not graduate from high school. One then could ask how educators can fail to understand how these programs, in reality, have such a minimal effect on the students they are meant to serve.

If New York City were an isolated case of a good program gone astray, we might have a right to be indignant and blame the players. But just as the educators in the New York situation too often place the onus on students and thereby "blame the victim," so we too often "blame the teacher" when educational programs are not properly implemented. The literature that describes change in education provides us a different message.

John Goodlad, in *A Place Called School* (1984), as well as in his earlier book *Behind the Classroom Door* (Goodlad & Klein, 1970), provides ample evidence of why blaming the teacher is too simple an explanation to account for the fact that programs designed to reach at-risk students usually have such a minimal effect on target populations. Goodlad reports on his observations in schools across the country for over two decades and concludes that unimaginative, routine, and standardized education is the rule rather than the exception. Furthermore, regardless of where one goes and regardless of the goals of the school, the education of at-risk students remains characteristically un-distinguished, although exceptions do exist, as Sarah Lightfoot (1985) and Joan Lipsitz (1983) have pointed out.

This rather dim picture is an accurate portrayal despite the presence of untold efforts through the development of educational programs designed to make things different. Basic educational routines in schools have remained unchanged over the past century, despite the fact that the demands on and purposes of schools have changed considerably during the same period of time. Today, the curriculum is much more extensive and complex, the services that schools provide are more varied, and the students in many of our schools represent a wider range of learning styles and experiences. Equally important, those students are required to be in school for a greater portion of their lives than were students 75 years ago. Yet the educational routines within our high schools and middle schools—that is, the basic core technology—remain quite uniform and based on approaches that have persisted for decades: teacher talk, whole group instruction, recitation, and recall.

It is clear, however, as Larry Cuban (1984, 1989) so ably points out, that the vast majority of teachers teach this way because the organizations in which they teach provide or encourage few other options. Teachers teach in classrooms with large numbers of students; there are only so many ways to organize learning for 35 or so students. Teachers teach in boxlike rooms; there are only so many configurations possible in a room of 1,000 square feet or so. Teachers at the secondary level teach 150 or so students a day; there are only so many "individual" contacts of much depth that a teacher can have with any of those students. These and other processes force teachers to engage in a subtle but powerfully dynamic negotiating process with students, thereby "arranging" for the teacher less variance that has to be managed (Sedlak, Wheeler, Pullin, & Cusick, 1988). The more standardized and routine the world of transaction, however, the more difficult it is for the school truly to adapt to individual differences. Compounding the scenario is the fact that teachers have minimal contact with other adults in the school, and thus most of their professional decisions are based on little or no consultation with other adults (Jackson, 1968).

There are only so many departures from the normal routine that a teacher will initiate, since such efforts generally require initiative beyond that of coping with what is. And few schools reward teachers for anything beyond coping with the expected. Given these conditions, then, there is little chance that most schools, for example, will create schooling that is more sensitive to the culture of Afro-American students.

These structural factors support, then, a schooling environment that fails to accommodate the special needs of at-risk students and thereby fosters disruptive behavior on the part of the students within it. Such structural elements raise for examination the manner in which school structure itself is "disruptive" for many students, since much of the student behavior that is troublesome for schools is bred by the very structure of schooling itself.

What Is to Be Done

In this chapter I have attempted to draw quite broad strokes. First I discussed briefly how the at-risk issue is fundamentally related to social class, and pointed to the fact that we are becoming an increasingly polarized society along these lines. Those who have, continue to have, and most likely will continue to have; those who never have had, have little now, and have little prospect of having. In our society, membership in this latter group is increasing, and society at large is faced with solving the problem of the educationally at risk. Surely, failure to take active steps aimed at reversing our perpetuation of a permanent under-class will doom us to increased class conflict. Finally, at the more micro level, the extent of "investment" that students have in schooling is a direct correlate of school structures that enhance that investment. Conversely, structures that do not enhance such personal investment usually are correlated with disruptive behavior.

I then went on to argue that a fundamental reason that schooling does not serve at-risk students well is that educators do not take into consideration, as they organize educational experiences, student culture and worldview. When students do not respond to our preformed educational agendas and subsequently fail, we blame them for their ineptitude. We turn then to "program" students—one activity that American education does readily. But our programs are too often ineffective, and there are good reasons for this. One reason is that we promise more than we can ever hope to deliver. Programs are created for political reasons as much as for substantial reasons; they often are "sold" to political groups and interests, all of whom are hungry for an easy solution to complex problems. This then leads to a more fundamental reason for the low success rate of our program initiatives, that programs serve as proxies for change rather than the changes themselves. Programs often serve as cosmetic veneers that are laid over an organizational form flawed from within. These forms are particularly flawed because the technology of schooling has not evolved in anticipation of variant outcomes.

William James once characterized education as the "flywheel of society." Our schools often serve that function, lumbering forward in a motion that was begun long ago for purposes that no longer are as important and in ways that do not work. It seems that we have uncritically accepted the function of the flywheel at a time when many are calling for reform. Yet reform is not truly possible given current organizational structures. Reform programs designed to assist at-risk students will continue, for the most part, to fail.

I am not so naive, however, as to believe that our current manner of organizing education is going to wither away and that a new arrangement will rise from the ashes. The reality is that we must work to transform our current schools through a series of "small revolutions." I want to close by noting just a few of these.

Those of us in schools of education have no small role to play in this process. All of the data about the persistent effects of instruction trace back to the fact that teachers are prepared for the way schools are. Part of the problem is that schools of education themselves are modeled after the ways schools are. When was the last time any of us experienced a teacher education program that emphasized critique, analytic problem solving, and, last but not least, the *modeling* of the instructional strategies that students are being exhorted to use? A training program should produce teachers trained in the craft, equipped with the intellectual skills designed to move teachers beyond survival and to alter what occurs in the usual classroom. Fundamental to such an educative experience would be the abilities to understand the structural antecedents to disruptive behavior and to diagnose student actions within that context.

Second, teachers have to begin to work together. The egg-crate, self-contained classroom is a throwback to the one-room schoolhouse and is not appropriate for the education of children with the complex learning challenges that at-risk students present. That design encourages routine, exacerbates management activities, and keeps teachers apart. There are few professions as lonely as teaching, and it is a tragedy that teachers know so much yet work together so little. Teacher associations could foster the development of the profession by light years if they could just find ways to negotiate away the isolation of teachers and *demand* collaborative educational environments. Such collaborative environments would, I believe, provide the underpinnings necessary to enable teachers to differentiate better between disruptive students and disruptive schools.

Finally, we need to get serious about experimenting with some well-conceived instructional strategies for disadvantaged youth that are operated by *teachers*. We have had years of ideas about the improvement of education from the federal government, state departments of education, private foundations, and university people. Is it not high time teachers had a chance? Let us, however, take into consideration some of the issues I have raised in this chapter. A small proposal along these lines may be in order: Have state departments suspend some of their patchwork programs and set aside 1% of their budget for two years, and 2% for the next three years, for proposals from teachers. The proposals would have to include the following elements:

- at least three teachers working together
- a significant challenge to some sacred organizational cow (e.g., only administrators know how to evaluate instruction, or kids from single-parent families do not have family support for schooling, or teachers cannot work together, or involving parents of at-risk kids in their schooling does not work) (The most deadly of all precepts in need of challenge might be, "We tried that once.")
- evidence of schooling that is adaptive to current client needs yet at the same time challenges clients to succeed in the world as it is

When we look at how unsuccessful we have been with the education of the poor and minorities in the past, these proposals seem worth consideration.

If we do not take this challenge seriously, then the plight of the disenfranchised in our society can rightfully join the degradation of the environment and the arms race as life-threatening problems that continue to exist because we do not care to resolve them before time has run out.

References

Boykin, A. W. (1986). The triple quandary and the schooling of Afro-American children. In U. Neisser (Ed.), *The school achievement of minority children* (pp. 57-92). Hillsdale, NJ: Lawrence Erlbaum.

Charters, W. W., Jr., & Pellegrin, R. J. (1973). Barriers to the innovation process: Four case studies of differentiated staffing. *Educational Administration Quarterly, 9*(1), 3-14.

Cuban, L. (1984). *How teachers taught.* New York: Longman.

Cuban, L. (1989, June). The "at-risk" label and the problem of urban school reform. *Phi Delta Kappan, 70*(10), 780-801.

Du Bois, W. E. B. (1903). *Souls of Black folk.* Chicago: McClurg.

Fordham, C. (1988, February). Racelessness as a factor in Black student school success: Pragmatic strategy or Pyrrhic victory. *Harvard Educational Review, 58,* 54-84.

Fuchs, E., & Havinghurst, R. J. (1973). *To live on this earth: American Indian education.* Garden City, NY: Doubleday.

Gerics, J., & Westheimer, M. (1988). Dropout prevention: Trinkets and gimmicks or Deweyean reconstruction. *Teachers College Record, 90*(1), 41-60.

Goodlad, J. (1984). *A place called school.* New York: McGraw-Hill.

Goodlad, J., & Klein, F. M. (1970). *Behind the classroom door.* Worthington, OH: C. A. Jones.

Grant, C. A. (1989, June). Urban teachers: Their new colleagues and curriculum. *Phi Delta Kappan, 70*(10), 764-770.

Hahn, A. (1987, December). Reaching out to America's dropouts: What to do? *Phi Delta Kappan, 69*(4), 257.

Hammack, F. M. (1987). Large school systems' dropout reports: An analysis of definitions, procedures, and findings. In G. Natriello (Ed.), *School dropouts: Patterns and policies* (pp. 20-37). New York: Teachers College Press.

Hodgkinson, H. L. (1986). Tomorrow's numbers, tomorrow's nation. *Education Week, 5*(34), 14-15.

Holland, S. H. (1987, March 25). A radical approach to educating young Black males. *Education Week, 6*(26), 24.

Jackson, P. (1968). *Life in classrooms.* New York: Holt, Rinehart & Winston.

Levin, H. M. (1986). *Education reform for disadvantaged students: An emerging crisis.* Washington, DC: National Education Association.

Lightfoot, S. (1985). *Good high schools: Portraits of character and culture.* New York: Basic.

Lipsitz, J. (1983). *Successful schools for young adolescents.* New York: Transaction.

Martin, D. M. (1988). Wake up: The American dream is fading, and our future is at risk. *American School Board Journal, 175*(2), 21-25.

McLeod, J. (1987). *Ain't no makin' it: Leveled aspirations in a low income neighborhood.* Boulder, CO: Westview.

Ogbu, J. U. (1978). *Minority education and caste.* New York: Academic Press.

Peters, T., & Waterman, R. H. (1982). *In search of excellence.* New York: Harper & Row.

San Miguel, G., Jr. (1986). *Let them all take heed: Mexican Americans and the campaign for educational equality in Texas, 1910-1981.* Austin: University of Texas Press.

Sedlak, M., Wheeler, C., Pullin, D., & Cusick, P. (1988, February). High school reform and the "bargain" to learn. *Education and Urban Society, 17*(2), 204-14.

Spicer, E. (Ed.). (1967). *Human problems in technological change.* New York: John Wiley.

Wehlage, G. G., & Rutter, R. A. (1987). Dropping out: How much do schools contribute to the problem? In G. Natriello (Ed.), *School dropouts: Patterns and policies* (pp. 70-88). New York: Teachers College Press.

Weinberg, M. (1977). *A chance to learn: A history of race and education in the United States*. New York: Cambridge University Press.

Williams, M. (1983). *On the street where I live*. New York: Holt, Rinehart & Winston.

Wilson, W. J. (1987). *The truly disadvantaged: The inner city, the underclass and public policy*. Chicago: University of Chicago Press.

14

Toward Integrated Responses
to Troubling Behavior

PETER E. LEONE
MARY BANNON WALTER
BRUCE I. WOLFORD

Understanding troubled and troubling youth, the nature of the problems they and we face, involves looking beyond the topography of specific acts and developing an understanding of the contexts within which behaviors can occur. Our understandings of "troubled" youth and "troubling" behavior are bound by our conceptualizations of deviant behavior as well as by the meanings we ascribe to specific acts. As the chapters in this book suggest, in addition to being shaped by individual responses to environmental events, behavior is influenced by interactions among individuals and others in their ecosystems over time, and by social, political, and cultural forces that give meaning to institutions and social groups. The contributors to this volume from varying theoretical, professional, and analytical perspectives have, through their discourse, data, and logical analysis, presented a diverse set of understandings concerning troubled youth and troubling behavior.

An adequate understanding of troubled and troubling behavior requires multilevel perspectives on the problem; responses to troubling behavior or interventions designed to prevent problem behavior should reflect our multifaceted understanding. Examining the range and mag-

AUTHORS' NOTE: Special thanks to Diane Greig, John Guthrie, and Ed Trickett for suggestions made on earlier drafts of this manuscript. We would also like to acknowledge the contributions of the participants at the Seminar on Troubled Youth, whose ideas influenced the development of this final chapter.

nitude of some of the problems currently faced by adolescents helps substantiate the need for broad conceptualizations of problem behavior and innovative responses to those problems.

Trouble in School and the Community

Early School Leaving

During the period from 1970 to 1985 there was a relatively steady decrease in the dropout rate among 16- to 24-year-olds in the general population. Data for 1985 indicate a 12.6% dropout rate for this age group. Statistics on the dropout rate for minority groups, though also on the decrease, are much higher, with 15.1% of Blacks and 27.6% of Hispanics in the same age range counted as dropouts (U.S. Department of Education, 1988a). Dropout rates are highest in the South, the West, and urban areas, where poor and minority populations are proportionally larger (Wetzel, 1987). Among students identified as learning disabled or emotionally disturbed in school settings the percentage of those who drop out is increasing dramatically. From the 1984-1985 school year to the 1985-1986 school year the dropout rate increased from 21% to 26.3% for 16- to 21-year-olds served in special education programs (U.S. Department of Education, 1988b). Special education students at highest risk for dropping out of school are Black youngsters identified as learning disabled or behaviorally disordered who have been previously released from school at least once and who are behind in earning graduation credits (Edgar, cited in U.S. Department of Education, 1988b). Among students identified as seriously emotionally disturbed, the dropout rate in 1985-1986 was estimated to be 41% (U.S. Department of Education, 1988b).

Juvenile Delinquency

The Bureau of Justice Statistics estimates that in 1986, 1.17 million juveniles were taken into police custody (U.S. Department of Justice, 1987). Of these, over 700,000 were referred to the juvenile court and over 64,000 to the adult or criminal court. The remaining youths were handled informally within police departments or by some other community agency. According to the U.S. Department of Justice (1989), the juvenile courts petitioned and formally disposed of approximately 535,000 delinquency cases in 1985, a 7% increase over the courts' work load in 1984. These increases were greater for males and non-White groups than for females or Whites (U.S. Department of Justice, 1989). Allen-Hagen (1988) notes that despite a decrease in the size of the U.S. juvenile population, there was a 10% increase in the number of youths confined in public juvenile facilities between 1983 and 1987. According to the most recent Children in Custody Census, 53,503 juveniles were held in public facilities in 1987 (Allen-Hagen, 1988). Of these, 54% were held for criminal (delinquent) offenses.

Overrepresentation of youth who are not members of the social, cultural, and educational mainstream in juvenile correctional facilities is an increasing problem. Approximately 29% of school-age youths belong to ethnic and racial minority groups, yet these groups account for more than half of all juveniles in public custody (Allen-Hagen, 1988). Educationally handicapped youths, who represent approximately 12% of the school-age population, make up 28-49% of individuals in juvenile correctional facilities (Casey & Keilitz, Chapter 5, this volume; Morgan, 1979; Rutherford, Nelson, & Wolford, 1985).

Use of Drugs and Alcohol

There is some evidence that the use of cocaine, marijuana, and stimulants is declining among high school seniors in recent years, although the diffusion of crack cocaine to new metropolitan areas continues (Johnston, O'Malley, & Bachman, 1988). Johnston et al.'s (1988) most recent survey of high school seniors indicates that approximately 66% used alcohol, 29% used cigarettes, 21% used marijuana or hashish, and 4.3% used hallucinogens in the 30-day period just prior to the survey. The actual use of drugs and alcohol among this age cohort may be much higher. The annual surveys of high school seniors do not include the large number of youths who leave school before graduation, those who are incarcerated, and those in residential or day-treatment settings (Allison, Leone, & Spero, Chapter 9, this volume). Further, evidence suggests that drug use is more prevalent among those who drop out (Friedman, Glickman, & Utada, 1985; Hawkins, Lishner, Jenson, & Catalano, 1987), youths hospitalized for psychiatric disorders (Klinge, Vaziri, & Lennox, 1976; Reichler, Clement, & Dunner, 1983), and individuals arrested and incarcerated for criminal offenses (U.S. Department of Justice, 1987, 1989).

Current Responses to Troubled and Troubling Youth

At the present time most interventions designed to assist troubled youth, and much of the research conducted on troublesome behavior, are based on implicit assumptions that the disorder, problem, or troublesomeness resides within the child (Leone, 1989). Accordingly, while we may acknowledge contextual, cultural, and organizational influences that shape the behavior of the individual, our frames of reference are predominantly person or problem centered. Responses to troubling behavior need not only to accommodate the range of individual differences that exist and the fluid, often overlapping nature of many problem behaviors, but also to examine and respond to the ecological and structural factors that have potential to exacerbate or mitigate troublesome behavior.

Chapters in this volume illustrate the importance of examining troubled behavior from multifaceted perspectives; when viewed as a whole they suggest that reliance on any one set of lenses for understanding troublesome behavior fails to inform us fully. While all perspectives implicitly or explicitly identify professional values and beliefs that direct attention to specific aspects of troubled or troubling behavior, differing points of view shed light on different aspects of problem behavior. For example, person- and problem-centered perspectives presented in Part I provide insight into the prevalence of specific problems and behavioral characteristics of groups of youth. Similarly, the social ecological perspectives presented in Part II illuminate the contextual and interactive nature of troubling behavior and the importance of understanding the multiple and interactive contexts within which behaviors occur. The structural and cultural perspectives presented in Part III illustrate the effects of organizational features and cultural factors on troubling behavior.

None of these perspectives alone can adequately inform those concerned with the prevention and treatment of troublesome behavior. For example, person-centered perspectives, in isolation, do not fully describe the complex nature of troublesome behavior as it develops within the context of institutional structures and cultural forces. In the same vein, social ecological or structural and cultural perspectives alone do not adequately inform practitioners, researchers, and others how to respond to troubled and troubling youth.

The development of appropriate services for troubled and troubling youth requires changes not only in the ways we think about troublesome behavior but in the structure of organizations as well as in the cultural forces and belief systems that maintain current ways of responding to children and youth. With regard to research, we need to examine the thorny, seemingly intractable problems not only with traditional empirical methods, but also with qualitative or interpretive studies and critical analyses that are based on differing assumptions about the nature of the problems being studied.

In the section that follows, a few programs are identified that have structures reflecting a multifaceted understanding of troubled youth and that serve adolescent clients through multimodal and collaborative approaches. While some programs have reconceptualized the range of services needed by specific client populations, others have changed the manner in which youths obtain access to services. The chapter concludes with a discussion of the implications of the integrated perspectives for research.

New Directions in Services for Youth

A few current programs have been recognized by the Office of Juvenile Justice and Delinquency Prevention (OJJDP) as providing multidisciplinary, community-based services for chronic status offenders and at the same time maintaining community support and high staff morale. The Orion Center, a Seattle program with multiagency sponsorship, serves youth at high risk for prostitution. Referrals come from counselor street networks and from social service and juvenile justice agencies. Services available to youths include food and medical attention, alcohol and substance abuse counseling, educational services, and preemployment training (Community Research Associates, 1987).

Another innovative, multidisciplinary street service operation, the Bridge, annually serves more than 4,000 youths in Boston. A medical van houses preventive health services, and education, job training, counseling, and referral to other community agencies are provided at the Bridge Center (Community Research Associates, 1987).

The intensive truancy project established in 1983 in St. Paul, Minnesota, is another example of a multiagency youth services program. Created to serve youth adjudicated for truancy who would otherwise

enter out-of-home placement, the program provides daily school attendance monitoring, supervised study time, and alternative educational
programming (Community Research Associates, 1987).

In responding to troubled or troubling youth, all three of these
programs illustrate the reconceptualization and multilevel perspectives
essential for the development of more appropriate services for youth.
In addition to focusing on individual client needs, the programs have
altered traditional relationships between clients and service providers.
In some instances these programs have taken services to the adolescents
and have changed traditional organizational structures by combining
the funding and administration of medical, educational, and counseling
services. While OJJDP has recognized these programs for youths with
multiple problems for their innovative efforts and community support,
at the present time little evidence is available on the impact of these
programs on clients.

Other examples of programs that reflect a multilevel understanding of troublesome behavior also exist. Gottfredson (see Chapter 12)
presents data on the effectiveness of differing school reform efforts to
meet the needs of youth at risk for delinquency and dropping out of
school. While the focus of her chapter is on the structural differences
among various programs, the interventions described also reflect person-
centered and social ecological perspectives on troubling behavior.

Another model that exemplifies integrated perspectives and responses to troubling behavior is Project Re-ED, developed during the
1960s. Known for its educational rather than psychodynamic emphasis,
Re-ED involves short-term residential care for troubled youths with
weekends at home and maintenance of family and community ties
(Hobbs, 1982). Evaluations of Re-ED suggest that in addition to altering the behavioral patterns of children in the program, the program
modified maladaptive family and school responses to troublesome
behavior (Hobbs, 1982; Weinstein, 1969).

In reviewing service models for children and adolescents with emotional and behavioral problems, Melton (n.d.) identifies characteristics
of programs that the research suggests have positive effects on troubled
and troubling youths. Briefly, Melton notes that effective programs (a)
integrate affective, cognitive, and social interventions; (b) are truly
community based; (c) have a well-developed system of case advocacy;
and (d) provide opportunities for youths' involvement in planning their
education and treatment.

Systems Change

In addition to programs whose structures and services reflect a multifaceted understanding of troubled and troubling youth, several projects have been developed to change the structures of current delivery systems. The Child and Adolescent Service System Program (CASSP), developed by the National Institutes of Mental Health in 1983, focuses on the improvement of multiagency service delivery systems for severely emotionally disturbed youth. However, in contrast to traditional initiatives that often develop model treatment centers or programs for children and adolescents, the CASSP system is designed to improve the systems through which services are currently delivered. In 1988, CASSP supported 28 state and 11 community-level grants (National Institute of Mental Health, 1988). In addition to focusing on improving the structure of service delivery systems to serve youth, CASSP has adopted a functional and proactive definition of youngsters who are eligible to receive services from systems that receive funding. Specifically, eligible youths can be defined by state and local agencies as those who need a specific level of service or those at risk for needing a specific level of service. Further, CASSP-eligible youth are those who "have service needs in two or more community services, such as mental health, health, education, juvenile justice, or social welfare" (National Institute of Mental Health, 1988). CASSP also requires that minority representatives and families of disturbed youth be involved in the planning and implementation of service systems appropriate to youth of diverse ethnic backgrounds.

Other major initiatives that have the potential for broad-based systemic change are the projects sponsored by the Robert Wood Johnson Foundation. Eleven states and the District of Columbia are currently developing systems to better coordinate and finance home- and community-based services for emotionally disturbed children. A major thrust of the initiatives is to eliminate fragmented and often ineffective systems of care in the various jurisdictions receiving support (Robert Wood Johnson Foundation, 1989).

Advocating a multiagency approach and structural changes to improve service deliver, CASSP and the Robert Wood Johnson Foundation initiatives suggest that although adequate treatment technologies exist, disturbed youth are underserved due to inadequacy of our current service delivery systems. The effectiveness of these macro-level strategies or structural changes will be realized to the extent that they can affect the belief systems associated with current means of providing services.

If professionals and others concerned with troubled and troubling youth rely primarily on person- and problem-centered perspectives and person- and problem-centered responses to deviance, then our current system of service delivery, although it fails to identify many youths who need service, needs only to fine-tune and improve its child-change technology. However, if we step back and adopt broader understandings on troubling behavior and believe that problems experienced by some youths suggest a poor fit between youths and their ecologies (and that we can alter those ecologies), or that institutions can and do create problems when their organizational structures are insensitive to diverse groups of students, then the current service delivery systems must change.

Along with changes in service delivery, those who systematically study troubled youths and troubling behavior need to broaden their investigations to include not only traditional person-centered perspectives but also studies of the social environments in which adolescents experience difficulties and the organizational structures and cultural forces associated with our current responses to troubling behavior. Broad, multifaceted perspectives on the genesis of deviant behaviors and integrated responses to those behaviors are essential for the development of a just and equitable system of services for all youth.

References

Allen-Hagen, B. (1988, October). Public juvenile facilities, 1987: Children in custody. *Juvenile Justice Bulletin.*

Community Research Associates, Inc. (1987). *Assessment of model programs for the chronic status offenders and their families* (Report prepared for the U.S. Department of Justice, Contract No. OJP-85-C-007). Champaign, IL: Author.

Friedman, A. S., Glickman, N., & Utada, A. (1985). Does drug and alcohol use lead to failure to graduate from high school? *Journal of Drug Education, 15*, 353-364.

Hawkins, J. D., Lishner, D. M., Jenson, J. M., & Catalano, R. F. (1987). What the evidence suggests about prevention and treatment programming. In B. S. Brown & A. R. Mills (Eds.), *Youth at risk for substance abuse* (DHHS Publication No. ADM 87-1537). Washington, DC: Government Printing Office.

Hobbs, N. (1982). *The troubled and troubling child: Reeducation in mental health, education, and human services programs for children and youth.* San Francisco: Jossey-Bass.

Johnston, L. D., O'Malley, P. M., & Bachman, J. G. (1988). *Illicit drug use, smoking, and drinking by America's high school students, college students, and young adults 1975-1987.* Rockville, MD: National Institute on Drug Abuse.

Klinge, V., Vaziri, H., & Lennox, K. (1976). Comparison of psychiatric inpatient male and female adolescent drug abusers. *International Journal of the Addictions, 11,* 309-323.

Leone, P. E. (1989). Beyond fixing bad behavior and bad boys: Multiple perspectives on education and treatment of troubled and troubling youth. *Monograph in Behavioral Disorders, 12,* 1-10.

Melton, G. B. (n.d.). *Service models in child and adolescent mental health: What works for whom?* (Report to the Nebraska Department of Public Institutions, Child and Adolescent Service System Program (CASSP), grant MH39884-02 from the National Institute of Mental Health).

Morgan, D. J. (1979). Prevalence and types of handicapping conditions found in juvenile correctional institutions: A national survey. *Journal of Special Education, 13,* 283-295.

National Institute of Mental Health. (1988). *The Child and Adolescent Service System Program (CASSP): Fiscal year '88 report.* Washington, DC: Author.

Reichler, B. D., Clement, J. L., & Dunner, D. L. (1983). Chart review of alcohol problems in adolescent psychiatric patients in an emergency room. *Journal of Clinical Psychiatry, 44,* 338-339.

Robert Wood Johnson Foundation. (1989, August). *News from the Robert Wood Johnson Foundation.* Princeton, NJ: Author.

Rutherford, R. B., Nelson, C. M., & Wolford, B. I. (1985). Special education in the most restrictive environment: Correctional special education. *Journal of Special Education, 19,* 59-71.

U.S. Department of Education. (1988a). *Youth indicators 1988: Trends in the well-being of American youth* (USDE Publication No. PIP 88-834). Washington, DC: Government Printing Office.

U.S. Department of Education. (1988b). *Tenth annual report to Congress on the implementation of the Education of the Handicapped Act.* Washington, DC: Author.

U.S. Department of Justice. (1987). *Sourcebook of criminal justice statistics: 1987* (NCJ Publication No. 111612). Washington, DC: Government Printing Office.

U.S. Department of Justice. (1989, March/April). *Cracking down on street drugs: New strategies* (NIJ Report No. 213). Washington, DC: Author.

Weinstein, L. (1969). Project Re-Ed schools for emotionally disturbed children: Effectiveness as viewed by referring agencies, parents, and teachers. *Exceptional Children, 35,* 703-711.

Wetzel, J. Q. (1987). *American youth: A statistical snapshot.* Washington, DC: Wm. T. Grant Foundation.

Author Index

Subject Index

About the Authors

Kevin Allison is an Assistant Professor in the Department of Psychology, Penn State University. Recently he was Clinical Director of City Lights, a community-based day treatment and young adult transition program in the District of Columbia. He received his M.A. and Ph.D. in clinical psychology from DePaul University. His research interests include identity development, stress, and substance abuse in ethnic adolescent populations.

Pamela Casey, a Staff Associate in the Research and Special Services Division of the National Center for State Courts since 1986, holds a doctoral degree in psychology from St. Louis University. Her primary research interests are in the area of judicial administration-mental health system interactions. Within this area, she has conducted research on expert mental health assistance for indigent criminal defendants, the use of information by juvenile court personnel in deciding cases, the management of information retained on central registries of child abuse and neglect, and the procedures involved in the involuntary civil commitment process.

Thomas J. Dishion, Ph.D., is a Research Scientist and a Child and Family Therapist at the Oregon Social Learning Center in Eugene,

Oregon. He is currently interested in research and clinical work focusing on antisocial behavior and substance abuse in children and adolescents. In his research efforts, he has examined the contribution of families to peer relations, as well as the joint contribution of peers and families to problem behavior. His clinical work has involved attempting to develop clinical intervention models based on developmental research. His methodological interests include multivariate statistics and behavior observation assessment.

Robert B. Everhart is Professor of Education and Sociology, School of Education, Portland State University. For 10 years prior to his current position, he served on the faculty at the University of California, Santa Barbara. His research interests are in the areas of the sociology of education and educational organization and policy. He is author of numerous articles and chapters, as well as *Reading, Writing, and Resistance: Education and Labor in a Junior High School* (Routledge & Kegan Paul, 1983) and *Practical Ideology and Symbolic Community* (Falmer, 1988).

Carolyn Molden Fink, a doctoral candidate in the Special Education Program at the University of Maryland, College Park, received her B.S. and M.A. in learning disabilities from Northwestern University. She has worked as a teacher and administrator in special programs for adolescents with severe learning and behavior problems. Her interests include disabled youth in the criminal justice system, computer-assisted instruction in special education, and transition of disabled students from school to community life.

Denise C. Gottfredson is an Assistant Professor at the Institute of Criminal Justice and Criminology at the University of Maryland, College Park. She conducts research on delinquent behavior and education, and specializes in applying research to problems faced by criminal justice and education practitioners. She has directed and evaluated several school- and community-based delinquency prevention efforts. Currently she is conducting an experiment, in collaboration with an urban school district, to reduce troublesome behavior among adolescents by altering the school and classroom environments. She has written several articles and book chapters on the causes of delinquency and strategies for reducing delinquency, and she is coauthor of *Victimization in Schools*.

Debra Huntley is an Assistant Professor of Psychology at Wichita State University in Wichita, Kansas. Since obtaining her Ph.D. in clinical psychology from the University of Houston in 1987, she has been actively involved in research on social support and depression, family interactions, and influences of single parenting on child psychopathology. Her clinical focus has been on children, adolescents, and family issues. Both her research and clinical work emphasize a community psychology perspective.

Ingo Keilitz is the Founding Director of the Institute on Mental Disability and the Law, an arm of the National Center for State Courts since 1981. He is also a Lecturer in Mental Health Law at the Marshall-Wythe School of Law, College of William and Mary. Dr. Keilitz has held professorships in psychology at Creighton University and in special education at the University of Missouri. He has published widely on topics in mental disability and the law, special education, psychology, and program evaluation. He is currently working on a book, *Uncertain Covenants: Mental Illness and the Ordinary Administration of Justice.*

Peter E. Leone is an Associate Professor in the Department of Special Education at the University of Maryland and has an affiliate faculty appointment in the Department of Psychology. He completed his Ph.D. in special education at the University of Washington. He has been involved as a teacher, consultant, and advocate with community-based programs serving troubled youths for a number of years. He has authored a number of research articles on troubled and troubling youth related to follow-up, juvenile corrections, and disciplinary exclusion from the public schools. His research interests include understanding the social ecology of troubled behavior, legal issues related to educational access and equity, and interpretive research methods.

John Lewis McAdoo is an Associate Professor in the School of Social Work and Community Planning at the University of Maryland at Baltimore. He received his master's degree in social work and his doctorate in educational psychology at the University of Michigan. His research interests include racial attitudes of preschool children, the role of the Black father, and the well-being of the urban elderly. He has done postgraduate work in mental health epidemiology at Johns Hopkins University and evaluation research at Harvard University. He is the coeditor of *Black Children: Social, Educational, and Parenting Environments* (Sage, 1985).

C. Michael Nelson, Ed.D., is a Professor with the Special Education Faculty at the University of Kentucky. He has worked as a teacher and as a child psychologist with children with learning and behavioral problems. He is coauthor of two books on children with behavioral problems and coeditor of *Special Education in the Criminal Justice System* (with Rutherford and Wolford). He is a Past President of the International Council for Children with Behavioral Disorders. His professional interests include school consultation, applied behavior analysis, and special education in correctional institutions.

William C. Rhodes is Research Professor, University of South Florida, and Professor Emeritus, University of Michigan. He received his Ph.D. in clinical psychology at Ohio State University, and later served as acting Mental Health Commissioner for Georgia and Associate Director of Children's Programs in Community Services at the National Institute of Mental Health. While on the faculty at George Peabody College in Nashville, he collaborated in the development of Project Re-ED. He is best known for *A Study of Child Variance*, a comprehensive four-volume study, completed in the early 1970s, of conceptual knowledge and service delivery for children identified as emotionally disturbed.

Robert B. Rutherford, Jr., is a Professor of Special Education at Arizona State University. He received his doctorate in special education from George Peabody College in 1971. He is President of the Council for Children with Behavioral Disorders and was the Director of the Correctional Special Education Training (C/SET) Project. He is the former editor of *Behavioral Disorders* and the current editor of the *Severe Behavior Disorders of Children and Youth* monograph series. He has written a number of journal articles and book chapters in the areas of behavioral disorders and special education in the criminal justice system.

Carole B. Shauffer has been a staff attorney at the Youth Law Center since 1981. She has also been an attorney at the Louisiana Center for the Public Interest and the American Civil Liberties Union of Louisiana, a teaching assistant, an instructor, a house parent, a welfare rights organizer, a file clerk, a research assistant, and a restaurant worker.

She is the daughter of Irving and Edith Shauffer, the wife of Russell Richeda, and the mother of Benjamin Daniel and Elizabeth Shauffer Richeda.

James Snyder is an Associate Professor of Psychology at Wichita State University in Wichita, Kansas. Since receiving his Ph.D. in clinical psychology from Southern Illinois University in 1977, he has been active in research on the contribution of peers and family to the development of conduct-disordered behavior in children and adolescents, and on observational methodology. He also has extensive experience in the clinical treatment of conduct-disordered children and adolescents using behavioral family therapy and self-instructional training. His research has been published in numerous journal articles and book chapters.

Ellen Rowse Spero received her undergraduate degree in psychology and sociology in 1986 from Brandeis University and her M.A. in education from the University of Maryland, College Park. She is now a teacher at A Different Drum, an alternative school in Alexandria, Virginia. Her areas of interest include adolescents with substance abuse problems, troubled and troubling adolescent girls, and alternative education.

Edison J. Trickett is Professor of Psychology at the University of Maryland, College Park. He received his Ph.D. from Ohio State University, did postdoctoral research at the Social Ecology Laboratory, Department of Psychiatry, Stanford University, and taught at Yale University before going to the faculty at Maryland in 1977. His research interests focus on the development of an ecological framework for research and intervention in community psychology, with particular emphasis on the adolescent-school relationship. Most recently his work has focused on how adolescents in need of special services and immigrant and refugee adolescents cope with the high school experience. He has coauthored a book on mental health consultation and has written numerous book chapters and articles on the ecology of school life and adolescent adaptation.

Mary Bannon Walter received her undergraduate degree in human ecology in 1971 and her M.A. in psychology in 1975 from Marywood College. She has worked with educationally handicapped youth as a teacher and as a school psychologist in public school and community mental health settings. Since completing her Ph.D. in special education at the University of Maryland, College Park, in 1988 she has worked as a Faculty Research Associate at the University of Maryland. Her research interests include issues in programming for exceptional youth in correctional settings and teacher training.

Loren M. Warboys is a staff attorney at the Youth Law Center in San Francisco, where he has worked since 1979. He has litigated cases throughout the country on behalf of children, particularly children confined in institutions. In addition to his work at the Youth Law Center, he has taught a course on law and the juvenile court at John F. Kennedy School of Law. He has published a number of articles on legal issues involving children and is coauthor of *Representing the Child Client* (Matthew Bender). He is a graduate of Syracuse University and Harvard Law School and is admitted to practice law in California and New York states.

Bruce I. Wolford, Ph.D., a Professor in the Department of Correctional Services, College of Law Enforcement, at Eastern Kentucky University, received his Ph.D. from the Ohio State University in 1979. He is currently the Director of the Training Resource Center Project, which serves as a professional development and training center. He has authored numerous publications in corrections and juvenile justice, and is a former President of the Correctional Education Association, member of the American Correctional Association Board of Governors, and former editor of the *Journal of Correctional Education*.

Susan F. Zlotlow is currently an Assistant to the Dean in Graduate Studies and Research at the University of Maryland. She received her B.A. in 1970 from the University of Rochester, and her M.A. and Ph.D. in clinical psychology from the University of Connecticut in 1977 and 1979, respectively. She has held a wide variety of positions, both applied and academic settings. She is a recent recipient of a national Individual Research Service Award from the National Institute of Mental Health to investigate the relationship between school and family environments during the transition from middle school to high school.